PENGUIN BOOKS

THE HIDDEN PLACES OF BRITAIN

Leslie Thomas was born in South Wales in 1931 and, when his parents died, he and his younger brother were brought up in an orphanage. His first book, *This Time Next Week*, is the story of that upbringing. At sixteen he became a reporter on a weekly newspaper in Essex and then did his National Service in Malaya during the Communist bandit war. *The Virgin Soldiers* tells of these days; it was an immediate bestseller and has been made into a film with Lynn Redgrave and Hywel Bennett.

Returning to civilian life, Leslie Thomas became a top Fleet Street feature writer and travelled throughout the world. His second novel, *Orange Wednesday*, was published in 1967. For nine months during that year he travelled around ten islands off the coast of Britain, the result of which was a lyrical travelogue, *Some Lovely Islands*, upon which the BBC based a television series. He has continued to travel a great deal and has also written a number of television plays. He is a director of a London publishing house. His hobbies include golf, cricket, music and antiques.

His other books include *Come to the War*, *His Lordship*, *Arthur McCann and All His Women*, *The Man With the Power*, *Onward Virgin Soldiers*, *Stand Up Virgin Soldiers*, *Tropic of Ruislip*, *Dangerous Davies: The Last Detective*, *Ormerod's Landing*, *That Old Gang of Mine*. Penguin also publish his latest bestselling novel, *The Magic Army*.

THE HIDDEN PLACES OF BRITAIN

Leslie Thomas

PHOTOGRAPHED BY PETER CHÈZE-BROWN

DECORATED BY SHIRLEY FELTS

PENGUIN BOOKS

Penguin Books Ltd, Harmondsworth, Middlesex, England
Penguin Books, 625 Madison Avenue, New York, New York 10022, U.S.A.
Penguin Books Australia Ltd, Ringwood, Victoria, Australia
Penguin Books Canada Ltd, 2801 John Street, Markham, Ontario, Canada L3R 1B4
Penguin Books (N.Z.) Ltd, 182–190 Wairau Road, Auckland 10, New Zealand

First published by Arlington Books 1981
Published in Penguin Books 1983

Made and printed in Great Britain by
Hazell Watson & Viney Ltd, Aylesbury, Bucks
Set in Bembo

Dedicated with love to my son, Matthew,
who was born on the day this book was begun

Such is the patriot's boast,
Where'er we roam,
His first, best country ever is,
At home.

Oliver Goldsmith, *The Traveller*

Contents

Introduction

This book – this story, as I like to think of it – was begun on the day my son, Matthew, was born. Now, at its conclusion, he is almost ten years old. The excuse for this tardiness is that I had other things to do. But between novels, screenplays and television scripts, I always went back to *The Hidden Places* – to travel to some new scene and to write about it. To do so was to breathe different air.

On reading the very title people will say, "But there *aren't* any hidden places in Britain! Not any longer." Their protest is, of course, justified. Nowhere described in these travels is wholly inaccessible. The motor-car can take us almost anywhere (as, indeed, it did me) and even islands can be reached with no more effort than is needed to propel a boat. Perhaps a better premise is that I have attempted to describe what are, perhaps, the less obvious parts of Britain. Some, like the island of Stroma, are remote, it is true; others, like the low and lonely marshes of the Hundred of Hoo, are within an hour or so's drive of London.

I think it best, at the outset, to declare myself as a simple traveller. The urge to go places has always been with me, but although I have journeyed the world and home again, the small horizons of my own country are those that call most insistently and satisfy me best. I can claim to be an expert in little or nothing. These observations on geography and topography are the product of someone who takes pleasure in maps, contours and the accidents of landscapes. What knowledge I have of natural history has only been gained by a layman's observation; history and archaeology are mysteries I love, but still mysterious. My talent, as I hope those good people I have waylaid on these journeys will agree, is the art of companionship.

How did I choose my *Hidden Places*? By, again, the simple method – by sitting at my fireside and enjoyably going through an atlas of the British Isles and marking down the places bisected with the least roads. It would, of course, have been easy to choose any number of areas in Scotland or even Wales. I attempted, however, to spread my travels over the whole country and to avoid, as far as possible, places that, although remote, were over-familiar to the holiday tourist. Thus Snowdonia and the Pennines were excluded. Cape Cornwall, which has more than its share of summer visitors, I saw in January for the reasons explained in that chapter. Islands I reluctantly kept to a minimum, only Stroma, the Summer Isles and Unst in Shetland coming into that category. Having already written a travelogue called *Some Lovely*

Islands, I felt that to overload this book with others would be self-indulgent and repetitive.

There were, naturally, other considerations. Some places, like the misty, magical Summer Isles, I had long dreamed about; others summoned me by their very mellifluence. Allendale Town was one – saying it was sufficient to make me want to go. Ross and Cromarty, a familiar line from that everyday poem, the weather forecast, was another. Shingle Street on the Suffolk coast called insistently. I had to sample the peace of Pennant Melangell. To say Achiltibuie was a triumph in itself.

Some places proved fruitless. A chapter to be called *On Ermine Street* about the Roman road that climbs straight as a ladder north of Lincoln, went unwritten after a preliminary exploration. Airfields and bungalows were responsible for my change of mind, which was a pity for some of the hamlets were suitably sleepy and Ermine Street itself runs for many miles with few interruptions, one of those being a village interestingly called Spital-in-the-Street.

Early in this protracted journey I met another disappointment. Surprisingly this was at Knoydart, Invernesshire where a hundred square miles of highland forest and glen is populated by a scattering of people. My intentions were a mistake from the start, for I had set my eyes on the place where the late Gavin Maxwell and his otters lived and which was the setting for his book, *Ring of Bright Water*. Called Camusfeàrna in that classic story I knew this was fictitious for Sandaig. Unfortunately – amateur that I am – I alighted on the wrong Sandaig! This settlement had only one house, inhabited by a bright octogenarian lady and her son – but it was two headlands south of the correct location, although both are on the Sound of Sleat.

I reached Mallaig, at the end of the narrow (and busy) Road to the Isles, accompanied by my wife. Her presence, we agreed, was a mistake. She has many qualities but the pioneer spirit is noticeably lacking. Having selected the wrong location, I found my error compounded by daunting rain and a soaking passage across Loch Nevis in an open fishing boat. My life companion began to regret her involvement when she was required to climb a rusty and seaweed-clothed ladder to the jetty at Inverie on the Knoydart peninsula. We were greeted by a cheerful young man, a son of the estate owner, who enquired as to whether I had come to look at a faulty telephone. Oddly enough, this telephone was one of the few fruitful aspects of the day since it was installed especially at the behest of Neville Chamberlain, who went to rest at Knoydart after his efforts at Munich in 1938. It actually rang while I was there and I had a curious thought that the ghost of Adolf Hitler might be on the other end.

In my travels I attempted to find landscapes as varied as possible. A canal, a marsh, mountains, a peninsula, an Atlantic village, a pebble beach, a small town held between a river and the North Sea. The accents of the people have been varied, their kindnesses differing, but still kindnesses. I scarcely met a harsh word or a harsh soul in the whole journey.

The many thousands of miles I travelled, from Cape Cornwall in the south-west to Muckle Flugga in the ultimate north (with Allendale Town in the very centre, so the inhabitants claim, of mainland Britain) were mainly accomplished by car. A defective hip joint makes long efforts on foot both difficult and painful, as I learned while climbing the hill that hides Twm Shon Catti's cave in Wales. For nine years I had a love affair with a beautiful, hooded Peugeot Cabriolle. Despite this affection, motors are yet another area of total ignorance to me. The one drawback, it seemed, in this admirable vehicle was the lack of a map-reading light. After many experiences on winter nights crouching in front of a headlight trying to ascertain the route, I discovered the perfectly reasonable light in the glove compartment when I was cleaning the car on the day I eventually sold it! A splendid replacement was an RX7 sports car which went in for servicing and was burned out in a fire at the garage on Christmas Eve, 1980. North Wales, the last safari, was explored in my wife's car which suffered two punctures in remote areas.

Each time I set off from my home in the south of England, clad in my cosy old clothes, throwing a bag in the back of the car, and driving away, I experienced an identical excitement. As I drove I listened to a variety of music, often matching the landscape: Delius for pastoral Dorset, Wagner for Wales, Vivaldi for the Vales of Oxfordshire and Warwickshire. I also sucked my way through yards of those mints with the holes.

There were times when I despaired of man's inhumanity to nature. He has chosen the most pleasant places for his baleful nuclear power stations and – not at all surprising I suppose – the most isolated locations for his secret defence establishments. But even these change like the seasons. When I made my first visit to Orfordness in Suffolk it was strung with wires and poles like some nightmarish hopfield. Early warning devices I understood. Eight years later when I returned, they had all gone. Outmoded.

Great oil pipes now bind Shetland like strangling ropes, but, thank God, the great cape of Herma Ness has been dedicated to the Arctic skuas and terns. A friend who has recently taken a post at the busy Sumburgh Airport is followed by grunting seals as he walks along the beach next to the runways. Hoo, in the wilder shores of Kent, has been mooted but (fortunately for its people and its herons) rejected as a site for the new London Airport; there is a diabolical threat to put a nuclear power station on the splendid Chesil Bank; an oil rig as big as a village has been built at Kishorn in remote Ross and Cromarty.

Places change, especially over ten years; people also. Some to whom I have talked in these adventures have moved on, others have died – most sadly for me, the lovely lady, Jill Brown, who kept the Altnaharrie Inn on the side of Loch Broom.

The great pleasure of making these explorations and of writing about them in this book will always remain with me. The privilege of being able to take a poetic name from the page of an atlas and then go off to transpose it into earth and sky and people is one of which I have been most conscious. I hope that this book brings some of the laughter and the wonder of my adventures to those who read it.

Leslie Thomas, 1981

ONE

A Hare And A Puffer Boat

On a June day, muddled with sun and glittering showers, I stood precariously inside the dome of the ruined mill at Napton-on-the-Hill in Warwickshire. My back was against the great wooden mill wheel, and I looked out to Edgehill, where they had the battle, to the shadowy spires of Coventry, to the Cotswolds, to the plump Oxfordshire farms, to the old canal which turns stiffly like bent tin through the Midland parishes.

This was the palm of England's hand. A spreading countryside, populated with fine trees and outstretched fields; a place with a measured life, bland and beautiful; comfortable between the restless south and the gritty northern places.

I suppose a fast man in a fast car could be in London in under two hours, but in this place the big city is not felt; there is no dependence on it, nor is it talked about unduly. In a pub in Priors Marston I heard a man say: "An' there she was, the old gel, in her armchair in the garden, right centre of the cabbages and looking nasty towards the house. It was coming on to rain too. 'It's 'e's at the flue,' she say, 'so I'm staying out.'

"I thought t'was being a bit off being out there just because old Percy was sweeping the chimney. Then there was this bang and all the soot shot up out of the pot and clouds of it came out of the windows and the door. And then old Percy, like the bloody devil, black all over, comes out laughing, and waving 'is twelve bore. He'd just shot it up the chimney. 'All right, Missus,' he says, 'I've done. You can come on in now.' "

It was the canal – the Oxford Canal – that first made me go there. It crept with a sort of crafty joy from Oxford to Napton and on to Birmingham, sneaking and sidling through fields and hamlets and meeting only one town, Banbury, on its way. The railway and the roads, which took away its commercial usefulness, charge north and south on their desperate journeys, but the canal yawns and ambles by green places that the rushing traveller neither sees nor suspects. You can almost hear it enjoying an elderly guffaw.

I first became aware of it from the road, north of Oxford, when I came upon the astonishing sight of a bright yellow boat apparently sailing through serene meadows. Its cabin, part of its coloured deck, and the snout of its bow were raised above the grass and it travelled gently from one hedgerow to the next, vanishing around the back of trees and emerging from the rump of a grazing cow.

For a hundred and seventy years the canal had been there but I still experienced that joyful jump that comes with discovery; that slow, self-satisfied, slightly idiotic smile that I know is spreading over my face at such moments. I had been looking for the canal, and – magically! – there it was. I couldn't see the water, but I could see that boat voyaging across the field. While the traffic rushed uncaringly behind my back, I stood and watched. I had the feeling that I, alone, was aware of it, and I felt as pleased as any man who discovered the source of the Amazon.

A mile further, and there opened a promising side road, suitably unkempt. It led obligingly to a little bowed bridge, beneath which the canal idled under alder trees, nudged by thistles and a rash of buttercups. The muddy water was midge-ridden and birds were sweeping low among the midges, banking and rolling a few inches from the surface and streaming like daredevil fliers beneath the cupid arch of the bridge.

To reach this place the canal wriggled in secret out of Oxford, away from snoring spires, car factories, parking meters, blocks of flats, and a garden suburb, whatever that is. At one point it curled artfully under three trunk roads in the space of a few yards, and then made a joyous run for the open fields. Even from the small bridge I could see the red faces of suburban houses looking towards me. But the alders shielded the canal, the day's uncertain sun had one of its moments, there was profound silence beneath the trees and I knew I had come to the right place.

James Brindley, who built the waterway, was not a romantic. He wanted to get the coal barges moving as soon as possible. On the forehead of the dreamy little bridge he fixed a metal plate saying no. 228 and left it at that. He required the sides of his canal to be dug sharp and straight, but he had a few rough edges himself. The board of the canal company, weighted with so many clergymen that notices of its meetings were always appended to Oxfordshire church doors, did not take to his ways and adopted a resolution that 'the Engineer, Surveyor and Clerks of This Company do not associate or drink with any of the inferior officers or workmen'.

The immediate countryside can have changed only little since they dug the last spadeful of earth out of the canal and let the water in. Apart from an inexplicable packet of Bird's Eye frozen peas (full) lying on the bank by the bridge, it was an eighteenth century scene. Black and white cattle, knee deep in clover and their own thoughts, hawthorn and elderberry bursting with birds, and the occasional *gal-lump* of some water creatures diving at my approach. Reeds thickened to a wall on the far bank and beyond that the meadows, patched and squared in different greens, extended to a grey farm squatting on a ring of trees. This is Civil War country. A Royalist stronghold with many a Cromwell's man stretched out beneath the turf, and the old houses still crouch low with eyebrows raised as though a cannon ball had passed recently overhead.

That rainy June had caused rivers to clamber over their banks and invade indignant fields. A middle-aged couple navigating a motor cruiser from the direction of Oxford said that the flooded Thames had not been merely uncomfortable but terrifying. And yet here, under the sleepy trees, with the hawthorn and elderberry hedges below them, and the tangled towpath weeds and flowers sheltering lower, it could not have been any time but June and nowhere but England. The canal, peacefully contained within its banks, was harmless as it was idle.

View of Somerton, Oxfordshire, looking west-south-west from the Somerton-Souldern road.

Across a reedy meadow I saw the railway which brought death and, in a way, life to the canals. A train rolled by heavily, humping its load of Leyland cars, wailing and rushing from Oxford, while the indolent waterway went quietly nowhere. Somewhere not very distant in the other direction, I knew that crowded traffic was chasing north and south, but I could not hear it for the racket of the birds.

It was close and cloudy, with the sun flickering through like some old magic lantern. Two water creatures were having a race from bank to bank some way ahead. I could see their jogging heads and the clean wake they left, but by the time I reached the spot they were safely hidden in the alcoves of the far bank.

Another bridge was arched over the water at the end of the straight towpath along which I was walking and, just short of it, a canal narrow boat, like an awkwardly tall man lying down, rested with its coloured cheek against the bank. There was no-one aboard. In this, the kernel of Oxfordshire, its name looked strange. It was called *Flower of Shannon*. A navigational error perhaps.

Bridge no. 228 between Yarnton on the Woodstock road and Kidlington on the Banbury road just north of Oxford. This view showing the towpath is from the north looking south.

* * *

A few more meadows, another bridge, and the canal performed one of its sly curls, burrowed beneath the main Banbury road, and made an elbow turn at a delectable hamlet called Thrupp where the Inland Waterways Executive – a pompous title, surely, for people concerned in the ancient and unofficial business of canals – maintains a depot in idyllic surroundings. Imagine being a man like Aubrey Jones, living in the thatched cottage where he was born, and occupying himself with the repair and well-being of this snug and secluded waterway. His name, like that of his employers, failed to give the sound of the entirely rural man that he was. Tall and heavy, he told me that his family always said he ought to be a policeman. Fortunately he preferred building lock gates. His house was in the enclosed yard at the very turn of the canal, reached by a drawbridge and scattered with the bits and parts of boats and barges. He bumped across the stony roads and lanes of his domain in a small van, and he knew every crease and bend of the waterway and all the people inhabiting its banks. To hear him recite, in his deep, careful voice, the names of all the locks and stopping places from Napton to Thrupp was to hear a poem.

"Been working here fifty years now, just over in fact," he said. Quiet afternoon sunlight wandered through the cottage windows, and caught the old lustre of a large Sunderland jug on the dresser. His wife was making tea. He said, "This house used to be a mill. I was born

The thatched cottage at Thrupp owned by the Inland Waterways Executive, where Aubrey Jones was born.

here and I used to help my father about the yard and on the canal. When I got old enough to work I went with him as an apprentice carpenter. I don't have to go far to see lock gates and such things, drawbridges and the like, that I helped my father to make when I was a boy.

"God, I can remember plenty of winters when the canal was frozen solid and they had to get horses hitched to an ice boat to pull it through. Some on the stern and some on the bow and those horses seemed to know just what to do. They'd steer the boat themselves through the ice and break it up. I've seen ten and twelve horses to a boat. My father used to tell me he'd seen sixteen in the hard winters when he was a boy.

"All the barges were working boats in those days. You'd never see a pleasure boat on the canal. They wouldn't allow them. Coal coming down from the Midlands, and the brewery in Oxford used to use it a lot too. I think they sent the last barge down just after the war, about 1947.

"At Bank Holidays it was a traditional thing that we used to drain some of the pounds, which is what we call the stretches of water between one lock and the next, and repair the lock gates. Three or four days every Easter and Whitsun, and the people working the boats used to take a bit of time off, go to Banbury Fair and that sort of thing, which they still do. Nowadays we can't do the locks in the holiday times because everything's topsy-turvy now. That's when the canal is busy. So we have to do the repairs in January and February when the weather is hardest.

"It's never been an easy life, but I suppose you choose what you choose. I had the chance to go into business years ago with a man who is very wealthy now. I didn't go. I suppose there was something about the canal that made me stay here. And I kept thinking about becoming a policeman, but I kept finding jobs to do here and by the time I'd got to the point where I had them all cleared up for a bit, I was too old to go in the force. So anyway, perhaps it was just as well."

We stood in the garden of his thatched house. Summer had settled for the evening at least. The boatyard was streaked with long shadows and there were round shadows among the tall, full trees. Through the far gate, the lock gate and drawbridge – imagine having a drawbridge to your house! – stood sturdy and white.

On the far side of the canal a run of cottages, demurely formal, faced the towpath. Rose Beauchamp lived there in the house where she was born. As an eight-year-old she scampered, black-faced, about a coal barge, journeying through the flat lands of England while others were at school. She never learned to read or write but she knew her geography of the Midland counties.

"I never was a scholar," she said. "The only school we ever got to was when Sister Harriet used to fetch us from the barges when we was tied up in Oxford; and she used to take us off to St Thomas' Sunday School. We used to sing and listen, but coming from the canal, and not being scholars, we only used to do the best we could."

Rose was a bright, tidy woman with a quick recall of those young roving days. She pronounced her name 'Beecham', like the best in the land of that illustrious family, and can look from the neat parcel of her front window onto the slow water she travelled so many times.

"First of all I was with my father and the rest," she remembered. "Then I had a canal boat along with my sister. I reckon I was about nineteen at the time, though it's a bit difficult to tell. Sometime about then, anyway. My sister, she would be about seventeen, and me had the boat 'tween us. We used to carry coal. We was like the minstrels, I can tell you!" She hooted happily at the memory.

Their voyages were from Oxford to what she poetically called Birnigam and back, three or four days for the journey, nudging their way through a countryside that was itself only moving slowly out of the nineteenth century. Like all the canal people, she delights in reciting the unconscious verse of the locks and stopping places – Tamworth, Tooley Hall, Griff Colliery, Napton and the rest. "Lovely," she sighed, to herself it seemed, "Ah, it was lovely. We had a mule called Bill who pulled the boat. He was a bit stubborn, but he was all right. He'd doze along all day pulling us, and when he got to the low bridges he'd scrouch down to get under. Lovely. We lived like lords because we had everything. At nights we'd be cosy and sweet in the cabin with our little stove. Didn't matter what it was like outside. And the pubs was full of life. The old melodeon going and the canal people tap-dancing. They used to be very good at that, tap-dancing. They didn't have much room on the boats to practise any other sort of dancing. You can't do a waltz on a narrow boat, can you? And they got very good at this tap-dancing, because if you lost your step over the side you'd go.

"Ha! Many's the time I've been in the canal. Never learned to swim, either. Never. My father was forever fishing me out with a hook. Somebody used to shout 'Rose is in again', and he'd hurry and get his hook.

"We didn't mind if it was hot in the summer or freezing cold in the winter. It was all the same to us. It was lovely. Lovely."

*   *   *

The church at Shipton-on-Cherwell, "almost tumbling into the green water". The footbridge to the right of the picture leads across the fields to the church and ruined manor of Hampton Gay.

Andrew Yarranton, writing in *England's Improvement By Land And Sea* which he published in 1677, put forward the suggestion that the River Cherwell should be made navigable from Oxford to Banbury (at what sounds the highly reasonable cost of £10,000) so that the corn from the Midland fields could be transported to London. It was never done, but just above Thrupp the canal and the river became confused among the water meadows, intermingling, touching and parting, or running as straight as railway lines alongside each other. At Shipton-on-Cherwell there was a churchyard almost tumbling into the green water, and across the fields a sort of castaway church at Hampton Gay; a church without a village, with no road or path, marooned in bright meadows.

The fields were boggy from a combination of cows and summer rain. I went across them to the old ruined house of Hampton Gay, almost buried in a copse that had grown from within its walls. Even now local legends are repeated about the night the house caught fire. It was nearly a century ago, but to go there is to get the feeling of a very mysterious place. It must have been handsome, white walls and mullioned windows, standing among its fields. It had tumbled in on itself, masonry and debris lying where they fell so long ago, trees and bushes thrusting strongly from its doors, windows and chimney places. Still nobody knows how or why it caught fire. The only certainty is that nobody has ever gone back to clear up the mess.

Following the thick, green course of the canal north, I found myself walking like some jungle explorer, some Oxfordshire Colonel Fawcett, in a damp world made warm by the incursion of sudden sunlight. Strongly it cut down through clustered branches hanging over the towpath, warming the muddy earth, making the moisture rise, streaks of steam like warm ghosts, from the grass and weeds and carelessly tumbling flowers. I was alone, closed in all around by walls and arches of almost solid greenery. The water lay heavy and undisturbed, a cloth of green across it; I would not have been surprised by an alligator or two.

The lock and lock keeper's cottage at Cropredy, showing a boat about to enter the lock to continue its journey towards Oxford.

Then, in this jungle I saw, rounding a bend, a great grey building, monstrously turretted, galleried, grown over with weeds, parcelled with creepers. There it stood, high but defeated, being swallowed by Nature.

It was like coming upon a decomposing Aztec temple in the fastness of a Brazilian rain forest. Were it not for huge painted messages on its side giving the news that "D.C. LOVES C.H." and "ROY JAMES WAS HERE", I might well have been the first man for a thousand years to set eyes upon it. Unfortunately it was only an abandoned cement works, left forlorn, like the rubbled manor house a few miles down the canal. One day Oxfordshire may grow over it completely and then it will look quite pretty.

Each lock on the canal has its own onlooking cottage and its edging garden spilling prettily to the bank. Other houses comfortably grouped themselves round about, and their gardens embroidered the towpath too.

At Cropredy there were lupins and lilac thick to the water's edge, many other flowers as well, and small circumspect trees and paved yards. The sun was warming them when I saw them that day. Only bees and birds and cats were to be seen, the bees working madly among the flowers, the cats, fat and polished, stretched in the shadiest places; so idle that the birds knew of their laziness and stalked brashly among the paths and bushes.

The lock there and its cottage were neat and sweet and surrounded by the mysterious gurgling of water that was a part of every place like this. Stand and listen and then follow the mumbles. You will find that the water sidles and sneaks away from the canal side through all manner of cracks and culverts, making a childishly joyful noise as it dives beneath the ground, heading for some secret place of its own.

Over page, the canal just north of Pigeon Lock.

Cropredy was not an entirely beautiful village, the builders have been at it; and those of other times left it with a somewhat sombre, square-shouldered, church. It had its own battle

in the Civil War, though, and nailed to the walls of the church was some of the armour that the soldiers left behind. There was a Roundhead breastplate and helmet, looking flimsy now. There was a gorgette, some arm pieces and a sword, spidery with all the years that had gone since it was last pointed in anger.

As the canal trundled from Oxfordshire into Warwickshire, so the accents of the people who lived on its banks changed. It was possible to detect the Midland vowels coming into their words within a few miles of Fenny Compton, on the border. There the waterway once wriggled through a tunnel where the canal boat children used to shout and sing and laugh and hear their voices bouncing from one county to the next. It was still called The Tunnel, although it had been open to the sky for many years. The cutting was deep, walled now with hawthorns flown by many colours of butterfly and moth, and the water was still, undisturbed by boats or people.

In the miles from Oxford to The Tunnel I had seen only three craft moving on the canal; the ghostly barge I saw apparently moving across the meadow, the couple with the motor cruiser below Thrupp and, at Upper Heyford, a strange and beautiful craft, a home-made puffer boat, which was carrying a young man from Reading on a voyage through England. He had thrown in his job as a salesman and simply set sail in his little iron boat, going he knew not where. His laundry was hanging on the deck and a kettle was hooting on the stove in his galley. On a canal you can always ask a sailor where he is heading because all you have to do is to trot along the bank at his side. I asked him when he expected to get back home again. It was like putting a question to Sir Francis Chichester. The young man shrugged and said: "I don't know. I'm in no hurry. I'll just keep going." He paused, then said: "Maybe I'll never go back home."

The gate house at Wormleighton.

The foundation blocks of the tunnel that Brindley cut for his canal below Fenny Compton were still to be seen, at surface level, riven with holes and wrapped in moss now, the convenient homes of voles, rats and other soggy creatures.

At one place a delicate iron bridge, dainty and gently bowed, almost Venetian, crossed the olive channel. After the robust stone of the other bridges it took the eye from far downstream. Its rails were carefully carved, its aspect entirely pleasing. It was only a footbridge and whatever its use in the past it was little trodden then. I cannot recall crossing a bridge lined and carpeted with mosses, grass, buttercups and clover as this one was. But, like all the other bridges, it had its prosaic number plate, except that this one said '137 *a*.' Either somebody overlooked it when they counted the bridges first time, or, more reasonably, it was put in as an afterthought and they did not want to mess up the numbers as far as Napton Junction.

A mile away was the village of Wormleighton, dun stone houses with fine fluted chimneys; a magnificently arched and towered gate house, a church with geese about the porch, and everywhere rich red beeches and great rotund oaks. This was a Warwickshire that Shakespeare would recognise without a blink. This deepest interior of England seemed an age and a million miles from the cities or the sea. I saw *two* thatchers at work in one afternoon.

One of them, Alfred Webb, a small, amused man, agile, it seemed, even when he stood still, was patching the roof of a cottage by the church. He was sure he had a job for life. "I've got three years work just about here," he said. "And I work all the year except when it's too frosty and the thatch gets too brittle and when I goes on my holidays to Cornwall, I like it down there. It's the only time I get to see the sea."

He showed me how he split and bound the pieces of witchhazel to pin the thatch in place. "I started on the Earl of Grafton's estate in Northampton," he said. "I was a lad working on the farm and a thatcher asked me to help him with a big barn. I said 'No, mister, I've never done that work' but he said he would show me how, and he did. I've been at it thirty years now. I reckon I know most of the roofs around the Midlands. I don't want to do anything else. It's very quiet here and I like it quiet. All I want to do is to go on thatching until I'm too old and rickety to climb the ladder. Thatch is the best roof you can have. Lovely and warm. I wouldn't mind having a roof like this myself, but I can't afford it."

The yews, planted by mediaeval village bowmen, still grew strongly in Wormleighton

Detail from the fifteenth century chancel screen inside the church at Wormleighton, showing this very early portrait of a man wearing spectacles.

churchyard. Geese squat in formation beneath the umbrella tree at the gate. It was a fine church, with a fifteenth century screen across its chancel, carved with the heads of various local notables, one whom, remarkably, wears spectacles. In the chancel are benches adorned with such wooden vignettes as two bishops, back to back, as though at the commencing of a duel, and a dog rudely sticking out its tongue.

The sniff of the Civil War is everywhere. The screen itself was smuggled from Southam before the Roundheads could get their hands on it. And, above the choir, its dates reflecting the confused calculations of those troubled times, is a memorial of almost cinemascope proportions which records:

> '*John Spencer Sonne and Heire of Sir Robert Spencer Which John Spencer Departed this life at Blois the Sixth of August after the computation of the Church of England and the Sixteenth after the newe computation in the yeare of Our Lord Christ 1610 Being 19 yeares old eight months and odd days Never maryed of whom his brother Richard Spencer hath made this epitaph.*'

A few stony paces away, at the altar rail, is another memento of the same family, this one anatomical and to the point. It says: '*Here lyeth the bowells of Robert Lord Spencer. The body is buried at Brington.*'

Going north again the road does a sort of dance with the canal, touching, crossing, backing away, with the canal performing the most complicated steps, staggering about the landscape in the strangest manner for something, which is by its nature, so sober and straightforward. The counties were spread out to each horizon, dark at the distant edges, tones lifting to cool green as the fields advanced towards me. It gathers itself into low, long hills, with the noblest trees in all England roaming across them like some tousle-headed army. Matronly clouds moved slowly, dragging their attendant shadows over the land. It would rain briskly and then the sun would flood out and light the white walls of the farms and their congregations of outbuildings. A farmer had mustered his sheep in a gully and his men were busy with the shearing. The road was as empty as the canal had been.

At Marston Doles Lock the customary little hamlet had sprouted around the canal, seeming to draw some profound quiet from it; a settlement within itself, apart from the rest of the village. There was a copse of giant rhubarb here, ridiculous among the hollyhocks and wallflowers. Fishermen, seeking roach and gudgeon skulking in the corridors of thick water, crouched below their green umbrellas, and on a wall by the lock gates was a dire notice making threats against anyone 'propelling bullets or missiles' or 'live or dead animals' into the canal.

The cottage gardens had the familiar coloured look of the patches seen all along the towpath. One had a little outhouse, perhaps a privy, so overgrown that it had a small, private, lawn on its roof, with pigeons peering as millionaires might look out from a penthouse garden.

From here I could look north into the modest hills of Warwickshire, to Napton-on-the-Hill, a village spread like a picnic teacloth across the green of a long flat mound; its cheese-coloured church sits among the raddish-coloured houses, and at one end, like a fat man enjoying an outdoor sandwich, is the bulk of Napton mill.

View towards the mill at Napton. The mill now stands without both sails, the second one having been destroyed in a storm, although the sails are in the process of being restored.

I left the canal, taking the road towards the mill, eventually meeting the ubiquitous waterway again at The Folly just below Napton. The pub there was called The Folly, and apparently a folly it was because it's no longer a pub, but somebody's house. The bridge, its aperture and reflection making a full moon, leads the road to a dead end.

A narrow boat was inching up the canal and waiting for it was Anita Adkins, a young woman who, with her husband, Ken, lived in one of the old canal farmhouses, Holt Farm, near Southam.

Years ago, in the working days of the waterway, the farm was used as overnight stabling for the barge horses and mules. Rose Beauchamp's mule, Bill, would have been familiar with its straw. The Adkins kept it as a provisions store for the canal users. That morning they had been out of bread so, when the loaves eventually arrived from the bakery, Anita Adkins drove across country to catch up with the barge, the occupants of which had needed the bread. The slowness of water travel and the kindness of canal people go to make a certain courtesy.

I went then to Napton, a mere dimple on the map of England, but a full-grown hill in that landscape. In the house at the skirt of the hill lived Miss Ethel Gill. She had been there for fifty-five years. Her parents died and the rest of the family moved away, but she remained with her dogs, making a living from her market garden on the very forehead of the Midland counties.

She said I could climb to the top of the mill if I liked, but if I broke my neck then it wasn't her fault. I agreed that it would not be and I went into the mill. It was like climbing up inside the body of the giant. Step by cautious step on the ladders until I reached the dome. The mill had fallen into ruin (although it was being restored), the one remaining sail hanging out like some scarecrow's arm, the great cogs within clogged with rust, the wooden axle and beam shot with beetle holes.

But what a remarkable place to look out and see. I stood, a mainland lighthouse-keeper, staring joyfully over Warwickshire, Oxfordshire and Northamptonshire. The damaged roof was wide open and a careful half turn took my face to another aspect of England. The wind made subdued moans and rattled the loose woodwork. Just above my head, the clouds roved in summer packs. Out there, where the green ran to grey, was the field of Edgehill, where they say you can still hear the clang and clatter of the battle on certain ghostly nights. There to the north was the bumpy outline of Coventry and the sharp fingers of its Cathedral spires; Banbury in the south; the Cotswolds, lumpy, to the south-west.

Almost beneath my feet Napton spread itself out among its several streets. Its church sat smugly among its well fed trees. The first hay was being cut on a shoulder of a field two miles away. The sound of sheep and a bicycle bell floated up to me.

But I was not finished with my journey. Not quite. I wanted to find the junction where the canal finally turns north to Birmingham and meets the Warwick and Napton Canal. I had imagined that this would show traces of a busy place, a major stage in the businesslike journeyings of the canals of past times. I thought that there I might find the signs of some industry, wharfs, jetties, warehouses, stables for the horses, a basin for the boats and a pub for the men.

But when I reached the spot, after being directed by a fisherman from the road, and walking through luxuriant meadows, I discovered that whatever had been was no more. There is a house, sitting daintily by the water, a small boat nosing against its front step. There is a bridge above the point where the canals join and then saunter out in three directions. But nothing else.

There were no people, but across the water, under a signpost (a strange sight on a canal, where you could hardly get lost, could you?) pointing importantly three ways to Oxford, London and Birmingham, was a large, stately hare. He sat unconcernedly in the open, inspecting a front paw. He may have seen me, but he knew he was safely across the water. We were there, the hare and I, at almost the centre of an England that has become increasingly grown with industry and its pollution, and there was no-one else. Just the two of us. The sun came out and warmed the fields, the canal contrived a dun little sparkle, and there were no

The bridge beside The Folly just north of Napton Lock.

sounds but the water, the birds and the insects. Eventually the hare finished whatever he was about and ambled away in the general direction of Northamptonshire. I walked back along the towpath to the road knowing that it had all been worthwhile.

TWO

Winter On The Cape

In some strange and contrary way I love the hollow days of early January. All the noises of the Christmas and New Year season are silenced. The air is sharp to the sniff, skies are flat and cold and black winter trees rattle against the wind.

I drove from London on the fourth day of the year, taking the wet road west: Surrey, Hampshire, Dorset, Somerset. Night came down, hardly giving the afternoon time to leave. I stopped at an inn on the Devon frontier, comfortable but decently subdued after the celebrations of the season. There was a fire and a paunchy dog lay in front of it. He looked as if he would never get up again. During the whole of the evening only a handful of customers arrived. The landlord and I talked about cricket, always a delight in January.

By noon the following day I was driving through the swirling Dartmoor rain. The entire population seemed to be indoors, as if it had recently heard some bad news. Afternoon lights were shining, but neglected, in towns and glimmering in cottages. I drove with the certainty that at the end of the journey I would surely find what I sought – a deserted Cornwall.

My destination was the extremity: Cape Cornwall and St Just, the last town in England. I wanted to experience it bereft of summer tourists, when it was at home by itself, as it were, hidden and again enclosed as it was many years ago.

Cornwall is very surprising and, as I drove down the final stretch of road to Penzance on that winter day, the rain and the mists were left behind clothing the moors, the sky cleared miraculously and I arrived at Mount's Bay on what could only be described as a perfect spring evening. Fading light over blue water, cormorants diving in the empty sea, the last of the sun on the shingle and children running and calling on the beach.

That night the western wind barged about the town like a drunkard, rattling at my window and whooping through the empty channels of the streets. But morning came with a great grin of sunshine and from my bed I could hear that free, salty sound of seagulls crying over the bay, a sound that can almost be smelled. I went to the window and lifted the sash and there it was again, like a vision, the wide, unruffled sea, the lambent sky, the unseasonal sun and the birds like paper in the breeze. It was January the sixth.

Before breakfast I took a walk along the shuttered promenade. It seemed a pity that all the people were away when the weather was so balmy. Or perhaps not. I've been in Penzance in

August when hundreds crowded into Woolworth's, refugees from rain. Now, here I was, in the first week of January walking with a topcoat, watching *The Scillonian* being unhurriedly – well, casually – prepared for her next crossing to St Mary's in the Isles of Scilly, squinting at the squalling seabirds, noting the quiet embroidery of the waves on the uninhabited beach, and looking out to where St Michael's Mount stood like a cardboard cut-out of Camelot next to the sky. It was so pleasant and summery I would have quite liked an ice-cream cone.

Watching the loading of *The Scillonian* at the quay I thought of friends of mine, Danny and Wendy Hick, who lived out there across the sea on their rocky little Scilly island called The Gugh, with their children, their dogs and cats and Cuckoo, their donkey, which had a deep but hopeless passion for that self-same vessel. *The Scillonian* would sail from the quay at Hugh Town on St Mary's in the Scillies, and head for the open sea and her home berth at Penzance. She would hoot her hooter, and Cuckoo, standing like a solitary god on the promontory of The Gugh, would bray back in the most heart-touching way, the only recorded love affair between a donkey and a steamship.

Few things are so satisfying as watching men load a small vessel. I sat on an iron bollard, the sun comfortable on my wintery face, and fell to talking with Peter Jenkin, a man who could come from nowhere else but Cornwall. He was short and bearded, a story-teller and a publican. What man could ask for more?

"Ah," he said nodding at the ship. "I remember the old *Scillonian*, the one before. Flat-bottomed, she was, and my God did she let you know it on a rough day out beyond the Wolf Rock. When I was a little kid, about five I suppose, I would be brought down here and put on board with a label tied around my neck. It said: 'Please deliver to St Agnes.' The captain

The Scillonian *preparing to depart for the Scilly Isles.*

always saw that I got ashore at St Mary's and then the local boat would take me across to my aunt on Agnes. I've had some rough crossings on the old tub, believe me, but I always managed to get there. Mind you, with that label around my neck, I always felt like some sort of walking parcel."

In these quiet places, through the winters when the summer visitors are away and cosseted in their towns, the art of the story-teller is respected and well-preserved. Jimmy-the-Night, the porter at my hotel, related to me how the countryside had been excited and impressed by a real Hollywood film unit working on location scenes there. Jimmy became quite an important man because, at night, it was his responsibility to get telephone connections to all parts of the world for the famous film people. Hollywood, Hong Kong, Hawaii were almost routine, and there were even more difficult and exotic places. He had enjoyed the prestige of asking the overseas operator – who remained annoyingly unimpressed – for these calls and one night he almost hugged himself when he was asked to get a number at Chiang Mai in Thailand. He recited the exchange and number, in an off-hand Cornish way, to the overseas operator who disconcerted him by immediately replying, in an equally casual fashion, "Now you just hang on a minute, m'dear, and I'll connect you."

The operator was apparently not only familiar with Chiang Mai, which he pronounced with considerable satisfaction, but he also knew the name of its province. Coolly he enquired of Jimmy, "Now, which number might you be speaking from?"

"Penzance 98765," muttered the disconsolate Jimmy.

"*Where?*" asked the man who knew perfectly well.

"PENZANCE!"

"Will you spell it?" sniffed the operator.

"My God!" howled Jimmy. "You know – Penzance! Penzance! Like . . . like *The Pirates of Penzance.*"

Came the reply, "Ah now, come on, I don't have time to read the sports pages. Spell it."

"That," said Jimmy as he told the story, "is why it's called Unknown Cornwall."

*   *   *

Mid-morning was adorned with sunshine. I left and took the road across the toe of Cornwall to St Just, the final town in England. Looking back, I could see Penzance arranged rather solemnly around the bay with St Michael's Mount humped like a preacher holding forth to an attentive congregation.

There was a rich, briny smell about the air reinforced, almost immediately I smelled it, by the curling aroma of a pig farm. The road hugged a stream, it hunched its shoulders and became a lane; banks rose on either side, walled and creepered. There were snowdrops under the trees and soon there would be primroses. Noon had the balm of spring.

These western walls were no haphazard matter. The granite was shaped and fitted with finesse, large boulders and interlocked stones, intended to last at least as long as Cornish things tend to last. Cottages were made in the same burly way, their doors and windows confidently looking towards the Atlantic; and churches too, gnarled ocean churches with winds frequenting their belfries. The January sun was benevolent enough to encourage dogs

Right, from Cape Cornwall looking towards Land's End shrouded in mist.

Left, St Michael's Mount seen from just west of Marazion and looking across Mount's Bay.

to sleep on walls and cats to sprawl on window ledges. Indeed, every wall seemed to have its dozing dog, as if today were some sort of canine holiday. Doors were open to the air and wives hung decent washing in direct competition with the stainless sky. Milk churns sat on little wooden stages like chessmen on a board, and seagulls stood on the milk churns. It was a truly beautiful day.

But all the cosiness, the intimacy of the place, vanished in a moment. For, on reaching the crest of a subdued hill, I was all at once confronted with the wide and utter magnificence of the untrammelled sea. It was spread gloriously around Cornwall, shining like new, incredibly and unjanuarably blue. The salt breeze came directly from it, getting into the eyes and the nose, enough to make your hair curl. The Longships lighthouse stood up straight, miles out. Ships crept like mice along the skyline.

I stood taking it all in, entranced for ten minutes or more, the breeze giving me an occasional jocular push. Thus engaged, I attracted the curiosity of a lady from a neighbouring house. She left her washing and came down her garden to join me in my gaze.

"What's the matter then?" she enquired eventually. "What's out there?"

It's asking too much, I suppose, to expect anyone to be entranced by something they see every day, especially when they're elbow-deep in soapsuds.

"It's the sea," I replied lamely. "I was looking at the sea."

"Oh," she said having a glance due west. "The sea, is it?" She smiled indulgently and went back to her laundering.

The encounter had embarrassed me somewhat; in former days down here they used to take people away for having conversations with mermaids and clouds. Perhaps they still did? Returning to the car, I headed it towards St Just.

Yellow gorse, so vivid it seemed luminous, covered the rising, curving land on one side of the road, while the other flank tumbled down to the great thrown-about rocks of the shore. I had read that traces of an Iron Age fortress called Chun Castle were to be found among the gorsey boulders on a hill thereabouts. From where I stood one hill looked much like another, so I stopped and asked an AA man who was sitting on his motor cycle watching two children conversing with a donkey in a roadside paddock.

"Ah, yes, now," he said, so slowly that each word came out like a separate sentence. "I reckon you'll find that 'un up there." He pointed decisively, then looked at me closely, the puzzlement that comes with the familiarity of a place spread on his face. "It's a climb," he said. "Further than it looks." Another pause. Then, "And there's nothing much up there to see when you gets there. Only stones." He returned to considering the donkey and the children. "Now that's a pretty sight," he said as though trying to get my interests in perspective.

After that I felt it would be almost rude to climb the hill despite his warning. In any event, it was nearing lunch-time and, the truth is, I would never make the grade as a real explorer. There would always need to be an inn on the horizon at twelve-thirty or thereabouts.

There was a granite pub within half a mile and there I had a miner's lunch, identical to a ploughman's lunch – bread and cheese and onion – except that it's served on a tin plate. The bar was hung with old lamps from the tin mines, miners' helmets and the tools of their troglodyte trade.

Down there, in the narrow land of western Cornwall, are the last ruins of the old mines; extraordinary skeletons, hollow engine houses, tottering chimneys of red brick, still erect above the rocks and the churning ocean. How they have remained standing although neglected all these years in the whistling south-westerly gales, is a tribute to the craftsmen who built them, not that they care now. The ancient burial mounds, the old formations of rocks, and the raddled mine buildings make up widely-spaced chapters in the stony history of Cornwall.

Some of the mines, or bals as they called them, reached like fingers far below the sea. Even today, in places, the ever-moving currents are stained red with seeping minerals. Naturally a

Left, Plan-an-Guare, known locally as The Plane, in St Just. Right, sunset from Cape Cornwall.

whole catalogue of disasters is still well remembered, together with the old, dreadful legends, the superstitions and the underground ghosts. Snails, rabbits and hobgoblins – called buccas and knackers – were objects of fear engendered in the distant darkness of the tunnels.

But it is the persistent story of the exiled Jews that pervades Cornwall and especially the tin-mining villages. Jew Street, Market Jew Street turn up in several towns; the smelting houses in the mines themselves were called Jews' Houses and there was an ore brought from the subterranean bogs called Jews' tin. The story is that the men of Jerusalem who engineered the Crucifixion were banished by the Romans to work in the Cornish mines and their anguished 'sperrats' still incant in the depths and the darkness. The name of the village of Marazion is said to derive from 'the bitterness of Zion'.

The Botallack Crown mines. The shafts go under the sea, and it is possible to hear the rocks rolling on the sea bed above.

Whatever the privations of the miners, however, there is no denying that, once released from their underground darkness, many of them surfaced to some of the most spectacular vistas in Britain, some small compensation for a hard, short and dangerous life.

Standing in the empty, eerie engine house of the old Botallack mine, the view through the holes and yawning windows was of the grandest rocks and the most regal ocean, bright blue, curling green, churning white. I wonder did the miners envy the sailors, or perhaps the sailors envy the miners?

On their infrequent holidays, which it seemed they gained only because they insisted that on certain religious days the mines were occupied by ghosts (a nice device not since used in trade unionism), the miners gathered in St Just for drinking and wrestling on the circus ring of grass, ancient in origin, called Plan-an-Guare, or locally, The Plane. Searching for it in the

A Cornish milestone near Land's End.

confined centre of the little town, I asked at a butcher's shop and was told to "look behind the Co-op". Sure enough, adjacent to the butter and fats department there it was, an amphitheatre of grass with some of the timeless granite blocks remaining, projecting like old molars. As if they did not have enough to work during the rest of their lives, the tin miners also had drilling contests on holidays in the granite blocks around The Plane. The holes they drilled are still there. Apart from this and the Cornish wrestling matches, Wesley used it for services during his West Country pilgrimage (a brilliantly successful venture judging by the size and frequency of churches he left in his wake). Today the children of St Just use the prehistoric area as a convenient playground. There is one of those stern notices warning that it is scheduled as an ancient monument and threatening considerable consequences to anyone who defaces it, but this patently carries little weight since there is a large and ragged hole in the notice-board itself.

The last street in England is called Cape Cornwall Street and runs prosaically from the shops of St Just down to the pounding sea. It has, rightly, a row of council houses and, even more rightly, a fish and chip shop which, bless its heart, does *not* proclaim itself as the first and last establishment of its nature in the kingdom. St Just tends to leave boasts of that nature to the commercial denizens of Land's End.

In an English summer, doubtless, St Just is as thick and as thronged with holidaymakers as the remainder of West Cornwall – and glad of it – but this was empty January and there was a mild charm about the prim place as it went about its unhurried business.

There is time for courtesy, too. As I was driving away, I enquired directions from an elderly fellow, bent and bearded, who was standing on the kerb, apparently about to launch himself across the town square to the pub opposite. He gave me intricate directions, so intricate that, within moments of setting off, I found myself in a front line of small, deep-set lanes which eventually led me back to the square again. My informant was still tottering across, an inch at a time. Embarrassed, I stopped and enquired again. Making no sign that he had ever seen me before in his long life, he provided the same detailed directions and off I went once more. Again I found myself in the maze of high-banked lanes, and once more back in the square. The old man had now reached the far pavement and the pub was in his sights. He turned and saw me. Without any change of expression (although this might have been difficult to detect through his full beard), he revolved and tottered towards the car. Once more he gave the directions. I explained that when I followed them I reached a signpost and, taking its information as gospel, ended up back where I had begun. Through his stormy whiskers a

The road to Cape Cornwall. Old cottages are sandwiched between the more modern coastguard cottages.

mouth appeared, agape in a soundless laugh. His eyes gleamed from his creased, red face. "Ah now, that signpost," he giggled. "You don' wan take no heed o' that. The little buccas is always turnin' that the wrong way!"

The interesting thing about the observation, apart from his courtesy, was that I *thought* he had used a well-worn swear-word, meaning that children had turned the post around. It is only now that I have come to write my notes that I realise he was using the old mining word – *buccas* – the spirits from the depths.

Eventually I turned in the somnolent square and went back down Cape Cornwall Street. Sun splashed across the faces of the houses and I thought how marvellous it must be to live in that street, with the Atlantic down at the end, the shops at the other and the winds and breezes coming straight up the pavements. On those pavements children played, even though there were rocks and beaches only running distance away. They might as well have been in Manchester. Still, children and dogs always prefer pavements.

The street plunged into the funnel of a twisting, narrow lane. The houses were left astern and were replaced by sturdy stone banks topped with mops of vivid yellow gorse. A final bend and there were the hefty shoulders of Cape Cornwall, the sea like ermine around them. The earliest sun of the year lay deliciously over the fineness of the waves, white birds curled and called, the breeze flew around me as if I were a lighthouse. My head reeled.

I could see a real lighthouse – the Longships – standing like the admonishing finger of a drowning man; further out was the Wolf Rock Light and beyond that, lying low like a raiding fleet on the horizon, were the pencilled outlines of the Isles of Scilly. Between the islands and where I stood, of course, is the drowned and legendary land of Lyonesse which, with its knights (who may have had no time to get out of their armour), its ladies, its chivalry and its castles, has been sunk forever since the time of King Arthur.

Now, long, long after, it remains a romantic place, unrefined and thrilling and made only slightly the less so by the exhortation 'Up Plymouth Argyle', daubed on one of its more accessible promontories.

This, of course, was the wreckers' coast. It had to be a Cornish parson who, announcing to his congregation that a helpless and laden ship was drifting ashore, instructed none to leave his

Pendeen lighthouse.

The mermaid of Zennor carving in the fifteenth century church of St Senara.

pew until he, the parson himself, was at the church door and rid of his cassock. "So we might all start even."

The inhabitants of the towns and villages traditionally regarded any distressed vessel driven to them as having been sent by God to provide their needs in much the same way as He provoked cabbages to grow in their gardens. In 1837, the judge at the Cornwall Quarter Sessions, in sentencing two young wreckers from St Just, said, "I am sorry that in your neighbourhood this has not been sufficiently regarded as an offence of the blackest dye. This infamous system of plundering from the unfortunate has been too long a stain on our County . . ."

I found that the sea passages off Cape Cornwall were watched from the coastguard station, perched like a precarious hen-house on a ledge above an inlet, where the fiercest rocks shred the incoming sea. Higher up the land was a row of coastguard cottages with a brave Union Jack, stiff as tin, standing out from a flagmast.

The climb up a steep, stair-like path to the coastguard station had to be taken unhurriedly. Despite the breeze the sun made me hot and I was glad when I reached the top. The young coastguard, a friendly man, apparently glad of some company, told me he had once lived in London but he preferred it here looking out on the sea. It was not difficult to see why. "On a real stormy day it's wonderful," he said quietly. "Non-stop foam all the way from here to Land's End, a fine sight, believe me. It's like an artillery bombardment. And then there are very calm days with all the colours in the sea, and nights when there's so many ships out there that their lights look like Brighton promenade."

His eyrie was full of charts and maps, emergency telephone numbers on a list on the wall, a compass and a pair of bulky binoculars. I was permitted to look through these and I moved them slowly along the seam of the horizon. Obedient ships were plodding north and south, the Scillies were firmer but still remote, twelve miles away the Wolf Rock Light stood up with uncompromising clarity, a small freighter voyaged behind the Longships Light and its attendant rocks. These rocks form a long, spiky tail and, with the lighthouse rising at one end, it looks like a mermaid sitting up combing her hair, as mermaids are wont to do.

I returned up the headland, mounted some rocks and then gained the cliff path where, to my astonishment, I met a sedate Chinaman walking daintily and sniffing the air. I wished him good-day (in English) and he gave a nice Oriental nod and passed on his way. What he was doing there I have no notion; I suppose I could have asked him. Perhaps he was making some foolhardy attempt to walk home.

At the top of the peninsula I was back among the gorse and the riven lanes again. On the walls the westerly dogs were still asleep. What a life.

Travelling on to Pendeen I stopped at one of those Cornish milestones, carved and corniced, beautiful and careful, little black hands pointing out the directions. This one had a finger pointed at St Just and another pointing the other way to Morvah, with the date 1886 beneath. Those were the days when people had time to carve out milestones. I could not help feeling that a man would not mind having a headstone on his grave like that. Very tasteful.

Pendeen lighthouse, like all its brothers along the coasts, is spruce and white with the two trumpets of its foghorn projecting from the top. They looked like the gramophone horns in the old-fashioned advertisements for His Master's Voice. The one with the dog. At Zennor there is a delectable fifteenth century church with a pert mermaid carved on the side of a tiny pew, enclosed and with accommodation for only one person. The mermaid has her traditional comb and looking-glass in her hand. She wears her fish tail with chic but is otherwise uncovered. She also has long tresses and a neat belly-button. She makes a nice change from angels.

The sea is present everywhere around here. The church door is stained with salt and the roof is wooden and rounded like the hull of a boat up-turned, with the ribs showing. Outside the church is a tombstone commemorating John Davie of Boswednack, who died in 1891, the last man to possess any wide knowledge of the ancient Cornish language. Beneath his name, in

Above, the prehistoric chamber tomb at Zennor Quoit.

Cornish, is a couplet from the Book of Proverbs.

Another tombstone relates: 'Here lies the mortal part of John Quick, of Wicka, Yeoman. He was hospitable, sociable, peaceable, humble, homely, honest and devout. In manners he excelled his equals, in piety he was their example. He met his death with composure, September 12th, 1784.' Few can have left this earth with better references. His wife Wilmot 'of spotless and virtuous character', is buried in the same grave. She predeceased him by twenty-two years, but they waited until he joined her before they made the headstone. So much for equality.

There are landed sailors and resting tin-miners lying side by side in the cossetted church-yard, near the sea and the seams where they worked. A timeless sundial looks down on them, made by Paul Quick in 1737. Sundials are a feature of Cornish churches. The one at St Wenn even has a small, eternal joke: it is inscribed 'Ye Know Not When.'

I left the little square-towered church and climbed to Zennor Quoit, a prehistoric chamber tomb on the hill overlooking the village. It was vandalised by farmers, centuries ago, and, as the AA man said of Chun, there's not a lot to see when you get there. Not of the tomb that is. But straighten up and look out across the glory of Cornwall, as I did that January afternoon. Rocks – no, boulders – like great, smooth buns lay all around and tumbling down the hillside incandescent with gorse. The tower of Zennor church looked up with curiosity from its valley.

A man, a roadmender with a shovel, walked steadily along the curved road far below, going towards the retreating day. He was in no hurry.

There was no skyline now. Darkness advanced with every roller from the sea. The distant lighthouses began to light up. From high on that hill at Zennor I could hear the headlong sound of the ocean. The sound of Cornwall.

Right, looking down from Zennor Quoit on the village and showing the Celtic field pattern so common in this area.

THREE

In Wildest Kent

Coming in from the estuary, the heron circled over the elms like a long-necked airliner. I could see the eel wriggling in its beak. It reached the high encampment of nests and dropped to its own, its wings folding with a mechanical awkwardness. The young were squealing for the food before the big bird had time to settle.

All above me in those trees were herons. They sat, grey as Presbyterian clergymen, or took off to the river and the wide-watered marshes. Their take-off, uncertain to the point of panic, gave the impression that they thought it might be their last. But once in flight they were sure and beautiful. There were more than three hundred in the wood, their raucous voices the only sounds for miles. That warm day I had walked for four hours without seeing another person.

This was the ancient Hundred of Hoo, the misty miles where foxes sit and watch, with apparent interest, the progress of liners and supertankers down the broad back of the seaway. Central London is forty miles distant.

I looked at a map of the Home Counties and saw that the northern edge of Kent, the Thames coastline, was scarcely touched by the red web of roads that pattern every other part. From Gravesend to Allhallows – sixteen miles – there was a path along the sea wall, roads reached up from Chatham and Rochester to the villages, and spindly paths pushed on a little further into the flatlands bordering the river, but that was all. It had always been a mysterious place, a coastland of creeks, fleets and inlets, secret bays and the odd brooding house deep in the marshes.

Coming to Hoo from the south, I began to prepare myself for disappointment. The everyday, flat-faced houses of the Medway towns straggled along the road, the fat transporters heading for the oil refinery at the Isle of Grain bellowed along the same roads. Then, at Allhallows, there were caravans and wooden holiday chalets and vendors selling hamburgers with tomato ketchup.

But there the sea wall begins and I took it, walking west with the Thames on my right, below me a haphazard broken beach of sand and shingle. Even the caravans at Allhallows took on a different aspect as I walked, the smoke of their chimneys fingering above the low trees. Now I was at once in vacant country. It lay low, wild, green-grey, flat ahead of me, shaggy with reeds and curly with waterways, rising slightly inland in more ordered fashion, sketched

Cooling Castle.

with fields and embossed with summer spinneys.

Then, to my right, to the seaward, the wide arm of the Thames reaching out towards the North Sea and across on its far bank to the hills and buildings of Essex. Large, thoughtful ships prowled through the water, their noses either sniffing the first salt of the open ocean or getting welcome land smells after a long voyage. A tanker, a mile long, went quietly east, a lisp of smoke at its yellow funnel, a cravat of lace foam at its business-like bow. A merchantman pushed thankfully towards port like a man going home from work and glad of it.

Beyond the ships, on the other coast, were the squatting oil tanks of the Essex refineries, silvery on this fine day, and ahead I could see a tall stack, an orange flame burning at its taper end, bright even against the sunny sky. Across there, more to the east, was Southend too, its pier staggering way out into the muddy estuary.

But on my side of the river I was already alone. Walking a few hundred yards along the sea wall and then onto the beaches and small, muddy juts of land, I went with every step further away from the world of caravans and hamburgers.

The history of this place is full of sneaks, pirates and other raiders, French and Spanish particularly, and before them, of course, the Danes who missed nothing, getting a whiff of plunder even across these unpromising marshes. It was an area not easily defended, although there was always a hope that the attackers might get stuck in Thames mud or drowned in unexpected creeks and inlets. If they stayed long enough, which they rarely did, then they might be conquered by marsh fever or any of the other numerous damp ailments that have afflicted the inhabitants over centuries. Cooling Castle, now decorated with lawns and hung with willow trees, was built as a garrison for the broad peninsula of Hoo, and General Gordon, later to find greater and wider horizons in China and the Sudan, built a series of little forts along the coast. But it was difficult to keep anyone out. A villager from High Halstow, out after a rabbit for the pot, might easily come upon a camp of furtive foreigners in one of the bends of Yantlet Creek.

Gordon's forts were followed in the 1940s by square-eyed, concrete pill-boxes waiting for the Germans who never came. One of these I found along the coast looking as though it had been shipwrecked. Solid though it was, the action of tide and sand and mud had lifted it over the years and thrown it at a steep angle, like the hull of a vessel driven upon the shore.

Now, in this place, I felt very isolated. Quiet sounds issued from all around me. The water gently elbowed the shore as though it were telling improper tales, the deep grasses and reeds hid piping birds, and the gentlest of sea winds moved across the marsh. A pair of oyster-catchers, the first I had seen since making a journey to Fair Isle the previous summer, dived low across the estuary sounding their panic-stricken warnings.

The first of the small leads and inlets cuts into the land here, a slippery little channel lined first with sand and shingle and then, abruptly, mud and moss and heavy weeds. The triangles of beach breaking occasionally into long, slim stretches, were surfaced with seashells, bright and small, lying about like buttons. Here, too, is the most fantastic collection of jetsam I have seen in a long experience of journeying around deserted coasts. In most places the tide takes away whatever it deposits, but there, in this land-trapped seaway, the rubbish of the sea is thrown up usually for good. In a hundred yards you can find enough wood to stock a timber yard, posts and spars and planks and boxes, encrusted with weed and salt, lengths of rope and strange, accidental iron sculptures. It was everywhere above the tide-line.

One crate announced that it contained the produce of Israel and another had held some commodity described in curly Arabic writing. And here they were, marooned together on an English beach. I found a length of knotted rope, so thick with seashells that it looked like a necklace of some huge mermaid. No-one would claim that it was a beautiful place, the grey-green marsh, lying low, the debris-strewn beach, the mud and the moss and the sand intermingled. But it was isolated, lonely, hidden. And that was what I was seeking.

Looking west across St Mary's Bay.

Looking upstream to where the diminishing Thames threaded itself through a small hole in the horizon, I took perverse comfort in the knowledge that only a few miles that way dusty people were jostling in London's Oxford Street, adding up piles of figures behind city windows or descending into a hole called the Piccadilly Line. Here there was only warmth, quietness and a salty whiff from the direction of The Nore.

I arrived at a longer beach between St Mary's Bay and Egypt Bay, and here the driftwood was piled so spectacularly that it might have been a barricade set up against imminent invasion. It was noon and the sun was lofty and hot. Alone on the beach I stretched myself out, my head on a cork-filled canvas fender with the indecipherable name of some vessel on it, and my feet resting royally on a crate which at one time had been dispatched by Señor Pascal Hermanos of Valencia and had contained *Produce de España*. I felt content and isolated, but I must have looked, from a distance, like some exhausted Crusoe because my sunny doze was broken by a shout of "Are you all right there?" from the direction of the sea.

Shuffling up onto my elbow, I saw a sailing dinghy just off-shore with two men gazing apprehensively towards me. "Are you all right?" one of them called again.

"Fine," I replied, "Just resting."

They seemed astounded that anyone should be sleeping in the sun on that deserted strand and among all that driftwood. I suppose from the sea I must have looked like a solitary, shipwrecked mariner. They sailed away with two puzzled waves and I settled back, letting the sun cover my face and pushing my fingers through the warm and brittle sand.

I must have looked odd, so alone and comfortable on that narrow beach, with skylarks

Looking upstream across the Cooling marshes towards Tilbury. Part of Decoy Farm is in the right middle distance.

hovering ecstatically above the bushy grass on my right hand; on my left, great silent ships were moving through the water and beyond them the oil tanks of Essex, piled like white drums.

Those delirious skylarks refused to let me drop into anything deeper than a doze. They rose and whistled from the grass and the reeded inlets. From my place on the beach I watched them soar and sing against the polished summer sky. Making a lazy half turn, I saw that a big tanker was abreast of me now. I wondered if the captain could see me lazing there from his bridge. It had twin red funnels, perched behind, like two liveried coachmen. Through the heat haze that curtained the more distant sea, I saw the bulwarks of a heavy merchant vessel coming into shape.

I got up and clambered over the driftwood, then through the loose sand to a concrete groyne and from there onto a single track wriggling along Egypt Bay. At Decoy Creek, a two-armed inlet, sidling in from the sea, a pair of swans cruised as mutely and gracefully as the big ships on the other side. Before me now the marsh spread, grey, dark green, light green, laced with ditches and secret streams. It looked impenetrable, but beyond it the land rose firmly and kindly, plumed with thick trees and modestly distributed with sheep and cattle.

The odd thing about this place was the absence of gulls. Never had I known a shore so free of their angular calling or the beating of their wings. Only the diminutive storm-petrel was apparent, skimming between the marsh and the open estuary. He was named petrel after St Peter, because he flies so low he sometimes seems to walk upon the water. A satisfied family of ducklings bobbed on the gentle waves, a dozen or more strung out in a line with the elder

Halstow marshes, Decoy Farm, viewed from near St Mary's Bay and looking across Egypt Bay.

ducks outriding on each flank. Across in the Decoy fleet another flotilla moved along on easier waters, their mother nagging them around the stern of one of the swans.

Before me, on the marsh itself, was a strange settlement of square buildings, white in the sun like some Mexican adobe village. It was not marked on the map and I went down across the sinky grass, by an untrustworthy path between the reeds, to investigate. Someone, for motives best known to themselves, had put a barbed wire fence across the land at this point. It went over the hump of the embankment and dipped uncompromisingly into the sea, seeking perhaps to corral both sheep and fish. Tufts of wool decorated it to the landward, the bladder-wrack and seaweed hung from its spikes at the water's edge.

Walking cautiously inland towards the Mexican village, I sent a flight of magpies chattering from almost beneath my feet, and then a brace of partridge took off with their sudden aero-engine whirr. Almost immediately I saw a fox, sitting like a householder in the sun on the doorstep of one of the buildings. I stopped, poised on the edge of a pool that blinked up through the rushes. I hoped he would not see me. He had. But he was in no special hurry.

He looked both well-fed and unafraid, his tail full, his coat a fine chestnut. He turned up his nose in a disdainful sniff and then quietly loped away into the midday marshes. Jumping awkwardly and muddily through the hidden pools, I went forward to get another sight of him, but he was gone.

The little buildings were of heavy concrete and they had great iron doors. One I opened with difficulty, and as it strained against its rust I saw a printed notice inside that instructed me to extinguish 'All lucifers and other lights' by order of A. Cooper Key, Her Majesty's Inspector of Explosives, dated 'this 14th Day of September, 1900.' My romantic adobe village had been an ammunition store.

Birds found the oblong buildings to be convenient homes, and dozens flew off through holes in the roof as I went into the first one. There was nothing inside except rotting wood and cossetted wild flowers pushing their way up the concrete walls. But no explosives.

Herons in flight.

Out there on that isolated shore was the ideal place, of course, to keep such things. It's a pity they didn't use the last few sticks of gunpowder to blow up the storehouses when they moved. Still, Mr A. Cooper Key might have been pleased to know that his wise regulations of 'this 14th Day of September, 1900' would still be preserved in that solitary place today. A sort of memorial.

Going back towards the Decoy fleet I was in time to see one of the swans returning from a flight. It came head-on towards me, braking in mid-air, neck craned, wings unsurely poised, flat feet stuck out tentatively as though afraid the water might be chilly.

Inland from Egypt Bay an uncertain path pushed its way between a deep marsh drain and flat saltings spreading away to the sea wall. The saltings were a pattern of pools and puddles, reflecting the bright sky and the reeds and stunted bushes which peered into them. A child's doll lay among the green like Moses in the rushes. Larks soared and sang deliriously and the petrels came in low from the Thames. I was still very much alone. I had not seen another soul in four hours. Then looking out into the estuary towards a piled container ship, a moving Manhattan, I saw my first heron cruising poetically from sea to land, low and languorous, making for the wood I could now see on the hill by High Halstow. It circled with a stalling slowness which seemed so deliberate that it was difficult to see how it could remain airborne. But it knew what it was doing. It changed course again and lazily its flight path dropped towards the heronry.

I followed the path for a mile inland, until the ground on either side became firm and farmed. A man with a red tractor was working in a distant field, the colour of his machine a vivid spot, like a ladybird, in the monochrome landscape.

The path curled about a ruff of trees bordering a house with a yard and a solid barn. The house had white windows staring out over the marsh and the grey tongue of the estuary. There was a chimney at each end of the house and I could hear a dog barking. I felt like a traveller coming out of a desert. The house had the earthy name of 'Swigshole' and Roger Boston, the warden of the nature reserve in the Norrards Wood, where I had seen the heron heading, lived there with his wife Gabrielle and daughter Kate.

"I come from the north," said Mrs Boston from her kitchen window. "I'm used to hills. I find it very strange living in a marsh like this. I don't suppose I see more than three or four people a week here. It's very isolated, just marsh and water. But looking out of the window at night is strange because you look over the darkness on this side and out to the oil tanks and the refineries on the other bank of the Thames – and they're all lit up. Millions of lights over there, blazing away like Blackpool. I don't know whether it's a comfort to us all alone here or whether it's an annoyance."

Every morning a taxi, paid for by the education authority, bumped down the lane to take Kate to school. But neither of the Bostons could drive and the groceries had to be manhandled through the deep and slippery wood. Roger Boston, a tall, bearded man who spent nights in the wood recording the song of the nightingale, shrugged it off as one of the disadvantages of his profession. They arrived at the house early in the year, just before the first herons and the first snow. The heronry is the largest in Britain, one hundred and fifty pairs making their homes at the summit of ancient elms in the very fastness of the Norrards Wood. Their ancestors have been nesting there since the Middle Ages.

Roger admired herons. "You should see them in the snow," he said. "God, they're fantastic. We had a good fall in the winter and the snow filled up the wood, and the herons were flying in and out. They'd arrived a bit early. Misjudged the weather. Beautiful, that's all you can say about them, beautiful."

The strange thing is he was once an actor, playing one of the leading parts in *Lock Up Your Daughters*, a great success at London's Mermaid Theatre. He confessed still to thinking about his days on the stage while he walked his lonely woods, or waited, crouching and alone at night to record the song of the nightingale.

"I don't honestly know why I quit the theatre," he ruminated. "I was doing very well, I suppose. And sometimes I miss it. But this has its compensations and its own excitements. I've always felt very close to this sort of thing, how everything depends for its life on something else. It's wonderful to see."

To me the woods, arching above us, filtering the sky and the sun, looked full of silence. The only movement I could catch, apart from the passage of the herons, was a small, brilliant butterfly busy among the ferns. But for Roger it was teeming with life. Carefully he turned back a curtain of ferns and set near the ground was a nest full of blindly hungry young birds.

"Blackcap warbler," he said quietly. He extended his index finger and pointed it towards the crouching family. Immediately every mouth was opened wide, like a quartet of contraltos going for a high note. He pulled his finger away and the beaks closed. Then he pushed it towards them again and they extended wide once more.

"They think it's their mum come back with the shopping," he laughed. "Nobody knows they're there but me, and now you. They're pretty rare, you know, so I keep quiet about them. That's half the thrill, finding something rare. There's been a golden oriel in these woods and that's next door to a miracle. He's got a song like an errand boy whistling. There's been an avocet on the marshes and a black-tailed godwit. But I'm interested in everything, in the balance of Nature, how everything depends on everything else to live."

There was a commotion above us in the branches. A wood pigeon took off with a confusion which suggested it had fallen out of the tree. We both laughed.

We walked through the thickening Norrards, a wood unchanged since it was named – the Northwards Wood – in the Middle Ages by the villagers of High Halstow. Roger knew every step of the way through what seemed to me to be the nearest thing to the Malay jungle to be found in England. We reached a break in the trees and three herons passed above us, one behind the other, a line of flapping washing. He said that he had discovered a rare slowworm; that he thought foxes were blamed for too many crimes; and that he missed the theatre so much that he couldn't even trust himself to go and see a play because he feared that he would want to go back to the stage and leave the woods. "I'm an individual," he said. "So much so that I occasionally get into trouble with Authority. You'd be surprised how much Authority has to do with the most remote places. I had another job, in the north, at a nature reserve and I almost got the sack in a terrible row over a sand lizard." He was serious.

Back at 'Swigshole' again, out of the deep blanket of the wood, the sun was full onto the house, and lit across the home field and then the marshes, to the silvery blue channel and its creeping ships.

Gabrielle had his lunch ready. "Other wives," she mused, "have their husbands coming

home talking about what happened at the office or the factory. Mine comes running like a small boy up the lane, absolutely jubilant, and when I go out to see what's happened, he'll shout, 'Guess what? I've just seen a *lobeluaquadrimetrica!*' Believe it or not, that's a rare sort of dragonfly.''

* * *

When the clouds travel across the Hundred of Hoo, like all marshland places it becomes introverted, sulky, mysterious. Strange things have happened there. Binney Farm squats broodingly on the crest of a formation of fields rising from the marshes. Even from a distance it looked a haunted place, low buildings, the long horizon brushed by the estuary wind and one shattered tree stump standing like a single, rotten tooth.

Feeling like some Hitchcock character, I walked towards it across the long, rising meads. Briefly the sun brushed the walls of the farmhouse but did nothing to dispel the sense of disquiet. Here, they say, long ago, some sailors came up from Yantlet Creek and murdered a woman, who still wails, weeps and wanders accusingly about the marshlands.

Some sheep and cattle were grazing on the upland grass but I was the only person on that landscape. It seemed miles, the farm buildings crouching against the sky, that shattered tree stump, the wind whimpering through the barns and buildings. When I reached the place I found it was deserted. The old house had been demolished, not too long before either, for the foundations looked newly exposed. It seemed quite ridiculous feeling so solitary and edgy in Kent, at midsummer, at midday, in the wide, open air. But it was an oddly spooky place. A sly

Left, view of the heronry at Norrards Wood.

Right, the shepherd, Rodney Moore, shows the oven door at Decoy Farm where a farmer's wife is said to have met a "nasty end".

rustle behind me and I spun around ready to confront the terrible apparition of that murdered lady. But all that came around the corner was a plastic bag being nosed along by the wind. Hurriedly I went down again across the fields and did not stop until I was in the bar of the pub in High Halstow.

At Decoy Farm, a cosier place, the farmhouse had also been demolished to be replaced by a new house, but they had cheerfully preserved the big, iron bread oven where yet another unfortunate farmer's wife is said to have met a nasty end.

It stood large, rusted and appropriately vault-like, with the rest of the farmhouse flattened around it. A young shepherd, Rodney Moore, who had just come in from the marshes, obligingly opened the door of the oven. It creeked uneasily and we looked down into the large iron cavity, copious enough to take three dozen loaves or a fair-sized farmer's wife. Apparently, after the awful deed was done, discovered and punished, they carried on baking the bread as if nothing had happened.

The passions of a place so cut-off, so introverted as the Hoo Peninsula come as no surprise. In the churchyard of St Werburgh is the epitaph of William White of Cockhand Farm, 'most inhumanely murdered in the bosom of his afflicted family by a gun discharged at him through the window while he was sitting by his own fireside'. Most inhumane indeed. The violent

St Werburgh, Hoo, where William White of Cockhand Farm is buried. His tombstone is the one in the far distance near the north transept to the right of the picture.

mortality rate among the agricultural population obviously reached alarming proportions.

Charles Dickens, following his nose for atmosphere, left his cosy Kentish house for the Hoo marshes, and came upon the row of thirteen pathetic gravestones, still to be seen, side by side like stone skittles in Cooling churchyard. Buried here are the thirteen children of a couple called Comport, who lived at Decoy Farm in the eighteenth century. They died of the virulent marsh fever, the eldest being only seventeen years. Dickens used the churchyard, mentioning five of the little graves, as the misty background to the opening of *Great Expectations*.

Nevertheless, Decoy Farm today is an optimistic place with prosperous geese arranged beautifully around its dainty pond, overhung with languorous summer trees and flowery shrubs. The marshes fall away to the sea and the Decoy Inlet, where they used to drive the water fowl in the shooting season, signals in the sun. At the lower end of the farmyard was a barn with a wooden staircase going to its upper floor. To my astonishment the upper floor was occupied with a fine little museum of the marshes, pieced together by the farm foreman, Mr Squires, and a friend, out of interest and affection for this odd corner of England. There were birds and bats, fossils, stuffed animals, old coins, strange flowers, curled up shells from the estuary, and a collection of ancient clay pipes found in the half-hidden houses of the place.

*   *   *

It seemed that in these broad and quiet parts there were surprises wherever I turned my head.

Cooling churchyard. Near the south door entrance to the church are the graves of the Comport family from Decoy Farm and their thirteen children.

The signpost which points in two opposite directions to Cliffe. On one arm the name has oddly been misspelt.

Cooling Castle, surely the most sweetly named fortress in Britain, is miniature, with toy-like turrets, lawns and flowers, and eponymous, cool willows between its elderly walls. At St Mary's Hoo is buried the Reverend Robert Burt, said to be the anonymous clergyman who joined the Prince of Wales and Mrs Fitzherbert in uncertain wedlock at a secret ceremony in Clark Street, London, on December the fifteenth, 1785. According to the story, he confessed to this function on his death bed, revealing that he received £500 for the job.

Directions in the Hoo Hundred are difficult, inclined to the haphazard, as when one is confronted with a signpost which has *both* outstretched arms pointing to 'Cliffe'. Stoke Creek is off the road at the southern turn of the peninsula. It was from the road that I saw, above the marshy reeds, a line of masts and rigging. At the end of a thin lane I found Mrs Sheila Berger building a small garden for her children, Elaine, aged two, and Paul, aged four. Behind them, moored against the mud of the creek was a magnificent Thames sailing barge that to them was home.

For ten years they had lived there, Sheila's husband, Michael, travelling to his job each day like any suburban husband, and Mary, their other daughter, going off to school in Strood with her friends who live in the ordered, semi-detached land of metropolitan Kent.

The barge, eighty-five feet long, was romantically splendid, black-hulled, a huge steering wheel, at the stern the strong, wooden bow jutting out over the waterway and some homely washing blowing in the creek breeze from the rigging. Called *The Anglia,* she was built in 1890 for the grain trade from the ports of Norfolk and Suffolk to London, carrying feed for the horses of the capital. Later in my journey through lesser-known Britain, I was to meet

The old barge, The
Anglia, *lies alongside
other barges.*

men in Suffolk who remembered her with affection, lying alongside the quay at Orford, fifty years ago. They were pleased to know that she had found a good anchorage.

"We've sailed her up and down the coast," said Sheila. "She's still a magnificent craft. My daughter Mary took part in her first sailing barge race when she was three months old. Michael is mad about boats and sailing, and so we decided to live on the barge."

She had a fresh, open-air face. The children were busy constructing their optimistic garden amid the whorls of the creek. An arrow of water-fowl leapt for the sky from the far bank, and I could see a pensive heron ruminating in the rushes.

"Oh, it has its disadvantages," she said with a woman's sense of the practical. "For a start, we have to make it a rule that the children never play on deck. They are either below or on shore. It would not be too difficult for them to go over the side.

"But it's marvellously peaceful. And free too. Very free. You have this feeling of spaciousness looking out from the deck, and yet the cosiness of living below. In the winter the wind is very sharp across the flats, straight off the North Sea, and the snow comes in horizontally. That's really worth seeing. You come out on deck in the morning and all this mud is like a lovely cake."

On three sides the land lies flat and silent, the creek paddling against the shore, the birds sounding in the reeds and the tufty grass. But on the fourth side, like a strong army with spears, distant but menacing, stand the chimneys of the great oil refinery on the Isle of Grain. "I try not to look that way," said Sheila Berger. "It seems that all the anchorages we knew are being fouled up by something like that, a refinery or a power station, all sorts of ugly things. They seem to choose the most beautiful places to put them. But what can we say? We're just one couple living on a barge. One day there may be nowhere left where you can anchor in peace. And that would be a great pity."

It was the children's lunch-time. They patted their spades finally around the wild flowers they had hopefully transplanted, and taking their mother's hand went aboard their wooden home. From the top of the gangway they all waved as though they were sailing away, and I went back across the fields to the road. Before I reached it I turned, in a strange way half-expecting them to be sailing down the little estuary heading for the open sea. But Sheila Berger would be spending the afternoon doing her chores, like any other housewife, and waiting for her husband to come home from the office.

*   *   *

The following day I went to the Isle of Grain, which juts out from the eastern extreme of the Hoo Peninsula. It is remote, but not by any stretch of the imagination either beautiful or hidden, its great tanks and towers take care of that.

But I wanted to go there because I believed that somewhere amid all this hot industry, somehow spared by the roads and the pipelines and the fat oil tanks, would be little Port Victoria. Look on any map now and you will not find it mentioned, but in the last century it was a notable little place with a special rail line from London and a fine jetty out into the River Medway. For it was from here that Queen Victoria and Prince Albert embarked when the royal yacht took them to visit their many relatives in Europe. Her Majesty would board the royal train at Liverpool Street and be conveyed to the jetty, where her special harbour master would welcome her and a band would play while the pennanted yacht cast off with the utmost gentility.

Port Victoria seems to be a piece of lost history, although part of a long reign which, goodness knows, has been recalled and rewritten enough times. They were notable occasions on this quiet inlet and yet not a vestige now remains.

There is, it is true, the trace of a single track railway line, even the buffer where it came to an end, but the jetty and everything else has vanished, replaced by deep berths for ponderous oil tankers. All around are the impersonal installations of industry and the derelict buildings of war-time, army billets, look-out points, pill-boxes and the like, which the military men, never known for their tidiness, left when they ran out of war.

Among all this, however, was a small shingle beach and, extraordinarily, a solitary man sitting on a deck-chair in the sun. It occurred to me that he must have the most exclusive beach in the south of England. Without much hope I asked him if he knew the location of Port Victoria. Immediately he pointed towards the tanker berths and said, "It used to be over there. During the war the little railway was still there and there was an old jetty and a pub called The

Queen Victoria. But they're all gone now." He looked carefully out into the enclosed Medway and said, "I used to be on a destroyer out there in the Medway and sometimes we used to come ashore here. Many a pint I've had in that pub. Actually it was being on that ship that makes me come to this beach now. I could see it from the deck and I used to think that if I was still alive when the war finished I would make a point of coming to this beach whenever I could. And I still do."

He settled back to his deck-chair on his exclusive beach – his war-time dream accomplished – and I went further along the waterline in the forlorn hope that even one plank or stay of the old jetty could be seen, that someone might have thought to mark the spot of Port Victoria. But wire barricades around the area prevented me getting through. As a final throw, I interrupted a tea-break of some Irishmen who were sinking a shaft near the sea wall. Had they heard of Port Victoria?

"Niver heard tell of it," replied one, munching into a slab of bread and cheese. "No, not niver." Neither had his friends in the hut behind him.

Feeling I owed some explanation, I related hesitantly, "Queen Victoria sailed just by here in the royal yacht."

The Irishman seemed impressed. He turned to the others within the crowded hut. "D'you know," he announced, "that Her Majesty the Queen Victoria went sailin' by here in the royal yacht."

"Jeeze," came a voice from within. "An' ter t'ink we're so busy drinkin' tea that we missed the sight o' her."

The Isle of Grain, showing the gravel beach and the pier near the site of Port Victoria, on the mouth of the River Medway where it meets the Thames Estuary.

FOUR

The Island They Left Behind

It was Saturday night in the Pentland Firth. An August Saturday night on a deserted island with a spooky, wet mist hanging everywhere, cold drizzle dripping from my nose and eyebrows, the distressed howl of a foghorn on hidden cliffs, and two muscovy-ducks waddling in procession behind me.

I was clad in a postman's overcoat, sagging to my ankles, a garment unworn for the past ten years, and a pair of gumboots fashioned for a man with feet three times my size. It was no place for elegance.

As I trudged the broken road from one end of Stroma island to the other, I had a passing thought of people dining in comfortable restaurants in London several hundred miles to the south or walking beneath the warm evening sky of Nice. It is at times like this that the explorer within me is asked, most irritably, "What the hell are we doing in this place?"

Stroma sits like a small and sober hat on top of Britain's head. It is three miles over the racing Pentland Firth from John O' Groats. Marooned there, by my own design, on this mournful summer evening, I found that, for once, I craved human company and had set out across the island to watch television with the lonely lighthouse keepers to the north, the only other inhabitants.

The muscovy-ducks, whom I had called Vladimir and Anastasia (under the mistaken impression that they came from Russia), had been given several pieces of stale cake and were now mine for life. They flopped after me with blatant, cross-eyed devotion along the stony path, giving off short snorts of adoration as they waddled. I don't always make friends so easily.

Vladimir's beak had tapped tentatively on the streaming door of the damp cottage which was my island home. In that foggy and isolated place, the measured tapping had raised some ghostly apprehension in my heart. Hesitatingly, I had gone to the door and thrown it quickly open, frightening poor Vladimir so that he jumped with nervousness, both red feet leaving the ground. He landed in a rubbery sort of fashion and stared at me with a squint that encompassed both hurt and pleading.

As muscovy-ducks go, he was a poor sight that Saturday night. The wet air had smarmed down his feathers as though he had been applying thick Brylcreem in preparation for his calling upon me. His face and crossed eyes had the red, smashed, transfixed expression of someone who has just been punched in the face in a saloon bar.

"Cruck," said Vladimir. He gave a brave waddle forward, thought the better of it and waddled back. He continued looking at me. I think.

I had been stacking my provisions in the kitchen cupboard and I took a piece of hard cake, which, by the worn look of it, had been lying there months, and lobbed it out to Vladimir.

Stale cake it might have been to me. To Vladimir it was ambrosia. He tried to swallow it whole and it bulged horribly in his scarlet cheeks, his eyes swivelled and he flapped his soggy wings with excitement and pleasure. Muscovy-ducks are easily pleased. There was more cake in the cupboard, left by Jimmy Simpson, the owner of the house and the island, when he had stayed overnight to watch over the ewes during the lambing season. Before I could take it from the shelf, Vladimir marched in with a flopping of wet feet and stood with open beak. He had no pride.

But there are even ducks – and he was one – who are not permitted to have a Saturday night out on their own. I had closed the door to keep the fog where it belonged, but while Vladimir was squatting on the fire-side rug, all crumbs and ecstacy, there came a further tapping at the door and there I discovered his wife, Anastasia, decidedly peevish, and she marched in without any invitation.

She was even dowdier than her mate, if that were possible. Just as damp and with the same incredible squint, she lacked his red markings and his optimistic manner. Still, when you're a muscovy-duck living on an island off the north of Scotland, and there's only one other muscovy-duck around, you haven't got a lot of choice. She nudged her husband uncompromisingly across the rug so she could snap up the crumbs that he had not yet cleared. I gave her a piece of cake and she at once manoeuvred so that she had her backside rudely facing her mate with her beak and the cake at the other end. As he tried to waddle in an outflanking movement, she merely pivoted, without even glancing behind, and kept him out of reach until she had finished. She was a mean duck, that Anastasia.

All the cake was now gone and I sat down and waited to see whether they would depart. They stood, side by side now, staring at me with those crazy, wild eyes, grinding out sounds. "Cruck. Cruck. Cruck."

"Nothing doing," I said. "It's all gone."

Aghast at this news, they immediately set up the most terrifying honking and hooting, their dank wings flailing, their red feet stamping with greed and frustration. I had been having a fry-up (the standard consolation for solitariness) and I gave them a selection of bacon rinds. They were delirious. After that I knew nothing would ever part us but the sea. They ate everything I pushed in their direction and Vladimir made a clumsy and foolhardy sally onto the table in an attempt to reach the food cupboard. I gave him a shove and he crash-landed on the stone floor. The treatment appeared to sober them both for they sat in a reasonably quiet manner for another half an hour while I attempted to wind the generator at the back of the television set. Nothing happened – no sound, no eerie image appeared. In the end I gave up, donned the postman's damp and ancient overcoat (which was hanging behind the door) and the huge boots, and set out for the lighthouse to share the crew's viewing. The muscovies followed me out and across the island. Anastasia nagged him all the way too. But at the

The chapel with Duncansby Head in the distance.

lighthouse they had to stay outside the door. The lighthousemen wouldn't let them in because they always made wet marks all over the clean floor.

*   *   *

Stroma abounds with rabbits and ghosts. The rabbits (including a black family bred from somebody's captive pets, kept in the days before the island was abandoned) peep from thousands of holes and run along every gully. They sit in the hollow schoolroom and have gnawed half way through the prophet Jeremiah in the Bible that was left behind in the church.

The ghosts are the sort who make you laugh. There is Murdoch Kennedy, for a start, who still guffaws down by the seashore over the ghoulish tricks he used to play with his poor dad's dead body. It happened two hundred years ago but he still thinks it's funny.

His father, Kennedy of Carnmuch, had built the chapel and vault which stand today on the south-east corner of Stroma, overlooking the cliffs where the terns nest in summer. The saline air of the Pentland Firth was so powerful that the island dead were never buried, but laid in the vault where the salt flying from the rapid tides preserved them. Families would make regular outings to see relatives who had not been around for years. The young Kennedy used to make an entertainment of it.

Bishop Forbes, who visited Caithness in 1762, relates in his journal that the remains of Kennedy of Carnmuch were to be seen in the vault for many years and 'would have been so still had it not been for his son Murdoch Kennedy who played such wretched tricks (*O facinus indignum! Referens tremisco!*) on the Body of his Father, for the Diversion of Strangers, as in

The rock formation near the chapel.

time it broke to pieces and the Head was the part that fell off first. He used to place Strangers at his Father's Feet, and by setting a Foot on one of his Father's made the Body spring up speedily and salute them, which surprized them greatly.' The young Kennedy also had an encore. '. . . After laying the Body down again,' relates the Bishop, 'he beat a march upon the Belly which sounded equally loud with a Drum.'

Another shady chuckle might be discerned by the careful listener coming from the ruined house of Donald Banks, the island poet and coffin maker, who had lived next to the cottage where I had made my temporary island home. Donald combined both his talents when ordering coffin planks from a man of Wick on the Caithness mainland. He wrote:

> *Dear Mr Sutherland,*
> *Would you be so good,*
> *To send eight planks of coffin wood.*
> *Half inch lining, (dear Mr Sutherland,)*
> *For those who are pining . . .*

Stroma seen from Huna. Donald's funereal humour was, it was said, occasionally replaced by downright bad temper

and once, having quarrelled bitterly with an island family, he was heard to utter the words, 'I'll no bury any more o' ye!' A terrible threat.

He was a bachelor and lived during the end years of Stroma's habitation in his little carpenter's house with his three sisters. One day he decided to brighten up their home by fixing a star, fashioned from wallpaper, to the ceiling of the sitting-room. He fell from the table, broke his leg and died. He was eighty-four.

He must have all but finished the job when he tumbled because Donald's star remains beaming from the sagging ceiling. I stood there in his room, sadly aware of the abandoned past about me. On the dust-crowded mantelshelf was a rank of family photographs, shades in Victorian dress staring out forever into a room now desolate and holed, but which had once held the life of a warm family. Few things are so sad. One man in a frock coat stood by his bustled wife, an assured hand on her shoulder, looking prosperous and proprietorial. How strange that they should have been left here to moulder on that solitary, foggy outpost. They had, however, distinguished company, for the largest photograph in the bare room was of Queen Victoria, predictably glum (and who could blame her?) gazing with disinterest from the damp wall as she must have been that day when old Donald took his last tumble and was carried out in a coffin, which he had prudently set aside for his own occupation.

Donald's workbench and vice, open-jawed as though in protest, are in the next room, left like so many other useful things on Stroma. That was what gave the place its melancholy. It was not the isolation, not the fog, nor even the foghorn crying as though it were itself in distress. It was the abandonment of life. The discarding of everyday things by a people who believed their days would be better elsewhere.

Outside Donald's cottage is a plough, its share thrust despairingly into the ground and all over the island are stilled wheels and rusting implements. They left the books in the school, the ink in the post office and the collection box (empty) in the church. Somebody, as a final

Donald's box bed in the room where he stuck the star to the ceiling, part of which can still be seen.

gesture of resignation, took the island telephone off the hook.

The population departed, leaving a brand-new harbour, which they had built with government help, hardly splashed by the wash of a boat. The day the people quit was the only busy day of that harbour's life. They went because, as they built the jetty and the mole and the anchorage, their eyes kept looking up, across at the motor cars moving on the mainland roads, and the smooth toadstool growth of the Dounreay atomic power station on the Caithness coast. Life is never easy on islands but they had been a close and happy people, bonded by their stocky home and their familiarity with each other, and with the wild, sea-strung world about them. When they went it was the affluent society which took them and now they are scattered in streets and towns; some, perhaps, happier but sometimes, too, thinking of the place that was their home.

Jimmy Simpson, who left Stroma in 1943 but returned and bought the deserted island for grazing in 1960, remembered the people. "We had about two hundred and fifty folks here when I was a boy," he recalled. "It never seemed a lonely place. There were always people going in and out of each others' houses, there were forty children at the school and there were two teachers. We had concerts; three concerts in the winter when you had to sing loud to get above the sound of the wind. The young people would meet at the shop in the long, long evenings in summer. Aye, it was a great place."

It was Jimmy who took me across to Stroma on a flat and indistinct morning, his fishing boat *Viking* taking little bites out of the calm sea as we went across the three mile strait. We left the old lifeboat slipway at Huna, tucked away by John O'Groats, a small and secret inlet, a landing unnoticed by those whose ambition is to reach what tradition holds to be the most northerly mainland point of Britain. It was hushed there, the old cracked slipway, the stones and the bladder-wrack, men preparing the boat with little said, the water lapping at the shore like a tired dog.

Jimmy Simpson was a strong reminder that these northern capes were more the realm of the Scandinavians than the Scots; tall, strong and quiet, with fair hair and blue eyes. His sons carry the same Norse look into the next generation. He lived and farmed on the mainland but went regularly across to Stroma where he kept his sheep. Each season the island disintegrates a little more, the houses and the places he knew tumble further into decay. It is like visiting an old and lingering relative.

We had a mixed cargo that August morning. For my part, I was provisioned with eggs, bacon, sausages, coffee, tea, sugar, tinned milk, and all the stodgy victuals that a boy or man instinctively takes on an expedition. Less juvenile was a bottle of Scotch I had added in case the nights got cold. We were also carrying a bulky spare part for the dynamo at the Stroma lighthouse, in the charge of Alan Wilson, a mechanic who travelled the outcrops and Isles of Scotland at the behest of the celestially-named Commissioners For Northern Lights. It was an essential part and they needed it badly. "They say they've been getting by with running repairs and a few Hail Marys," he commented.

Well wrapped against the cold touches of the Pentland mist, we watched Stroma change shape, almost unroll, as islands do when you approach them. It had looked long and flat from Huna, tethered out there beyond Dunnet Head – which is true land's end – looking as though it were brooding over secrets it would never tell. Now, as we voyaged on the vacant channel, it stretched itself like a sleeping animal disturbed. Arms and legs of rocks stretched out seaward on either side, the harbour could be seen in its niche, and the first houses blinked nervously at our intrusion from behind the green banks topping the cliffs.

Jimmy and the *Viking* now have almost exclusive use of the harbour that cost £30,000 to build in the early 1950s, one of the luxuries of owning a deserted island. Landing there it was as though we were the first humans ever to arrive in a country of birds. They were all over the sky, the cliffs and the harbour itself, shouting and inquiring and screaming in their salty fashion; terns, skuas, shag, powerful gulls, shrill oyster-catchers and the jolly puffins, each one its own private joke, striding, sitting, flying; button-eyed and orange-beaked, black-coated, white-vested.

Willie Mathieson, the Stroma lighthouse keeper, had sent one of his assistants, John Boath,

Plough shares near the homes in Nethertown.

across the island with a tractor and trailer to collect Alan Wilson and the dynamo part. I gathered my books and provisions and stepped ashore onto the concrete wharf, expecting now to start trekking. But Jimmy, a reticent man, smiled and said, "No, there's no need for walking. I'll get the car."

He meant it too. From a shed at the waterside he trundled a shy but serviceable Morris Minor. "Starting," he admitted, "can be a wee bit difficult." He meant that also. I sat on the bare springs of the passenger seat, fighting the temptation to close my eyes, clutching my bacon and books, while we ran silently, terrifyingly, down the slope towards the deep green water of the harbour. She fired just as it appeared we must topple over, and a foot from the edge we stopped while Jimmy revved the engine. "Never failed me yet," he smiled.

Once the car was truly alive he turned it along the wharf, and then we coughed and shuddered up the steep gradient from the sheltered inlet to the broad back of the island. "Aye," mused Jimmy, "she's no' a bad vehicle. And cheap to run. No road tax to pay."

Now I could see it all around me, the slopes and grassland, the modest island flowers, the birds against the clouds, skipping rabbits by the thousand, sheep looking up, dull-eyed, at the car, and everywhere the fallen houses of the spreading settlement. As on most islands there had been no village as such, but dwellings distributed about the landscape apparently at random, so that each man had his land, his home and his privacy. By some curious juxtaposition the homesteads on the lower part of the island, nearest the mainland, were called Uppertown and those in the north, Nethertown. But it was at the fringe of the sea, where the

Left, the war memorial and church with the Union Jack flying.

waves broke, where much of life itself happened for the people, that the strange and graphic names were strung out as in a poem. From Swilkie Point, opposite the giant whirlpool in the ocean to the north, to Mell Head nudging the firth in the south-west corner, the sharp, riven inlets are a catalogue of names, the history and reason of which are mostly forgotten – Cully Geo, Finnies Haven, Sea Cave Hole, Hamar, Bay of Sluggs, Scar Craggan, Button Geo, The Altars and the Scope o' Camm.

There is also The Gloup. "While ye wander around the place," warned Jimmy, sending fifty rabbits scattering as we turned the corner by the church and the telephone box, "watch out for The Gloup."

"What's The Gloup?" I asked.

"A hole," he replied. "A great big damn hole. Ye'll know it if you see it. If you walk into it in the fog, ye'll know it too. Watch for The Gloup."

"I'll watch for The Gloup," I promised.

Jimmy's croft in the centre of the island was the sort of house you read about in childhood books, and remember forever. I realised I had arrived there years too late. But the place and its contents still gave out an adventurous whiff. He explained apologetically that it might be a trifle damp for it was only used once in a while, when he lodged there during the lambing season, or when the Pentland Firth became so untidy that he was unable to get back to his home on the mainland.

Hanging on a line across the living-room-cum-kitchen were a dozen dried fish. When I got

Right, Stroma lighthouse at Swilkie Point; in the distance can be seen the Orkney Islands.

the calor-gas stove going and the place warmed up, they began to drip on the floor. It became a bit disconcerting, dodging in and out of the drops, but I did not feel I could move the suspended fish. It would have been like taking somebody's washing from the line without permission.

There were some ancient but comfortable chairs and a broad table. On the mantelshelf was a pretty American cottage clock, which had stopped at three thirty-five, years before, and in one corner a stack of guns and fishing tackle. It was, in every aspect, the complete castaway's cottage, with the comforts every Robinson Crusoe seems eventually to provide, by ingenuity, for himself. In the bedroom was a hunched harmonium, presumably to be used if you felt like a quick song at twilight, and once you got into the great rolling bed (the sort in which you journey about during the night), there was a magic contraption of string and pulleys which, when operated, turned out the gas light.

There was also a lovely telescope and a chart showing the effects of the various forces of winds at sea which gave illustrations of how waves behaved when confronted with every blow from a mere zephyr up to a bullying force ten gale. One morning I awoke to find the wind banging around the house as if it were looking for the door, and from the window I could see it churning the ocean. Rain hurtled across Stroma. I took the telescope and examined the mighty and ominous Pentland Firth, checked the chart and decided it was at least force eight. I went back to bed.

Apart from the wind and the foghorn (never heard together, of course, which is just as well), the other noisy entity on Stroma is the wild stag which runs the island looking for his two lost wives with growing despair not to say disbelief. He must have thought they were his, all his, on an island with three miles of turbulent sea separating it from the next land. But, obeying some female instinct that women's liberation ladies would know of and undoubtedly approve, they plunged off the southern shore and swam successfully to Caithness, leaving behind their joint husband to search in puzzlement, wrath, and then eventual sadness. Jimmy told me that the stag had followed the hinds' trail to the seashore and then stood there gazing at the waves and the distant Scottish coast. Apparently, deciding that no woman could dislike him that much, he turned back inland and has spent the rest of his life trying to work out the mystery.

The folk of Stroma, in the former days, must have been compact and comfortable. To walk into some of their houses and to see the beds fitted into the wood of the walls as though they were in a huge cupboard, was suddenly to hear the night winds of long ago and to realise how tight and snug the people must have been while the shutters rattled and the sea howled.

There was one large house near the upper anchorage – the haven used by the fishermen before they built the new harbour – and it rose substantially above the grey of the rocks and the bright green of the grass. Inside it was just a shell, but the size of the rooms and the fineness of the hall, its staircase now rotting, testified to its former shape and elegance. Outside was a tangle of weeds and brambles trapped in what had been a walled garden. Some of the flowers that had bloomed there in the sea air were still stirring among the weeds and stones, some pale roses and a colony of half-hidden marigolds. There was a boat lying like a coffin in the grass and a grinding wheel that would never turn again. The place had been inherited by the rabbits and the gulls.

Stroma seen from near the seal colony, Gills Bay.

That day had fallen into mildness with the fog sloping off on some errand of its own across the sea. Looking inland, I could see the easily rising spread of the island with the many abandoned houses standing dumbly about it. I felt like the cowboy in the film who turns to find himself surrounded by silent and hostile redskins.

The sea had become grey and benign now, and the day was breathless. Visibility reached as far as the Orkneys when I looked out from the head of Stroma. On the horizon were the sheer faces of the highest cliffs in Britain lit by fitful, dramatic sunlight. Stroma lighthouse, clean as a whistle, stands peering down at the great race of the Swilkie whirlpool, a huge and turning potter's wheel in the ocean.

Alan Wilson, who had finished fitting the awaited component to the lighthouse machinery, came from the engine-room and indicated the out-lying islands of the neighbouring Orkneys to me. Two tankers, large and sure of themselves, pushed by on their way towards Scandinavia. The sea looked agreeable.

"There's been nights," ruminated the lighthouse engineer, "when this sea has been unfit for any ship. Out there a ship was wrecked a couple of years ago – and the lifeboatmen from Longhope went out and never got back alive. And yon whirlpool – I've seen boats going backwards with the tide, race down there."

Oyster-catchers, cormorants and gulls were whooping about in their normal, everyday panic and collections of puffins sat studiously on the rocks and observed the antics of the other birds like ornithologists. Across a blade of channel was another low island, green with the single white patch of a house on its flank.

*Duncansby Head
seagulls nesting.*

"Swona," said Alan pointing that way. "There's a man and his two sisters live there and they're strange, quiet folk. One of the women broke her leg some time ago and she had to be taken to the mainland to get it set. It was the first time she had been off the island in nineteen years. A chap from one of the Sunday newspapers got across there once, wanted to interview the three of them. But they hid and they wouldn't come out until he'd cleared off. They're a bit private."

With Alan Wilson I walked down to the lighthouse. I love lighthouses. In wild places I have come across them, strong and cosy, a refuge for those within and caution for those without. Stroma lighthouse had a beautiful grandfather clock just inside the front door. John Boath, the young assistant keeper, enjoys it for the same reasons. "I was born and brought up in a slum," he said. "Here I've got a fine job and a grand house."

The Commissioners For Northern Lights require unusual qualities in their keepers. They must be both quiet and cheerful, companionable but content in isolation. They go about their traditional and unique routine, tending the light, watching sky-change and sea-change, and living their outlandish lives. Among the things they learn is the art of lighthouse conversation. A good topic is looked after. It is never gobbled up in one rush, but spun out, explored, thought over, and discussed in single sentences over many weeks. Three men – the third on Stroma was a young student called Rob – moving carefully about a tower on the edge of the ocean recognise and acknowledge the conversational routine. A joke may take three weeks to tell, the punch line not coming until two Thursdays hence. Likewise, talk within the sitting-room on foggy nights has to be tailored and timed to the demands of the rowdy foghorn.

The night I went to the lighthouse to watch the television, leaving the muscovy-ducks

Jimmy Simpson, his son and friend loading sheep in the harbour to transport them to market on the mainland.

disgruntled outside the door, I sat with Willie Mathieson, the keeper, studying the technique of *not* arriving at the point of a story at the moment the foghorn emits its blast. Few things leave you feeling so shipwrecked as that. Either you finish the tale, jamming it into the silence between the hoots or you divide it into episodes, filling in the blank period while the horn is operating with dumbshow. For the same reasons, watching television requires a novel technique for, as the foghorn sounds, so you have to lip-read. Bad timing in a murder drama could mean that you alone may never ever know who-dun-it.

Willie was a serene and comfortable man from Unst, the most northerly of the Shetlands. Later, a long time later, I saw his home in that uttermost island. He had the distinction of knowing the man who lived in the last house in Britain. He sat that night, watching from the edge of his eye, the beam from his lighthouse reflected in a shaving mirror propped up at the window. It was not his duty watch but he liked to know it was revolving and shining. Not that it shone very far that night. Normally it swings its arm like a gymnast for miles around the seas, but in that closing sea fog it was pressing impotently into a vaporous wall only yards off the rocks. The warning had to come from the hooting hooter that night.

"Ye get used to it, the fog signal," Willie said. "But it takes a wee bit o' getting used to." With only a grave smile, he related what happened to the captain of a Danish cargo ship which had the odd misfortune to go onto the rocks almost directly below the lighthouse windows. " 'T'was the captain's duty, of course, to stay aboard her, but that foghorn was right next to his cabin and the poor man had to get out. He'd have gone deaf and mad ha' he not."

The Gloup.

"It sounds an odd sort of wreck," I suggested carefully as a land-lubber should. "Right under the nose of a lighthouse."

"Aye," he agreed, "t'was odd in a few ways too. We brought two injured men ashore, but it turned out it wasn't the collision with the rocks had hurt them. They'd been knocked over by a tram-car in Copenhagen."

The next day I found The Gloup about which Jimmy Simpson had warned me. He was not exaggerating. The Gloup is a great hole in the island's skin, a horizontal cave as big as a football field, with enormous slabs of rock as its walls, dropping sheer down into a great, deep dungeon and a cave – like a door that lets in the rushing ocean. Prudently lying flat out on my stomach, I gazed down into the innards of the thing, hearing the hidden collision of the sea and the land and then watching the swooshing waves come pounding through the deep archway, sending salty spray into my nostrils a hundred feet above. Today when the Pentland Firth was resting, it looked a dangerous place and in a storm it must have boiled terrifyingly. The story is that the islanders used The Gloup to bring in their illicit whisky. There must have been easier ways.

Channels of northern sunlight roved, wide-striped, across the island, picking out the scattered but vivid colours of sea-nurtured flowers; sending flocks of rabbits tumbling and tossing through the hummocky grass. I walked across the wide shoulder of the land to where the schoolhouse stands silenced. The playground has been used as a sheep-pen and there were seabirds thick above the eaves. A well-nourished skua was sitting on the moss-grown pump in the schoolhouse yard. I walked to each window and peeped in. Books, dusty but tidy, some tables and chairs, gas lamps and a dead old fire. And yet another harmonium. They were fond of the harmonium in these parts.

It was Sunday morning and, strangely, it could be felt. Only sheep and rabbits moved in this place and spread out, clear and apparently unattended, was the Scottish coast, Dunnet Head, John O'Groats, a lighthouse, the grain of the sea, the peace of the sky.

At the top of the track leading from the schoolhouse is a still-bright, red telephone box, its telephone long gone, standing outside the church which, astonishingly, does not appear on the Ordnance Survey map of Stroma. Not that it matters now for no-one wants to find it. Within all is dereliction and holes. On this Sunday morning twenty rabbits formed the congregation and they left as soon as I walked in the door. Stroma's church does not have the dignity of being ruined. It is abandoned, neglected, a shambles. But if there is anything sadder than a neglected pub, it's a neglected church.

The organ had been transported to the mainland years before (judging by the harmoniums left behind on the island it was the one that got away), but the pulpit remained, dumb and hung with ragged red tassles. The pews had been dismantled and were piled along one side of the nave like random driftwood. Windows looked in, open-mouthed, on the desolate scene. On the pulpit was a book, *The Commentary on the Holy Bible* by Thomas Scott, apparently left behind by the Reverend J. R. Russell of Glasgow, because his name was in the fly-leaf. There was also a prayer book, formerly owned by Barbara Allan of Stroma, and a pile of others left to be trampled upon by heathen sheep and nibbled by rabbits and rats.

I was glad to go out again into the wide air to see, suddenly, as one can only see from islands and mountains, a breathless spread of earth and sea, dappled, remote, quiet. I walked next to what had been the post office and peered in the windows. It was, as one might expect, clean and ordered but it, too, had that air of everybody-gone. On the counter were some forms and licence applications, a board praising the percentage rate of the Post Office Savings Bank and a bottle of dried ink. At the back of the little building was a room still comfortably furnished with a nice dresser, upon which stood a teapot and a jug and some sheet music: 'Red Sails in the Sunset', 'The General's Fast Asleep' and 'You Can't Do That There 'Ere.' Nobody on Stroma will ever sing those songs now.

At the end I wasn't sorry when I saw Jimmy Simpson's boat coming to fetch me off the island. Of all the out-of-the-way places I have known, this was the saddest. It seemed as though its life had been ended in a fit of pique.

"Aye, it used to be a fine place," repeated Jimmy as we went out of the new, mouldering harbour. "But things and people change."

I looked back. Sheep grazed and rabbits sat on the jetty and watched our departure. The sky was occupied with birds and a fresh Pentland wind blew over the channel and stroked the grasses of Stroma. Perhaps, one day, people, some people, may go back and find it and live there and make it alive again. I hope they do.

FIVE

The Russians Have Landed!

The last house in Britain is called The Haa, and is at a sweet and solitary place known as Skaw, on the island of Unst at the top of the Shetlands. Alison and Bertie Priest, who lived there, could walk out on to the breezy beach, almost at their door, look north across the sea and know there was nothing between them and the pack ice of the Arctic Ocean.

It is fair to say that neither was in the least impressed by their geographical peculiarity. They were a young couple with a baby – the most northerly child in Britain! – but they scarcely gave their outlandishness a second thought. Bertie liked to go out fishing and Alison knitted and (as when I first called) listened to Jimmy Young on the radio, like everyday housewives all over the kingdom.

Unusual things did occur, of course. Great winds (a blast of 177 miles per hour has been recorded) and storms, amazing sunsets, the Northern Lights, and . . . armed Russians.

I had gone to Shetland to fulfil a long ambition to travel on the bus that rattles the length of the islands, leap-frogging from one to another by ferry, a total distance equivalent to a journey from London to Southampton. Once before I had been briefly in Shetland, en route to the lonely outpost of Fair Isle, and, this time, when I arrived at Sumburgh on the plane from Glasgow that benevolent June morning, the first thing I did was to make my way towards the shore and the hidden inlet harbour of Grutness, to see again the great and wonderful shadow of Fair Isle crouched on the ocean twenty-three miles away. Fair Isle, my old friend. I could not resist a wave.

It takes only moments to detect the change in Shetland. The airport at Sumburgh which used to be a relic of war-time RAF days, and where I once helped to push a small Icelandic airliner out of the mud, is now swell and swelling every day. New terminal buildings, new runway, new car parks where once they only required room to reverse the local bus. The oil man cometh and goeth from his North Sea platforms all the time, returning from his wild locations, his pockets stuffed with money, descending beneath the swinging arms of a helicopter.

My heart fell when I saw it all. If there is anything more disconcerting than progress, it's abrupt progress. Was I to be too late in Shetland? Was it all gone? The bus to Lerwick, the stony capital, was at least reassuring. It was the same senile conveyance that I remembered

Looking north-north-east with The Haa facing its private beach and bay in the foreground.

from days past. Its seats were stiff, its gears ground horribly, and the clock above the driver, like Rupert Brooke's at Grantchester, was stuck irrevocably at ten to three.

As we left for the twisting journey up the long island the Shetlanders call Mainland, another helicopter, a great flying cow, came across from the ocean, its shadow sweeping across us, its champing engines deafening. I glanced at my fellow passengers. They numbered only half a dozen and they did not look remotely like wealthy oil men. One was rolling his own cigarettes.

It would be straining the imagination of the most dedicated poet to call Mainland a pretty place. It has never been. There are no trees, for a start, and few wild flowers. Wind ruffles the landscape. Rocks and peat bogs are scarcely delicate and the islanders' inbred habit of dumping everything from old beer bottles to disintegrating cars in the nearest convenient place is unendearing. (I once worked with a somewhat unromantic television director on a remote island where all I could see was grandeur and beauty. He, however, noted the dumped rubbish, left, as a matter of course, by the islanders. "This place," he remarked to my chagrin, "is nothing but a slum in the sea.")

There is, however, some poetic consolation in the catalogue of place-names that are scattered through the Shetlands from Fitful Head in the south to Muckle Flugga at the upper extremity: Scousburgh, Sandwick, Mousa, Burra, Scalloway, Bressay, Noss, Bixter, Papa Stour, Muckle Roe, Tofts Voe, Sullom Voe, Gutcher and Mid Yell (surely there is a joke there somewhere?) Baltasound, Saxa Vord and Mavis Grind.

Thankfully, the little capital town of Lerwick brought the reassurance I needed. It's as straight-faced as a piano tuner. And has always been. Perhaps it is unchangeable, which is a blessing. At its centre, where the thin and cobbled streets converge, there is an obelisk, around which all traffic is obliged to circulate with as much of a performance as that at Piccadilly Circus. The shops are slow, comfortable and slightly disordered, like shops I recall from the

1930s. They sell sensible woollen garments. There is a contrary cafe which closes at lunchtime, and I was told at The Grand Hotel that dinner began sharp at six-thirty. "Until when?" I enquired, of a lady behind a peephole. I should have known better. "Seven o'clock," she snapped before slamming down the shutter.

The harbour smells of fish and salt. Gourmet gulls were sitting on the decks of the Lerwick trawlers, pedantically selecting only the choicest morsels from the remnants of the previous night's fishing. Notices along the quayside are in English, Russian, Norwegian and Danish, a testimony to the nature of traffic in the port.

Large fishermen tramp with ponderous quietness about the jetties, becoming more vocal at evening after the bars have been open a while. They tell the story in Lerwick of a lusty Scandinavian who, rolling out at closing time, saw a concertina displayed in a shop window. He gazed at it lovingly for a while, then broke the window and helped himself. The police had no difficulty in finding him. They went down to the silent harbour and listened. The notes from the squeezebox came plaintively over the water and they merely had to follow them to the appropriate fishing boat. They found the young man in his bunk playing the songs of home.

I stepped over the ropes and nets of the quay. It was a mild afternoon for those latitudes, with the water slopping languidly in the dock and running lazily out in the Sound between the town and the green back of the close island of Bressay, which so conveniently shelters Lerwick harbour.

Beyond Bressay is a pimple islet called the Holm of Noss, unvisited by man for a hundred years. It used to be tethered to its parent island of Noss by a primitive rope-walk, which was prudently dismantled after a party of intrepid Victorians were left hanging in mid-air after something broke. They were rescued but nobody has asked to go there since.

*   *   *

Two thousand years ago Tacitus wrote of the feeling the Romans found in Shetland, a picture that remains unchanged today: 'Nowhere does the sea hold wider sway. It carries to and fro in its motions a mass of currents and in its ebb and flow, it is not held by the coast, but penetrates deep into the land and winds about the hills, as if in its own domain.'

To be in Shetland is to have the sea around every corner. It wraps the islands in a bright ribbon. Colours and shapes vary with the seasons and the tides and the time of day. In summer, day goes on for most of the night too, and on my first evening I climbed the hill from Lerwick town in clear sunshine that had only turned to burnished twilight when I returned at midnight. It was like the wick of a lamp being turned down, but slowly.

I had discovered a new hotel, where it was permissible to have dinner beyond seven o'clock and I had stayed in the lively bar with the company of oil men and others who now travel to Shetland on business connected with the North Sea rigs. A young man paid for half a pint of beer with a Bank of Scotland hundred pound note (I thought he might have bought a round!), and a Lerwick fisherman told me how his father had gone out one misty morning in his boat and, for the first time, had seen one of the great oil rigs come into view through the fog. "Dear God, Jamie," the old man said to his son, "I can see a cathedral in the sea."

Above, gulls in Lerwick harbour.

Left, the fishing boats in the harbour of Lerwick, Mainland.

In the glimmer–dim, as they call the unending dusk of midsummer, I returned down the hill towards the creaking wharfs and the silent town. It was gone midnight and it would have been easy to read a newspaper. It was strange, eerie even, to see the light, deserted streets. There was a dusty feel about the air and the sea looked flat and bronze. A single piping bird sounded from the seashore.

In Lerwick, at the Queen's Hotel, I had been accommodated in an annexe a few steps across the road from the main building, which was in the throes of undergoing such major alterations that its interior appeared to be just rubble, ladders and scaffolding. At night it was locked up like a construction site.

I went to my bed in the annexe, somewhat anxiously because I needed to rise early to start the journey to Unst in the far north. The daily bus left at eight o'clock. Not being in the habit of wearing a watch, there being no-one in the main hotel to call me, and it being daylight *all night*, I began to wonder how I was going to know what time to get up.

Right, looking west-north-west from Holm Skaw, an island just north of The Haa and used by Bertie and Charlie Priest. The islands of Muckle Flugga and Out Stack can be seen in the distance.

It had been a full day and I'd taken a few whiskies, so I went to sleep at once. When I awoke I had no idea what time of the day or night it was. I went to the window but it looked out on a narrow alley. For all I knew it could have been noon – and I had missed the Shetland bus. In my pyjamas I went to the bedroom door and poked my head out. Nobody about. There was only a short flight of stairs to the street, so I thought I would go and see if there was anyone abroad. As I reached the street door I heard my bedroom door close sedately behind me. Frantically I ran up the stairs. It was locked.

Returning to the front door, I tentatively looked out. Deserted. Broad daylight but not a movement, not a soul. There was no-one in the hotel from whom I could get a key and my fellow sleepers in the annexe would hardly be of any use. I crept out to see if I would be able to get back into my room by the window.

What a situation! There was I, in the uppermost town of Great Britain, as far north as Siberia, in the thin hours of the morning – and in my pyjamas. I clutched myself to stop my shivering and then, with great relief, perceived a sauntering policeman. He appeared at the end of the light, cobbled street, halted and considered my embarrassment. The northern breeze whistled up the legs of my pyjama trousers, the stones were clammy under my soles. "Officer, I'm locked out," I said pathetically.

"Aye, it happens," he shrugged philosophically. "How would you be thinking of getting back in?"

"The window?" I suggested doubtfully.

"Aye, it'll have to be the window," he nodded, as if he had considered every possibility. "I'll give you a hand."

He crouched and, at his invitation, I stood on his shoulders. He rose and I wobbled, putting

Left, looking down Commercial Street, the main street in Lerwick.

my hands on the granite wall for support. Like some unusual circus act, the policeman and the man in pyjamas stood there in that hushed, northern street. I got a grip on the window and hauled myself over the sash and into the room. Returning to the window I looked down and thanked my helper. He gave a nice salute and wished me good morning.

Gratefully I returned to my bed and slept. When I woke up at ten o'clock I found I had missed the bus.

Gutcher, seen from the pier, and showing the post office and tea room.

*　　*　　*

Going north from Lerwick, towards the Isle of Yell in the car I had been required to hire because of my oversleeping, it began to rain. It was forthright maritime rain, no polite inland shower, a squall that came in like a ruffian from the ocean. It suited the landscape, the low foreheads of the bald hills, the stooping of the rocky road. The sea, which came into view on cue every few minutes, was at its irritable best, rolling grey, white-crowned, running bent-backed beneath the low-hung clouds.

In these latitudes the temperament of the ocean is even less predictable than in many others. The neat museum in Lerwick has a touching array of personal belongings which have at various times floated pathetically onto a Shetland beach from some off-shore disasters. The brave islanders themselves went far off to sea in the most apparently fragile of boats, the sixern, a low-slung craft with oars and a single splinter of sail. When the fishermen went out in the sixerns (and this within the last century), the odds on their return were not heavy. The men took with them a curious little cooking stove and supplies for several days. They took also their ludders, trumpets made from animal horns which they blew to call comfort to each other in the twin voids of night and sea and to herald, eventually, their return to the home harbour. Each family had a different call on the ludder horn so that the waiting wives and children would know that their own fisherman was coming back to them. Sometimes there came no sound and the family would wait, listening with dropping hearts to the unbroken monotony of the waves running to shore.

The ferry that bore me across to Yell, and the twin vessel that later bridged the isthmus between Yell and Unst, looked, by contrast to the frail sixerns, to be as tough and buoyant as any ocean freighter. Bright red, blue and white, with a pert funnel and a busy engine, she looked as if she could bravely tackle the Atlantic. I have sometimes thought of the frustrations of being a ferry captain. Just to and fro over the same stretch of water, short and familiar. How wonderful it would be to say 'damn it!', turn sharp to starboard and head for the rolling main!

Yell was quiet. The rain had eased and some green flowed into the private patterns of the sea. Driving from the ferry I discovered that I had the luxury of *two* roads going north. The first veered to the east through Burra Voe and Otterswick, and the other headed due north to West Sandwick in mid-island. This one I took.

Here the landscape looked less unkempt than in the south, on Mainland. There were tidy cottages and white settlements, gardens and people looking over front gates, gazing at the sky as if wondering where the rain had gone. There were increasing numbers of seabirds, oystercatchers, with their orange spindle beaks and their constant calls of alarm; they always seem to have heard some dreadful news and to be anxious to spread it. Then there is the dear, comical puffin, called the Tammy Norie by the Shetlanders, and of course the ghostly swooping gulls, the Scories.

So absorbing had my surroundings become that I failed to pay due attention to the road. I had hardly seen another vehicle since leaving Lerwick and I was enthralled to see my first flight of Arctic tern. Anyway I was not watching the road and I bumped over a short, sharp hill to be confronted on the single track by nothing less than a parked steamroller!

What might have made an item of interest (to others if not to me) in the columns of *The Shetland Times* was averted by a smart swerve across a peat bog, which fortunately held firm until I managed to wrestle the car back on to the road. Even as I swung around it I noticed, with what might easily have been my last glance, that the steamroller had the design of the famous white horse on its nose. It came from Kent. I wonder how long it had taken to get up there?

As I reached the next ferry at Gutcher the sun abruptly found some real space in which to display itself. Looking across at Unst I knew at once, and with some relief, that I had not been mistaken in making the journey. It was green and shelving nicely into the sea, with settled white houses and the sound of dogs barking across the water. To the east was a whole herd of small islands in Uyeasound and the bigger back of the island of Fetlar, where a few years ago there was a miraculous nesting of a pair of Snowy Owls. The nest was hidden and protected with the peculiar jealousy that consumes ornithologists. But matters went wrong. When I arrived at Uyeasound there were still two Snowy Owls on Fetlar. But both were male.

At Gutcher I sensed, at last, that I was now seeing Shetland as I had imagined it; serene, unmolested, content with what has always been. There were some trees here too, so rare in these uppermost islands, sheltered by sturdy walls, cossetted like the precious possessions they are. Some islanders in Orkney and Shetland are oddly suspicious, even frightened of trees. I was once told by a lady at Hoy that when she had visited Scotland she had disliked the trees. "They spoil the view," she said with quaint logic. "They get in the way." Then she added darkly, "and creepy creatures, insects, you know . . ." she made a spider with her hand ". . . fall from them and into your hair."

There is a post office at Gutcher where a Shetland lady sells stamps and packets of Smiths Crisps. I bought some of each while awaiting the ferry. By the time I had finished my crisps and attached the stamps to some postcards of seals and puffins ('Up here with seal and pouting puffin – the people live right next to nuffin'), the sun had gone mad and was shining blatantly, warming the appearance, if not the actual temperature, of the sea. The opposite flank of Unst was shining bright green and the houses as white as well-washed sheets. It looked a welcoming place.

I had decided to make my headquarters on Unst at Uyeasound, tucked immediately under the elbow of the channel between Yell and the northern island. Leaving the ferry, I turned down the curling road that balances itself between the sea and a salty lagoon, a haven for resting seabirds and indolent fish. The settlement of Uyeasound, as is the custom of the scene in those parts, unfolds itself without hurry around the fringe of the bay, its houses not crammed together, but a decent distance apart, indicative of the privacy that the people treasure. But not so far apart that it's too far to walk to your neighbour for a dram.

There is a small hotel, with a careful garden of sheltered plants and trees, and behind it the curiously Mexican bell tower of a small church. There were seagulls shouting from the roof, a

Muckle Flugga lighthouse, seen from Hermaness Hill.

Looking north to Haroldswick. Topping the distant hills are the golf balls (RAF early warning stations) at Saxa Vord, which overlooks the Burra Firth and Muckle Flugga.

boy in a boat on the lagoon. Nothing else disturbed the air. That was where I stayed.

That evening, as the day began its long journey into the brief night, I went to fulfil an ambition – to look down on the most northerly part of these British Isles, the rocky lighthouse at Muckle Flugga. It was an odd, even eerie, experience, walking over the springing grass through the grey, late light. It was as if something had suspended the time of the earth, holding it in a vacuum; all was silent apart from the metronomic washing of the sea and the piping of a single, twilight bird. Rarely have I felt so solitary.

Seabirds, sitting on their exposed nests like parents at picnics, began to protest as I walked higher towards the great cliffs at the end of Britain. The long rising land is called Hermaness. It sloped upwards gradually from my feet, seeming to disappear far off into the evening. Half an hour from the start I came to a bird-watcher's hut, equipped with a rough bed and some rudimentary cooking utensils. It was intended for adventurers caught out there on that defenceless headland in bad weather. A visitors' book contained some lively humour (surprisingly naughty, some of it – for bird watchers!) and there were two entries for one night – one a student from Jerusalem, the other a Jordanian. I wager they had a night of interesting discussions and parted at day-light the best of aliens.

Also prudently provided were some yard-long canes and, remembering previous episodes on Stroma island and elsewhere, I gladly took one. It was not long before I needed it. The enormous skuas and the fulmars, now angry at my intrusion in their nesting grounds, began to attack me, swooping like wide-winged dive-bombers, trying to hit me with their wings

and their feet, an unnerving experience when you are negotiating a cliff several hundred feet above the boiling sea.

Fortunately I knew the drill. I tied a handkerchief to the end of the cane and held it above my head. Thereafter their attacking swoops ended at the extremity of the cane. It felt more than a little ridiculous to be walking in this remote corner, with not a soul for miles, a white flag held high – like some pathetic and defected soldier seeking someone to whom he could surrender.

Eventually, I was there – at the veritable conclusion of Britain – standing, like a disem-bodied spirit, looking down from the most dramatic and frightening precipice, almost onto the apex of the Muckle Flugga lighthouse.

It stands offshore, set upon a spray of rocks, its regular beam shining north towards the Arctic, so far, so powerful that it would have been no surprise to have seen it reflected back from the pack ice. The sea washed lazily about its feet and slopped over the neighbouring

Above, a colony of gannets on the west coast of Hermaness. The rock in the distance is known as Natural Arch.

Right, looking south from above the cliffs across the little bay of Norwick showing the village of Norwick in the middle distance.

islets. Sitting far above it, in that remote gloaming, I felt very alone and very happy. Even the skuas and fulmars had gone home. This is one of the occasional things for which I reach. This is why I had gone to that place. I sat on the top of the cliff for an hour. The grey, gritty twilight seemed constant, showing no sign of going away. So I went first, winding my way down and inland, back again to the homely houses of the settlement of Uyeasound. It had been a good evening.

*   *   *

On the following morning I went to Baltasound and Haroldswick, where the Vikings made their first grateful land-falls. It was not difficult to see the attraction of Baltasound for men who had journeyed perilously across the seas of the savage latitudes. It is all but landlocked, with the anchorage protected by the arms of low, clean hills, swept by the wind. The dwellings here are again decently spread out so that no man may poke his nose over another's fence. There are ruined crofts on the uplands, tombstones to industry that never got its reward, inhabited now by sheep and dog-like Shetland ponies.

At Haroldswick the fierce king Harold Hardrada came ashore to change the course of this country's history. He and his warriors would recognise the place today, the wide, flat-lying bay, the naked hills, the pale sky, the silence.

Norwick is the northernmost village on Unst (and, therefore, in the British Isles), again a scattering of white, precise houses with enclosed flower gardens, and the final place to post a letter in Britain; beyond that the road leads to the last house in the kingdom.

The sun was out when I reached that house over the hilly track. It squats beside a stream full of fish and marsh marigolds, a wooden bridge, a gully leading to the vacant beach with its long-armed rollers. The house – called The Haa – is of one storey, white, with a red roof, and an upturned boat – used as a storehouse – by its side. Two sheepdogs lay in the friendly sun beside a wooden fence. From the gate there was a view to the beach with the violently blue sea coming in at a regular rush, its waves forming spaced, white bands, its roar always available, its breeze salty to the taste.

Strangely enough, this house was formerly occupied by Willie Sinclair, who was a friend of Willie Mathieson, the lighthouse keeper I met on the island of Stroma when undergoing one of the other adventures in this book. Now Alison and Bertie Priest lived there.

Alison, a young woman, with the native modesty of the ladies of those regions, was friendly enough in her greeting but suggested I returned in the evening when her husband was at home. I said I would and I did. And I was very glad because Bertie Priest, the last man in Britain, told me one of the most amazing stories I had ever heard during my travels in remote parts.

"One winter night," he said in the best tradition of the island storyteller, "we looked out and saw rockets being fired towards the north of Unst." He was sitting in the enclosed room, a slim, lithe, young man with a reputation as a strong fisherman. Alison sat listening and knitting in the Shetland style. We had two drams of whisky poured.

"It was her," said Bertie nodding across to the far wall. "That one." I went across the room and bent to look at a framed photograph. It was of a wrecked vessel, spread-eagled across

Right, the small bay and the cliffs, just north of Norwick. The road above the cliffs leads to The Haa.

some stormy rocks. "A Russian trawler," he nodded. "And a terrible night it was, you can believe me. I grabbed a rope and went up to the cliffs. The other men from Norwick and some from Haroldswick were there. There was a big sea but nobody was lost. Some of the Russians got themselves ashore and we pulled some out. But they were all right. The ship was a loss. You could see that without looking twice. She was never going to get off those rocks."

He smiled quietly. "Ach, there was some queer stuff appearing on the island after that," he said. "Maps and plans and charts. Charts of *Boston Harbour*! Now what would a *fishing* boat be doing with them? Some men came up from London and took a lot of the stuff away and, of course, we never knew what happened to it. But the steering wheel went missing too . . ."

"Things do," I agreed quietly, "from wrecks."

"Aye, yes. It was around on Unst. A nice wheel with brass." He paused and refilled the

*Charlie Priest (standing)
and Bertie Priest, outside
The Haa with the wheel
from the Russian boat.*

glasses. I sensed there was more to the story. "Then, about a couple of weeks after the wreck, my brother was ploughing the field on the top of the cliff, just above where the trawler lay. And as he was ploughing he saw these Russians walk over the horizon. They had come up the cliff path and they appeared, about ten of them and came towards him. There were two officers in uniform, and a civilian, and the rest were sailors – *armed with submachine-guns and rifles.*"

I stared into the steady eyes. "Armed," he nodded genuinely. "Here in Shetland. Russians. Just imagine what my brother felt like. They came towards him. He stopped ploughing and just waited for them. He guessed they'd come from one of the big Russian ships that are with the trawler fleet. So they walked towards him with their guns. The civilian stepped forward and the others stopped and he said 'Do you think I could use your telephone?'"

I burst into laughter. Bertie did too. "It's true," he swore. "So my brother brought them to the house here and the man who spoke English telephoned a shipping agent in Lerwick or Aberdeen and reversed the charges. Then, when the business was done, the Russians asked where they could buy some whisky. I took the officers and the civilian to the shop in Norwick and they bought the entire stock. Every last drop. They started to drink it even before they'd got back here.

"They were all blind drunk in no time! All the sailors as well. They were outside here shooting down seabirds, skuas and fulmars, with their submachine-guns. Just shooting them out of the sky. And they're *protected* birds, you know. They were having a great time.

"Then before they went, the chief officer said to me that somebody had stolen the steering wheel from the wrecked ship and that if they did not get it back they would report it to the police!"

It was all getting a bit *Alice in Wonderland*. "The police?" I echoed, thinking of the island's only constable.

"Aye, they're here shooting down protected birds like havoc and they're going to report the steering wheel to the police," he nodded. "I thought there was going to be trouble, so I said I would get the wheel back for them. I knew where it was. In the RAF camp."

"The RAF camp," I repeated weakly. "The RAF had stolen the Russians' wheel?"

"Correct," said Bertie. "That's the radar camp at SaxaVord. So I telephoned the commanding officer and he got the wheel back. He found out where it was. It was given to me and I ran down to the beach with my brother to return it to the Russians. By the time we had got there they had already pushed off in their boats and were heading for the trawlers. There was quite a bit of a swell running and it would have been difficult for them to get back. The man who spoke English shouted that they would come back the next day. So we stuck the spokes of the wheel into the sand and left it there. The next morning the weather was bad and so it was for the next few days. The wheel stayed there and they never came back for it. Never."

By now I was staring unbelievingly. But his face was straight and sincere. Armed Russians on British soil? Shooting the Queen's protected seabirds? A stolen steering wheel in an RAF radar camp? Bertie Priest stood up. "I'll show you," he said. He led me out of the room and into the evening light. He undid the door of his storehouse, the hull of the upturned boat next to his house. "There," he said pointing.

And there it was. Standing at the far end, a fine brass and wooden steering wheel.

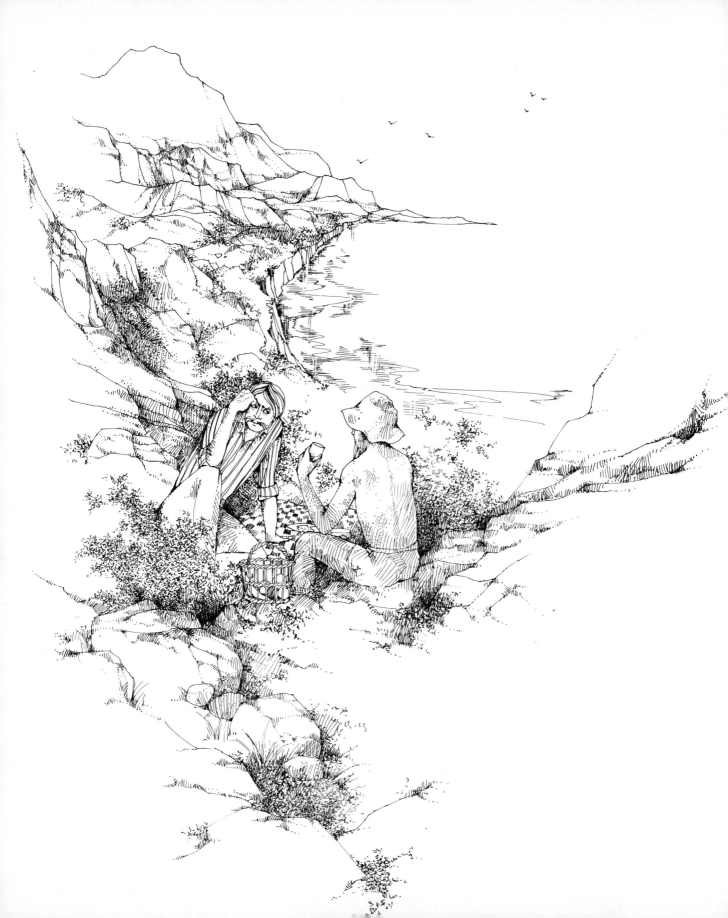

SIX

An Eagle In Wester Ross

The day you see your first eagle is the day you know that, now, you've seen everything. I saw my first eagle at Loch Broom, on the seafringe of the silent fastness of Ross and Cromarty, on a light and limpid day in early summer. As I watched, I wanted to shout.

The eagle loitered in the polished sky. Drifting down, wings akimbo, it was abruptly and presumptuously attacked by a rowdy crowd of commonplace herring-gulls. They mobbed it as it cruised at a hundred or so feet, shouting and screaming like washerwomen cursing a king. The eagle flapped them away with a languid, bored beat of wings, and then (you could imagine it yawning) rose without haste through the gull tribe, until it soared into a sky higher than they could ever dream. Far away, up there it cruised around like God.

Loch Broom is a cleft in the inletted, islanded coast of Wester Ross now called, perhaps less romantically, Highland. On its northern shore is the little white town of Ullapool, with its transluscent harbour, the comely houses in its street looking directly at the loch and across to a long, humped peninsula, purple and green, with a single inn delectably alone on the shore. Little Loch Broom is to the south, on the far flank of the peninsula and to the north-west, out to sea, a misty archipelago called The Summer Isles.

When I was a boy and I spent my time travelling in books, I made a collection of the places I most wanted to visit. Among these were The Summer Isles, because of their very sound, and the village of Applecross, described then as the most isolated mainland settlement in Britain, reached by a rocky road so high it journeyed through the clouds, and was attained, as one explorer put it 'with a sense of achievement'. Applecross was lower on the western coast than The Summer Isles, across the granite barrier of the Torridon Mountains. It was many years before I made that journey. I had been waiting and, in moments of thinking about them, I liked to believe, oddly, that they were also waiting for me.

Once I had actually attempted to telephone The Summer Isles (which were uninhabited). Not such a pointless operation as might be imagined since I have seen serviceable public telephone boxes on many depopulated islands. It's a ghostly thought to imagine the ring-ring issuing out into the mists, disturbing oyster-catchers and causing complacent rabbits to raise their heads. At the time I wanted to make the call to The Summer Isles I was working as a reporter on a newspaper in London. It had been a drizzling summer and our features editor, with a flash of inspiration which was perhaps less than vivid, instructed me to write an article about the weather. Dolefully, I thought that every aspect of this commonplace subject had been covered. So, instead of going through the routine of telephoning the soggy seaside resorts, or speaking to anguished organisers of fated fetes, cricket festivals and regattas, I enjoyed myself by looking up in the gazetteer all the place names in Britain that had some connection with meteorology – Windrush (Gloucestershire), Cold Kirby (Yorkshire), various Winterbournes in Dorset, and a place somewhere, I swear, called Rain. (It seems to have disappeared from the maps, perhaps washed away.) Everywhere the day was dismal. Then I tried to discover if there was anyone I could call on The Summer Isles. There was not but I eventually talked to a shepherd on the mainland who reported that the weather was beautiful, that the islands were basking in a blue sea. "There's no soul over there now," he said. "Only the sheep. It's a grand day for sheep."

I remember sitting at my city desk watching the rain curling down the window, my mind full of the imagination of them – The Summer Isles, green and tranquil in a coloured sea. And I was here, and up there were only sheep. Lucky sheep. There was no justice. But one day . . .

Years later the 'one day' arrived. The journey began in Glasgow where, the previous night, Mr Andro Linklater and I had engaged in a deplorable, not to say juvenile, contest of standing on our heads in the middle of a very good restaurant, an exhibition which concluded in our riotous departure from the establishment on the trolley that normally transports expensive puddings. Everyone applauded (so I was later assured): customers, staff and the lonely man who played the piano on a romantic little balcony. The next day, beset with worries that the restaurant might well have its four stars reduced to two spanners and a breakdown truck, I felt ill and dreadful, and I have not seen Mr Linklater since. I do hope he's all right.

As if to compound the error of this rare lapse from decency and sobriety, I had chosen to make the journey to the remoteness of Ross and Cromarty with another writer, my long-time friend, Brian Freemantle, a novelist of much talent whose mode of life, however, makes him singularly unsuited for anywhere that does not have – at least – a choice of luxury hotels; the sort of man who treats the label of a bottle of wine in a Scots ale bar to a disgruntled knitting of the eyebrows. He has, in addition, a fastidiousness about his clothes and personal appearance which scarcely fits him for adventures in the wild, open air; the sort of man who, wearing Gucci shoes, risks his life on a three-hundred-foot cliff to recover a dropped comb.

However, there is no more amiable companion, and we drove from Glasgow on a splendid day, pausing only three or four times for lunch and liquid refurbishment in the first two hours. As we left the streets and houses and pushed the nose of the car towards the green uplands, I extolled the freedom and isolation we were now entering, only to be disconcertingly interrupted by a traffic jam. The road was tight and there had been a collision a couple of miles ahead. When we finally restarted, Freemantle discovered he'd left his Parisian sunglasses in the last waterhole, and, being unable to turn, I parked and waited until he had gone back on foot and recovered them. A sour woman scolded me for stopping in front of her house, presumably because it ruined the bed and breakfast trade. It was not an auspicious beginning.

Gradually we moved beyond the traffic, leaving behind orchards and shops and rows of houses, driving on the rise to where the evening sun warmed upland meadows, neatly arranged with grazing sheep. We stopped eventually at a small but fine baronial hotel.

Looking south-east down Loch Broom and showing the villages of Ardindrean and Letters.

Freemantle, who looks for stars on hotels with much the same diligence as an astronomer seeks them in the firmament, mentioned that while it was not a patch on the George Cinq in Paris, it did appear to be comfortable in a primitive fashion. We ate, and drank, a good dinner and then walked in the lingering sunlight to the village inn which, we had been assured, was the centre of social activity in the locality.

Whatever the normal nature of that social activity, it had ceased on that evening. We entered a bare, square room, with a bar crossing its width at the distant end. Its furnishings and decoration would have scarcely enhanced a condemned cell. It was the clients, however, who

The small harbour at Ullapool.

immediately provoked attention; twenty or so customers, plus one barman and one barmaid, sprawled on the floor and over the bare furniture as if smitten by a death-ray from space. "That's what alcohol does for you," mentioned Freemantle sagely. He sniffed. "I think this is our sort of place."

As we walked among the mayhem, one man, wild of eye and accent, got to his elbow and bleated, "Scotland . . . lost . . . in the name of God – TO PERU!"

"It's the World Cup," I whispered to my companion who tends towards *chemin de fer* when it comes to sport. "Scotland lost to Peru."

"What would it be like if they'd won?" he murmured wisely. He reached the bar and managed to jack up the barmaid from her prone position across the beer handles. The sound of his money on the counter brought several of the slaughtered customers to within a glimmer of life. The man who had first howled the terrible news now sat up. Cross-eyed to the point of brilliance, he managed to smile a toothless greeting in our direction and then, as though his duty was as a cabaret artist, he took his shoes off and did a little singing dance in toeless socks before sinking with a renewed moan to the recumbent attitude. We applauded decently and I went over to him and, lifting his head, asked if he would like a drink. Those haunted eyes focused briefly and he managed to assemble a nod. As I was about to leave for the bar, he grasped my leg and said, "But I'll no' be able to return the compliment, due to several years of unemployment."

After that we had an absorbing, if not entirely happy, evening. The vanquishing of the Scots blue lions by some South American midgets was a dreadful and terrible blow. When we left, going on down the road through the glimmer-din, as they call the long end of the day, they were trying to revive their national spirit with some singing. It had to be a dirge and it floated on the cool air to us, as sad and poignant as any lonely piper playing a lament.

*   *   *

The next day was wonderful. A polished morning, sunlight high and early, clothing the mountains and reflecting from windows and water. Scottish weather lies in waiting, a grin on its face no doubt, to surprise you. Once, in February, I went to Dunoon on Holy Loch, prepared as if I was journeying to Ultima Thule. Out came the sun, brilliantly warm, bringing out the Argyll lasses in their summer frocks and causing American sailors from the nuclear submarine base to strip to the waists and beat their chests in a jungular sort of way. I've been in Aberdeen when it was as humid as Port Said, except Port Said doesn't have the aroma of fish. And once, in Glasgow, there were Christmas lights in the trees and the city basked like Biarritz.

On that day in Wester Ross, driving north and west the temperature was established in the seventies by mid-morning. We put down the hood of the car (my old and faithful Peugeot Cabriolle) and journeyed towards Loch Broom, with a fine sense of freedom and enjoyment, through the climbing glens, over bridges sitting like bonnets above waterfalls, along the smiling miles of the Caledonian Canal. I once knew a man who had the original plans, sketches and specifications for the construction of the Caledonian Canal. They were like Leonardo drawings.

The highest mountains rose before us, at this season still robed in snow. We skirted west through the green glens until in the late afternoon we rounded a final turn and shouted with the sheer enjoyment of our first view of the small town of Ullapool. It evoked at once a sensation of well-being, its white houses carefully but casually set alongside the banks of the reflecting Loch Broom. Our road curved at the blunt end of the loch, on one side of the water the high, humped back of the lonely peninsula, on our side the houses sitting smugly in the sun. Purple and green, blue, white and bronze, the scene filled the windscreen of the car. "Makes you feel like a drink, doesn't it?" murmured Freemantle.

Evening was the best time. The light sidled away to the western sea, leaving a late, quiet greyness. Drowsy seabirds flew unhurriedly a little above the satin surface of the loch, fish came up making dartboards all over the harbour. People loitered by the waterfront, not wanting to miss a moment of the air. Others waited, with no impatience, for the arrival of the steamer from the Hebrides. Some were meeting passengers or goods, but most were simply waiting to see it; each berthing, each sailing, unique.

For myself, I could hardly wait to set eyes on The Summer Isles. They were out at the mouth of the loch and slightly around the corner to the north-west, so they were hidden from Ullapool. "Ye'll need ta gao ta Achiltibuie," said one of the Ullapool fishermen, my first hearing of that deliciously pronounced name ('A-kill-ti-booee'). "There ye'll see yon Summer Isles." He paused reflectively. "Like a wee fleet o' ships."

It was further than we thought, a wild and winding road of twenty-six miles, single track, with a white village first, sheep in the vivid green fields, then a rising ride to gorse and heather,

Looking north-north-west across Loch Broom towards Ullapool with the village of Letters on the left.

and finally an exhilarating journey beneath the limbs of granite mountains supporting the pale sky. After leaving the village we saw only one house.

It was still warm enough to keep the hood of the car down. The road rose and dipped, the sea appeared, then vanished, and eventually we arrived at what might have been the end of the world – Achiltibuie, a sedate place with a few houses, a store and a post office, and, to my companion's huge gratification, a splendid inn and Egon Ronay-recommended restaurant! Here of all places!

He stood, his back to the sea, gazing at the place, in his eyes the gladness of a man who knows he has both luck and instinct. But my eyes were looking for only one thing – the islands. There they sat, mist-touched, lying low in the darkening sea, like something from a Norse legend – my Summer Isles. They were a mile or so out in the bay like, as the man said, 'a wee fleet o' ships.' "I'm going to have to go out there," I said to Freemantle. "Now I've seen them I've got to land on them."

He stared at them for a full ten seconds, his gin hardly touching his lips. "It's wonderful," he breathed.

"They certainly are," I said, my eyes out to the islands.

"I mean the restaurant," he said.

It used to be the village inn. At one time they held a sheep fair at Achiltibuie, an important once-a-year event which was planned and discussed through all the dead, dark winter and then mulled over and enjoyed again through the following autumn and into the spring.

By the time we left (Egon Ronay having been borne out) the evening had finally made up its mind to go, and calm darkness touched the landscape. The road was of a nature that makes you, too late, have second thoughts about the pleasures of a good wine at dinner. It looped and twisted, climbed and then contrarily swooped to sea level again. It had not seemed like that on the outward journey. Perhaps it moved once it was dark? There were sounds in the mountains. We had put the hood up but the windows were rolled down.

My friend, full of that special smugness that comes after an excellent dinner, sank down in the passenger seat and only opened one eyelid at my shout when a fearsome Scots wildcat abruptly sprang from the rocks at one side of the road, and, eyes ablaze in the lights, jumped into the heather on the other side. It was so thrilling, I howled with excitement.

"That," said Freemantle with the cautious assessment of a zoologist, "looked like a pussy cat."

You can't take him anywhere.

To reach the Loch Broom Peninsula (or the Scoraig Peninsula as it is also called) it was necessary to drive south-east from Ullapool to the blunt end of the loch, and then turn up a narrow road at Loch Broom Church and go back along the other side of the wide waterway, through the collections of small, half-concealed houses at Letters, Ardindrean, Rhiroy, Blarnalevloch and Loggie. The road peters out entirely before it gets to any of the last four. Transport is by boat, on foot or a bumpy bicycle ride. At Letters, needless to say, there is a little postbox under the trees.

A friend of mine, David Ross, tells the story of walking across this peninsula on a summer's day and seeing an old man working in a field. They paused for conversation. "Do they still have the little jaunting cars in Ireland?" asked the Loch Broom man. Puzzled, David said: "I'm not from Ireland, I'm from Inverness-shire." Inverness-shire was the next county.

"Aye," said the man. "I've heard of it. But it's a long way away."

David added that, in fact, he came from Dingwall. "Ach," sighed the man, "an' a dirty hole that is." David thought that the fact that he then lived in London had better go unsaid.

The only way to traverse the peninsula to its southern shore is by a high and narrow track from the inn at Altnaharrie, opposite Ullapool. It can also be reached by a big detour on the main road bringing you to Dundonnell, where a slim, steely waterfall slides deep down through ferns into an echoing cleft in the granite. There is a wooden bridge across the gorge that seems to sway with the very sound of the fall; spray rises through the bright green ferns and trees cling to the rocks, hanging down their heads towards the cataract like suicides who have yet to make up their minds.

At Scoraig, at the very tip of the long jut of land, out where the heather dips straight down to the Atlantic Ocean, there was, we were told, a colony of castaways; people who had turned their faces from the attributes of civilisation, including roads, and lived in harmony and isolation. Fifty-strong, they had occupied a deserted village and repaired it, farming the forgotten meadows, making their own tools and furniture, renovating the schoolhouse and teaching their children. They had become adept enough with boats to evoke favourable comment from the local fishermen. Their contact with the outside world was a public telephone box which the post office had obligingly reconnected for them.

To reach them meant a powerful trek of five miles or more along a path, thin as a piece of cotton, straggling along the cheeks of hills and the foreheads of cliffs. I was frankly astonished that Freemantle had not only agreed to accompany me on my projected arduous journey to reach these remote people at the end of the peninsula, but had insisted on making the arrangements for provisioning the adventure. This, I thought at the time, was much the same as Beau Brummell, offering to go in place of Stanley to find Livingstone in Africa. But at least it promised a quality packed-lunch, and so it turned out to be. Paté, chicken drumsticks, various tasty sandwiches, and coleslaw, with salad kept fresh in appropriate containers, plus no fewer than eight tins of beer. Wine, he had decided, was not the beverage of men on an expedition.

It was another remarkable morning when we set out. There was hardly a seam in the water of the loch, the sky was so high you could not see it, sun growing everywhere across the lovely landscape of hill and heather. We drove to Dundonnell and then along the thin road through a cossetted valley frothy with trees, an elderly and elegant church, and finally to the place on the shoulder of Little Loch Broom, on the southern side of the peninsula, where the road vanished into gorse and there was nothing for it but to walk.

My companion's cooperation, even eagerness, had encouraged my enthusiasm for the trip. In front of us the giant finger of land projected in the general direction of America. The sun was high and full now and we set out in the necessary single file along the slender track. The air was clean to the nostril and the warmth welcome on the face. Below, far below, we could see great rocks, like the hulls of sunken ships, lying clearly in the calm and empty water. Silence filled the whole world, a deep quietness that lay across the water, that curled in the clefts of the hills, that seemed to touch us as we walked. It was broken only in intervals by the call of a cuckoo, seeming to reach us from many miles away, far across the water perhaps.

There was no other birdsong, not even any shouting of gulls. Our footsteps sounded like drumbeats on the stony path.

Unfortunately, while the pleasures of this place were far from unappreciated, it was undeniably hot. The sun got to its zenith and burned on our heads, the going became more

Looking down into the valley of the River Broom towards Ullapool. Loch Broom can be seen in the distance.

Altnaharrie Inn seen across Loch Broom from Ullapool. Note the path over the hill which leads to Little Loch Broom.

difficult, and the drop down over the tumbling rocks more sheerly impressive as we went on. "I think my head's beginning to swim," mentioned my intrepid friend who was foraging ahead. "Perhaps we had better rest and have a beer."

We did. Sitting on a couch of granite we simultaneously drank in the scene and two pints of McEwan's Ale. "How far do you think we've travelled?" asked Freemantle in a tone which should have warned me he was losing interest.

"A mile, I should think," I guessed. "Certainly not more."

Falls of Measach in the early morning, showing the foot bridge across the gorge.

"It's taken nearly an hour," he returned, looking at his Cartier watch. "How far did you say it is?"

"Another three or four miles," I said.

"That's what I thought," he replied. "That's another three or four hours."

"Yes."

"And then we've got to get back."

"Yes. We do have to get back."

I knew I shouldn't have come with him. He pointed with a trembling finger towards the indistinct horizon. "Out there," he said plaintively. "Right out there. All . . . that way?"

"All that way."

"Look," he said indicating he was doing me a favour. "Why don't we sit down here, eat the lunch and drink the beer, and go back?"

"Oh, all right," I sighed. We opened the picnic basket and another two cans of beer and did just that. Stanley and Livingstone would never have approved. Beau Brummell would.

*   *   *

No man with half an ounce of romance in his soul, having seen the little inn at Altnaharrie, could fail to visit it. It beckons like a single finger across the waters of Loch Broom, a solitary patch of white against the dark shades of the high and humped Scoraig Peninsula. Viewed from Ullapool, it seems almost touchable. Pale birds drift across the face of bulky land over there and the eagles live in the crannies above.

The news that a palatable lunch, with a decent wine, had been known to be available at this isolated place induced a proper enthusiasm in my friend Freemantle, who, somewhat shame-faced after our strategic retreat of the previous day, was eager to make the crossing. "I hear they have a good variety of cheeses," he muttered. Had he been old enough to fight in the war, which he was not by a decade, I feel he would have merited distinction in the battles around the Champagne country or possibly in the saving of Gouda, a fancy counterbalanced by the added knowledge that he is also partial to the gourmet aspects of the Rhine Valley, although, in fairness, I cannot believe that he would have ever contemplated desertion or treachery on this score.

Another morning of wispy beauty emerged, the water of the loch almost seeming to float on the air. We were at the Ullapool harbour early, in time to witness the overnight steamer from the Hebrides materialise through mist hanging like a gauze curtain between Loch Broom and the wide sea. The water trembled and ran away in feathers as the rotund vessel made its way with genial importance towards the landing stage. Its radar scanner whirled above its bridge like a large rattle swung by an exuberant football supporter. The people in the quay watched it with impassive Highland anticipation, waiting in little groups for people or parcels coming ashore. They shifted their feet and agreed quietly that she was a bonnie sight an'all on such a fair morning. Vans began to draw up to claim their share of the cargo, the seagulls congregated expectantly, anticipating the oddments that seagulls expect as their due when ships arrive in port.

The ferry curved like a scimitar from the centre of the wide channel, turning quite abruptly when she had seemed almost past the jetty. Perhaps the captain's thoughts were elsewhere, like a dreaming bus driver who almost misses a stop.

However, he appeared to be quite cool and in command, looking down from his bridge as the vessel sidled to the quay and settled there with the sort of sigh that comes from a good journey and a satisfied arrival. We sat on some fish crates near the ice container – used to stock the fishing boats and called locally 'the piggy bank' – and indulged ourselves with that most happy of all occupations, watching the unloading of a small ship.

People disembarked with their parcels and string bags, their dogs, and in one case a cat whose black head projected stoically from a Dolcis shoe box. Some were greeted with grave friendliness by those who had waited and others trotted along the cobbles to where the buses departed for mysteriously-called places far up in the Highlands. But everybody seemed to know everybody and there were handshakes and proper greetings in the morning sunshine.

Our watching was interrupted by a call from behind us and below. We turned to see a pretty woman standing in a boat, a vessel small, white and curved like a duck. "Are you the passengers for Altnaharrie?" she called cheerfully. She was wearing a blue fisherman's smock. Her face was clear and her smile bright. We confirmed that we were indeed for Altnaharrie although we couldn't say it as well as she did.

Landlubbers that we were, we managed to get down the steps and into the boat, the lady helping us aboard as though we were two old biddies out for a day's whelking. It seemed a very condensed vessel for what appeared to be a quite considerable crossing. It was piled with merchandise and several other passengers clambered down the steps to join us. Freemantle, who fits quite elegantly into a luxury liner or a white-flanneled yacht, leaned over and whispered worriedly, "There don't appear to be any cabins."

Altnaharrie Inn seen from Loch Broom.

There were not. We set out of the harbour with the lady captain whose name was Jill Brown. Her husband was a veterinary surgeon and they ran the inn at Altnaharrie together. She said the name meant Boundary Burn, after a stream that hangs like a spider's web down the steep side of the Scoraig Peninsula.

Nothing changes more quickly than a landscape approached from the seaward. What seems to be a flat hill becomes wrinkled with valleys and gulleys, a rock becomes a little cape, a slender brown strand a curved beach. We watched from the smoothly moving boat as the object of our journey became more apparent. The inn, which from the other side looked as square and expressionless as a postage stamp, began to smile at us, its windows bright in the sun, its door wide open. Dogs barked, their voices travelling strangely as they always do across flat, still water.

Silver birches streaked the rocks rising at the back of the inn, intrepid mountain-ash clung to the merest foothold, the gorse splashed vibrant yellow and the heather purple. More intimate flowers bloomed beautifully in the shelter of the inn. Roses and honeysuckle hung on the washed walls; fuschia and geraniums edged their way from the lawn in front of the door down to the shingle of the beach, growing almost among the seashells.

Our boat, nodding like a homing hound, eased itself towards the fragile wooden jetty, Jill Brown guiding it surely alongside, between the shoals of sand and rock, as she had done many times before. We landed with a feeling of near exultation; the warmth of the air closed around us, the smell of the flowers and the sea everywhere, the springy grass under our steps and giant bees roaming gleefully among the thick climbers, like us it seemed, hardly able to believe their luck.

Two black dogs ran from the house, jumping and barking with the excitement of our

Fred Brown, vet and proprietor of the Altnaharrie Inn, standing in his garden.

Right, looking north-north-west in the direction of The Summer Isles across Loch Broom with Ullapool in the foreground.

disembarkation, although it could hardly have been a novelty. I took it all in; the huge backdrop of the mountain, the edging of blue sky, the glittering water and the intimacy of that tight, summery place. At that moment I felt I could have stayed there for ever. Freemantle was examining the inn, possibly trying to detect its star rating. Fortunately it had none.

Jill Brown and her husband Fred admitted that they had hugged themselves when they had found Altnaharrie. They had searched the west coast for such a place. "It wasn't difficult to choose," smiled Jill. They chartered boats and ran the inn for a few fortunate guests, and Fred still did his rounds as a vet. They originally came from the chimneys of suburban London, first going to live in the far north of Scotland before finding the inn and moving there.

We sat on the patch of lawn and looked across the painted water to the sedate, regular houses of Ullapool, strung like a train along the far shore. The black dogs had stretched out in the shade of two keel-up boats on the pebbles just below the garden. There was still no wisp of cloud anywhere. The urban Freemantle was trying to reach civilisation by telephone, paying for the call with the quotation of his credit card number. "I especially love the winter here," said Jill Brown. "We get wonderful still days and we're by ourselves and able to get on with the jobs that seem to pile up through the summer. It never seems as cold to me as it does in London. We don't get a lot of snow because the loch is very sheltered, but we have marvellous storms. Gales and the sea rushing almost at the front door. It's spectacular. One of the great luxuries of living in a place like this is lying in bed at night and listening to the wind and the weather."

On the other hand, recrossing Loch Broom on a dark night with a force ten thrusting in from the Atlantic can be uncomfortable. "We've had some interesting trips like that," she recalled. "But it's not often the weather deters us from visiting friends or going over to the

Left, Ullapool harbour with fishing nets in the foreground.

cinema club in the hotel at Ullapool. We go out by boat as naturally as most people use their car. It's part of our everyday life."

They cannot receive television at Altnaharrie so the evenings are spent reading and listening to music or eating and talking with friends and visitors. Wild animals roam the empty heights of the peninsula, red deer who sometimes come to nibble in the garden, pine-martens and wild cats and, of course, the pair of eagles. They come back to Loch Broom every year to nest.

Jill went off to prepare lunch and my fellow writer and I climbed up the steep path behind the inn. We were now almost level, but on the other side of the peninsula, to the place where we so pusillanimously abandoned our journey the previous day. Now I knew better than to try and encourage Freemantle to travel anywhere beyond the frontiers of civilisation or to a place where he might fail to hear the lunch gong. We climbed the gorge, had a competition throwing stones at a slim birch tree, the loser to pay for lunch. I won. The Altnaharrie stream slips and tumbles through the brushwood and the gorse up there, and then mutters over rocks between the birches and the mountain ash. Sometimes it rests itself in smooth basins before trickling over a jug-like lip to continue its wandering. The water in these pools looked pale brown, cool and tempting and the day continued hot. I clambered over some bun-shaped boulders and squatted. Freemantle descended also. "It looks like beer," I suggested. We cupped our hands and tasted it. "It tastes like beer too," grunted my friend. He is not a beer man.

Two days later my companion left for Inverness, there to return by train to the soft south. I walked with him to the early bus which left from the quay and he departed with his customary sang-froid and an elegant tip-up movement of his hand, which indicated that he would dispatch a campari and soda as soon as he reached a decent hotel in licensing hours.

In truth I was not all that sorry to see him go, old friend and amiable companion that he is, for this was the day I had planned to sail privately to The Summer Isles.

I voyaged down the full arm's length of Loch Broom in Ian McLean's new boat *Islander*, under the great forehead of the Scoraig Peninsula. Almost at the ocean, the granite cliffs are surprisingly replaced by a low, fertile valley where cattle loitered, the livestock of the commune which had isolated itself far out in that nose of Scotland.

On the other side of the loch was the curving land and the single road that ended at Achiltibuie. It looked just as wild from the sea as it had the night we drove along it. Ian McLean was careful with his new boat, all paint and varnished wood. It was the first day he had sailed in her. Alongside him in the wheelhouse stood John Murdo; two quiet men nursing a vessel along like maids with a new baby carriage. Ian's family came from Achiltibuie. His father was a stonemason. "He's got memorials all over the Highlands," he joked quietly. The loch opened out. He nodded to the northern shore. "The deportations never happened here," he said, mentioning a subject that is still enough to raise the wrath of Highland people today – the wholesale depopulation of the region by greedy landowners in the nineteenth century. Livestock, they had decided, were more profitable than people. "They say that at Achiltibuie," he related "the folk refused to move and when soldiers were sent by boat, the women all went down to the shore and repelled them with stones. The men stayed back in the village. After a little while the soldiers decided they'd had enough and they went back in their boats. They never returned to Achiltibuie."

John Murdo has the startling blue eyes of the Scandinavian. He comes from the Isle of Lewis, but married a girl from Wester Ross and settled by the loch. He said that his grandfather and father had told him that much of Lewis and this area around Loch Broom was, in their lifetimes, populated by many people who were tall, fair-haired and blue-eyed, the descendants of the Viking raiders of distant centuries.

In remote and romantic places such as this the power of superstition and the myths of magic never fade. There are fairies in the streams and giants in the hills. Nobody makes light of the evil eye, nor ignores the curled lip or the muttered curse or incantation.

Serious-faced people will tell you that fairies are in residence in the abandoned and ruined crofts in the hidden parts of the hills. The thick grass that seems to take over the stone is their protection against the eyes of humans. On small islands, and in deserted places on the wild mainland, elfin lights are seen at night – dancing. A man living on the shores of Loch Broom told me that he had a brother who was cursed by the fairies and could not shake the curse away for years. People also believe that mighty horses rise from the sea and gallop madly along the loch shores on certain nights. Some people in Ullapool still recall a woman who was said to have been taken off by the fairies and had to live with them for a year. Sprites from the hills are also said to have taught a shepherd boy to play the bagpipes – in the course of a single night. They have something for which to answer.

Water kelpies and mermaids are well respected, and people believe that the rowan tree will keep witches from their door, witches who have power to turn milk sour or to make frogs of human beings. But the rowan must not be planted at the wane of the moon because it will lose its disenchantment and die. Those who have the power of the Sian can make ordinary folk invisible, sometimes for ever.

It would not be difficult to imagine an enchantment cast upon The Summer Isles. They appeared in the misty sun as we drew away from the enclosing arms of the loch, isolated, silent, wrapped in their own thoughts. They seemed to move towards us, rather than we towards them, a ghostly fleet sailing on a spellbound sea.

Now I was lost in happiness. Here I was and here were they. Just as I had always known they would be. Scattered over a square mile of water, they now came from the mist, as though throwing off their cloaks. Seabirds began to circle them like crowns. Seals were sounding somewhere in an echoing cave. This was it.

"Which one would you be wanting to go ashore?" asked Ian McLean. I was lost for choice. Tanera More, Eilean Dubh, Glas Leac Beag. Then I saw the sea-pinks blushing all down the face of one island. It had a curved and sandy beach and bay. I could have sworn it winked at me. "That one," I decided.

"Aye," he nodded, turning the wheel of the boat. "That's Càrn Nan Sgeir. It's a fine little island."

They eased the *Islander* into a platform of flat rock that conveniently became a landing stage. Elated, I scrambled ashore. The boat pushed off and went for an hour's fishing leaving me alone, marooned, on an island in The Summer Isles. How wonderful!

In the tradition of every castaway my first reaction was to explore. I scrambled up a steep incline from the landing rock and stood surveying. My goodness, what a place! The islands were sitting all around me in the pleasant sun, the sea stretched like bales of satin, unrolling on each quarter, far out to where the great Scottish mountains shouldered the stainless and distant sky.

My island – it was immediately claimed – was about two acres in extent, a large isle attached

by the shell-strewn beach to a smaller one, like a letter 'H' with one leg shorter than the other. I was on the highest point of the larger portion, with thick moss, salty campion and sea-pinks, covering all but the largest rocks. These rocks protruded like the noses of people buried in flowers. The sea lolled all around, easing itself into the joining bay, flopping indolently against the steeper rocks with such lack of effort that you could almost hear it yawn. It was clearer than any water I have ever seen in this world, not excluding the bays of the West Indies and the lagoons of the South Pacific. The seabed was easily visible, patterned with shells lying on smooth sand. Fish idled in the little bays and nosed about the gardens of coloured weed. The water looked so transluscent and the sun gave it such a benevolence that you felt that, despite the latitude, it had to be warm. I leaned over and ran my hands through it. Freezing.

As I began to walk down from the slope towards the band of beach that tethered the two parts of the island, I disturbed nesting seabirds, terns and gulls, so that they rose incensed and screeching into the silent day. My old friends from a dozen deserted shores, the oyster-catchers, zoomed around, low and apparently panic-stricken, shouting their unending bad tidings, the newspaper vendors of the bird world.

As the birds reluctantly, and vocally, left their nests set openly on the moss and tight grass, I

The Summer Isles seen from Polbain.

saw there were many with a clutch of eggs. I half expected the terns, particularly, to come back and commence their harrying, their dive-bombing, as I had experienced before in the furthest north, at Unst in the Shetlands. But they confined their displeasure to circling and shouting, going back to the nests as soon as I had crossed the sandbar to the smaller leg of the island.

The rocks were a different colour here, almost rose, with wigs of bright yellow lichen clinging to them. A new pattern of islands lay off this flank. The sea was turquoise. I sat down, content and grateful. Amazingly the cuckoo's call came across the water, apparently from the far mainland, unless there is a marine cuckoo who roams the Atlantic fringes, or one shipwrecked on an outcrop in The Summer Isles.

Ian's bright new boat came around the headland and I waved and called, my voice bouncing across the water. People do odd things on islands. Ian and John sportingly answered and waved. They were slowly rounding the island, fishing as they went. I settled back on the warm moss and marine grass, the sun on my face and surveyed it all. The cuckoo's call still sounded, the seals honked somewhere deep and echoing, the seabirds whirled white against the blue of the sky, and there I was, somewhere where I had long wanted to be – King of The Summer Isles.

The eagle we saw on the return journey. Ever since Jill Brown had told me that the pair were nesting on the highest hump of the peninsula, I had spent much time looking in that direction in the hope of seeing them. It was getting towards evening, although the sun hardly seemed past its zenith, as the *Islander* returned to Loch Broom, leaving The Summer Isles far beyond its sedate wake in the smooth channel.

Ullapool had just appeared, a few dots on our port beam, and my eyes were on the other arm of the loch to where the inn at Altnaharrie now came into view, a white square against the huge land. Almost automatically I looked up. At first I saw only the gulls, a whole cloud of them like a crowd of waved handkerchiefs. Ian said something quietly and nodded. "See, the eagle," he said.

My heart jumped. I almost went over the side of the boat in my eagerness to get a better viewing place. I could still see only the gulls. "Where?" I asked urgently. "I can't spot it."

"Yon gulls are mobbing it," he said. "Look now, it's among them." Obligingly he turned the head of the boat so that I could see better. Yes! Glory be, there it was! Wings arched, it was making its way through the clamouring gulls, like a grand duke easing aside pushy courtiers. The gulls screamed and circled. None of them had the bravery, or the foolishness, to close into it. The eagle swooped to within a few feet of the loch, leaving the gulls staggering in mid-air. Then it abruptly changed gear and rose up, no . . . ascended, through them, higher and higher, until they were left far below, and there it sat, in the sky, looking over all the world, majestic and free, before turning and swooping away towards the purple mountain and its home.

I arrived back in Ullapool, besotted with my day. I almost staggered up the steps from the boat to the quay, and then walked slowly along the waterfront, now soft with late light. I went into the hotel and had a contemplative drink at the bar. The Islands, the sea, the sun, and the eagle. The thoughts crowded my mind.

If I never have a better day than that I just don't care.

SEVEN

The Road In The Clouds

The peaks of Torridon are among the mightiest and grandest in the whole of Britain. During my stay in Wester Ross they were always on the distant horizon like a large man looking over a wall. I drove south from Loch Broom towards them and eventually to the village of Applecross, another place that had called me from the days of my childhood reading.

But first I took a detour, for there was one more sight I wanted to see – Gruinard Island, the forbidden place, the isle where no man may set foot until the middle of the next century.

It lies in its bay just around Stattic Point, the headland on the southern extremity of Little Loch Broom, reached by a winding road through Dundonnell Forest, through Gruinard Forest and under the two and a half thousand foot haunch of Sàil Mhór. The road bends west then south before Badluarach, the hamlet from whence you can telephone the commune at Scoraig on the peninsula, and those people's nearest contact with the outside world. You simply go to the telephone box, dial 269, and one of the people on Scoraig leaves his or her work and comes to the phone. I had several conversations with them but they were guarded about sending a boat for me. In the end I did not go at all. They enjoy and apparently deserve the isolation and the peace they have found.

When the road bends south it dips towards the sea at Mungasdale and Gruinard Island comes into view. Man, with his great gift for inflicting hurt on the most innocent and beautiful, isolated this island for a hundred years by using it during the Second World War for experiments in germ warfare. It was sprayed with the most virulent of killers and since then no-one has been permitted there. It will be the year 2040 before another boat lands on that green shore. I wonder what its crew will find. Thousands of seabird skeletons? It seems doubtful for even the gulls and gannets give it a wide berth now. It waits in loneliness for the day of deliverance.

Seeing it was a surprise. I had imagined that any forbidden isle would be Wagnerian in proportions, high cliffs, great rocks and sullen seas, and I thought it would be far off the coast, right out in the ocean, solitary, unapproachable. But when I turned the car down the coastal hill and Gruinard came into view, I saw that it was only a mile or so off-shore, sitting forlornly like a dog outside a door. Its meadows shone green, its low rocks were harmless and the clean, easy sea washed against it in the most affectionate fashion. I stopped and stood on the edge of

the Atlantic and looked sadly at it for several minutes. Nothing moved out there, only the shadow of a cloud passing across the empty pastures.

Because I had started late in the day I stopped for the night at Poolewe and made an early beginning the next morning. It had been light for three hours when I set out at seven but there was a scarf of mist lying along Loch Maree, giving it the look of its reputation, the enchanted place. The mountains either side and their clothing forests were only there because I could feel they were. The clouds hung about them and the mist made the road wet alongside the lake. Turning a corner I came across a man with a milk van. He had stopped his vehicle by the side of the water and was staring anxiously down the dim road. He seemed relieved that I had

The Torridon mountains and Upper Loch Torridon in the distance. The entrance to Loch Shieldaig is in the right foreground and the south-eastern extremity of Loch Torridon is on the left.

arrived. White-faced, he beckoned me from the car and I left the driving seat to find out what troubled him. There were two churns in the back of the battered van. "I'm just taking the milk," he said as if his presence needed some explanation. Then, wordlessly, he nodded along the road. I looked and for a moment I had an uncomfortable feeling that indeed there were fairies and this was a haunted spot.

Three men had stopped their car about a hundred and fifty yards ahead and were apparently dancing in the middle of the road. *Dancing!* They performed a slow, girating saraband, moving their arms and legs in a strange, slow manner. "What d'ye make o' that?" asked the milkman nervously.

I hesitated. Then I had another look. They were still at it. But they were certainly not wearing green suits, curly shoes, nor caps with bells. "I'll go and see," I offered. He held my arm. I thought he was going to warn me about the enchantments of Loch Maree, but instead he swallowed heavily and said, "I'll be looking after your wee car for you."

My advance, I have to admit, was begun with caution, but I pulled myself together after a few yards. After all, their car was patently a Morris Minor. Fairies don't drive Morris Minors. As I neared them through the mist I saw what had happened. The car had skidded and run into a telegraph post, which was at that moment lying across the vehicle's bonnet. All the cables had fallen across the car and the passengers, in getting out, had become entangled in the mesh of wire. Their apparently slow dance was the result of their efforts to disentangle themselves!

Looking due south in the direction of Applecross and showing the new road recently opened.

This mystery solved, the men assisted, and the milkman reassured that anybody could make that sort of mistake on the side of a fairy lake in the enchanted mists of dawn, I continued on my journey.

The sun came out in time for breakfast and the great peaks of Torridon, snow on their roofs, appeared through the clouds and looked down on the world as they have done since they saw the Ice Age slide by. The run of Beinn Eighe has each of its peaks topping three thousand feet, and the higher cones of Liathach glower down to Loch Torridon. They may be mere mounds compared to some of this world's mountains, but, for me, there are none more spectacular, more powerful, none nearer to the sky and yet to the earth than these.

It was again wonderfully warm and I drove to Torridon itself and spent the day there, wandering along the lake, sitting among the pleasant pines, watching flights of duck, and conversing with benign and shaggy highland cattle, who, beneath their fringes, seem to have eyes that understand your remarks and are themselves desperately trying to tell you something. That night in a bar I listened to the local stories. It appeared that there had been a run of salmon poaching and the police had been informed that a certain van travelling on a certain lonely road at a certain hour was loaded with salmon. A highland ambush was set, the van stopped and investigated. Sure enough it was full of salmon – all *tinned*.

The amazing road to Applecross which I took next day, rises to over 2000 feet, the highest in all Britain. At one time the long snows of winter made the small village on its Atlantic promontory the most remote mainland settlement in the country; the rough winter ocean on one side and the white barrier on the others. It was certainly cut off by land for weeks at a time, the supply route to the outside world being on less stormy days across Loch Carron from Lochalsh, to the hamlet and harbour of Toscaig just south of Applecross.

Now a new road, long promised, has been painstakingly put together around the bulbous nose of the Applecross peninsula, tight against the sea for much of its way. It means that the remote western village is now approachable by land for most of the year anyway. The question its people ask is: Will it make Applecross a better or a happier place?

There had been an operatic thunderstorm in the night, beginning before dark when curtains of spectacular rain blew across Torridon's mountains and water. A loud battle appeared to be going on in the fastness of the hills and the pines were lit with lightning. It was well beyond midnight when it diminished to a whimper and by daybreak the world was washed and bright with sun again.

On the initial section of the road I was taking from Torridon to Shieldaig, the scenery is so hypnotic as to make you wonder whether it would count as a defence in a case of driving without due care and attention. The first fields were bright after the rain, populated by immobile cattle, each one like a hairy sofa. The loch blazed blue against the zooming mountains. Before Shieldaig there is a gorge, a giant's bite from the landscape, and then a riot of rhododendrons alongside the road. Always ahead, the upper peaks, each with its slap of snow, rose like a barrier, scree-scattered down the lower slopes and then tumbling birch woods falling to the fringe of the water.

Peaty streams struggle through holes and crevices in the rock; there are small glades of pine and rowan. Then, just short of Kishorn, the road appears to hunch its shoulders, like a man girding himself for a stiff climb, and then rises into the granite mountains. A roadside notice

Looking due west on the road from Loch Carron towards Kishorn. In the distance are the Applecross mountains; the stream in the foreground flows west into Loch Kishorn.

warns that the highway ascends to 2053 feet with 'numerous and dangerous bends'. I remember from my reading long ago how Applecross was only reached 'with a sense of achievement'.

The route runs for twelve miles, beginning modestly enough over some steep but short ascents, and then continues over a couple of stony bridges with small rivers hurrying towards Loch Kishorn as if their life depended upon it. From the rising road you can look down the treed slopes to the sandy lining of the loch, vacant except for strolling seabirds. Another bend and the extent of the barrier in front is apparent; great pudding-like mountains, black even in the sun. The road quickly settles for being a single track, green is lost in grey; on each flank of the route huge, rounded boulders stand at random as if some gigantic game was started in the days before history and never finished. This was the way the glaciers took, crunching through the mountain to cover half the earth. The scars they caused are still unhealed on every mountainside.

After another bend the road soars steeply. Soon the whole panorama of this singular place opens out, the traveller looking up at the peaks on one side and dizzily down to the scattered small islands in the loch on the other. Here a narrow cleft holds a tiny path – called The Coffin Path because in the days when the winter cut off the peninsula, coffins were sometimes brought by a tenuous track around the coast on the shoulders of strong men. It was a labour of love and most people preferred to be buried in the churchyards of the isolated villages; those who made it known that they would require to be buried in some place outside were eyed with apprehension through the long, remote winters. A suspicious cough was enough for suggestions to be made that perhaps they might like to move elsewhere before it was too late. This was the story I got from an old man at Toscaig, but he was reluctant to elaborate. Coffins are not a popular subject of conversation in those places.

Left, the view over the Highlands looking south-east from the top of the Bealach na Ba pass – the path of the cattle – with Loch Kishorn in the foreground. Right, the strange, rocky roof of the Applecross range looking east.

Another airy mile, the road pointing to the lower regions of the sky, and again the colours changed. Now I drove through the sort of sliced valley that is familiar from a hundred Western films, the red-rocked gulch. The landscape varies from copper to crimson, the rocks standing up like somebody's tonsils. The route zig-zags alarmingly every few yards, as if fully expecting to be ambushed, clinging to the skin of the mountains. Looking down, far down now, the wide Kishorn Loch has been reduced to size, trapped into a distant triangle. Aeroplanes have changed our ideas about heights, I think. My small son, on top of the World Trade Centre in New York, looked down on the river and the points of the city and asked in a mildly disappointed tone, "Daddy, won't it go any higher?" When you've frequently viewed the world from thirty thousand feet, what's a mere drop like that? But there, in the Torridon heights, it was possible to retain a good measure of awe for the altitude and the depths to which you could plunge if you were careless. The triangle of the loch looked far away indeed.

Looking east along the River Toscaig; the Coffin Path runs parallel with the river at this point.

At the apex of the climb the mountains flattened into a surface as bare, sharp and unwelcoming as the horizon of a dead planet. Rocks become black, studded with small, cold lakes, icily reflecting the sky. A wind pushed against the car. I could hear it howling through the hollows and natural pipes of that forbidding place. Then Nature did one of her tricks and, just as I was thinking that this was the most desolate prospect I had ever seen, a classic herd of deer, led by a finely antlered stag, came sprinting across the lean landscape. I had to stop the car to watch them. They ran beautifully, leaping rocks and water, finely outlined against the wash of the sky. Then they went, just vanished, plunging down the side of the scree into some valley known only to them. What a moment.

Now, as if it had come to the end of its act, the mountain range began to descend on the long, rolling slope to Applecross. Immediately, on this the western flank, the scene softened.

Kenny McKenzie outside his house in Shore Street, Applecross.

Distant peaks became hazy with sun, there was more green beside the road, mountain flowers showed and the lakes and tarns smiled with a warmer smile.

Half way down, a creamy mountain stream jumped and hurried through a valley it had fashioned for itself. There was a peat bog here with signs that it was still used to supply fuel, the straight, black spade marks that I had so often seen in remote islands and other places. The water of the stream, when it was not in a froth, was as brown as beer. I stopped and clambered down to it. I heard a bird piping. The air felt a shade warmer. There were some upland gnats mooching about one of the pools that the stream formed when it stopped to take a rest. It seemed an opportunity to be taken. I rolled up my trousers and took off my shoes and socks. Then sitting on a flat chair of rock, I plunged both feet into the lovely water. *God, it was freezing!*

From this place I could see far away into the valleys and the flat places of the Applecross peninsula. Green fields grinned down there and I could see collections of trees and people's roofs.

I returned to the patient car. Its windscreen was bright with sunshine. Down went the top and I descended with enjoyable anticipation into the opening vales. A line of white houses came into view, spaced along a sandy bay. Nicely rounded trees began to appear, oaks and horse chestnuts, and every now and then a rowan, of course, to keep the witches away.

Applecross is a single white street – Shore Street – alongside the Atlantic Ocean. The beach is lined with enormous flat rocks, like pieces of a disturbed mosaic. Fat gulls, occasionally raucous in the empty morning, sat on the boulders; the sea rolled quietly onto the land. All along the beach are washing lines where the village women hang their laundry to dry in the maritime wind. There is an inn, a post office and a sense of peace.

Looking out from the shore I could see Raasay island and the great blue back of Skye, its silver skirt of sea, hooped and puckered, stretched around it. There were no ships in sight on the water, nor people on the shore where I stood. Only myself and the gulls. The walls of the low houses in Shore Street were benign in the sun, their flowers glowed from their pots and window boxes, some sheets and pillow cases and a formidable pair of bloomers decorated the washing lines on the beach, but nothing else moved. It was the least occupied and most alluring main street I have ever seen.

I walked slowly, enjoying every step of the tranquillity. Small-seamed summer waves came in with their comfortable liquid roll and plopping sound. The morning was again warm on the face, the air clear in the nose. There was a low stone wall running along the shore-side of the street, worn smooth on top by the generations of villagers who have sat out there on light evenings to exchange wisdom and gossip. As I walked I saw that I had been mistaken in thinking I was the only visible inhabitant of Applecross. A neat, grey man with a bright face, perched on the wall, almost hidden by the sheets hanging on his neighbour's washing line. He looked like the ancient mariner sitting beneath the sails of a ship. He bade me a considered good morning and, curiously, made room on the wall for me to sit down. The fact that there was an unoccupied length of wall running the length of the street did not prevent the courtesy. He smoked a pipe and seemed glad of someone to join in conversation. His name was Kenny McKenzie and he was seventy-five years old. From his front door he looks directly out on to the Atlantic Ocean, knowing all its moods from a sweet day like this to the howling tantrum of a winter's night.

Aye, he'd spent most of his life there, he agreed. And it had not changed much. Mind, the new road around the coast was going to alter things. Folks were already coming into Applecross with their motor-cars and picnic hampers. Still the road was a blessing. Now, at least, they could get out in the winter.

"It took them a hundred years, ye ken, to build that road," he said. "When my father was a wee boy they talked about building it and now it's there. One time, when the mountain road was full with snow, you could only get over the hills by the motor-bike track. We had some good motor-bike riders and it was a good job we did too."

For forty-five years, he recalled, the ferry between Stornoway and the Kyle of Lochalsh made a weekly call at Applecross. "There was no landing here where it could put the people

Toscaig viewed from the east and showing Loch Toscaig.

Left, the harbour with the modern houses reflected in the water.

ashore or take them off," he said. "They had to go out in a wee boat. And it was three o'clock in the morning. In winter that was no' an easy journey. Cold and rough it would be and the ferry always came in at three o'clock. Folks used to wait alongside the shore and watch for the lights. But in forty-five years there was never once an accident. We had a grand ferryman, ye ken. I can see it now, each man taking an oar and rowing out to the big boat, and sometimes the waves coming in very high and rough. But we never lost a soul."

In Kenny McKenzie's younger days Applecross was not infrequently cut off for three months at a stretch. "But it was a happy time," he said. "Everybody helped each other in those days. Being a boy here was a wonderful thing. Now there are only four families left who remember, four families of the old stock. The fishing here used to be grand. There was so much fish in this bay that you didn't need bait. I've seen men go out and just spear the flounders. With no bait. And even only a few years ago the herring around here filled the boat. Fine fish it was too. I've seen this bay full of herring drifters at night, all their lights shining as bright as London. But now it's all gone. The fish just went away. And the fishing boats left. It's strange that when we used to be cut off in Applecross we used to be so busy, and now we've got a new road there's nothing."

Right, Applecross seen from across the bay.

I asked him about shipwrecks. Aye, they'd had their share of wrecks. There was the hull of a trawler broken half a mile down the coast. That was a stormy night, but every man had made it to the shore.

"In the war before the last war," he recalled, "there was a ship going through the channel here and, so it's said, the officer of the watch had gone to sleep at his post. The ship, she ended up on the beach just below Lonbain. Everybody went to help and she was lucky because she was floated on the high tide. After that every time she sailed by here she would sound her hooter and we would all wave. Then she didn't come by any more and we heard she'd been torpedoed in the Irish Sea."

Applecross always was, and still is, a place of sober, religious folk. On the day after I spoke to Kenny McKenzie, a Thursday, it was a special day, and there was no-one to be found in the village because they were at church for twelve hours, three long services with tea and sober talk at each other's houses. At one time, it is said, even to go out strolling on a Sunday in Applecross was frowned upon. A stranger is supposed to have been interrupted in this innocent pursuit by a villager who upbraided him for taking a walk on the Sabbath. The visitor knew his Bible. "It says in the Testament," he pointed out, "that Jesus Himself walked in Jerusalem on the Sabbath."

"Aye," came the bleak reply. "That may be so. But this is Applecross – not Jerusalem."

Going out towards the miniature harbour at Toscaig, a couple of miles from Applecross and once its connection to the outside world, I saw the crowds in front of three small churches; all wearing quiet clothes. A black-backed minister shook various hands. All around the sun shone and the seabirds shouted.

Toscaig harbour is sweet and small, a few boats lying against its flank, its mouth pursed narrowly. There were some shy houses and a crystal stream lined with vivid marsh-marigolds and marsh-irises. There was no-one there. Only the birds and the sheep on the slopes; only the light, mossy grass under my feet, the smell of the seaweed. Far, far out the high Hebrides pushed against the sky. Skye itself was sprawled along the horizon like a large man somehow sleeping on a clothes line. Islands and islets congregated in the bay. It was so warm and so beautiful that it seemed a shame that I had no-one with whom to share it. Then, bright red against the rising green of the land, I saw an outcast telephone box. Hooray for the GPO! So I entered and telephoned my wife in the distant south (where it was raining) to tell her how beautiful was the sight set before me.

Toscaig has a trio of small neighbours, Culduie, Camasterach and Camusteel, sitting like children on the shore. Each has its small, entrancing harbour, a few boats, cottages ruminating by the water, little groves of nut trees, and sheep and hens nibbling away on the mud of the anchorage as the tide backs out. The sheep gnaw the seaweed and the hens pick and peck at the various morsels left in the pools and eddies. I wager the lamb chops and the eggs have a fishy taste.

I sat down at Camusteel, enjoying the well-being of the summer's day. Nothing moved except the sheep and the chickens. The sky was out of sight. Then from the open door of one of the cottages I heard the Australian tones of Richie Benaud, describing play in the Test Match many miles to the south. My enjoyment was complete.

When I reached Applecross village again on the return journey, there was a noticeable increase in activity. Mrs Marget McKinnon, who runs the post office in the village, was sitting on the sea wall industriously knitting. She came to the place from Glasgow nine years ago with her husband, John, who was born in the village. They used to run a general store as well as the post office, but they closed it down. As she uncompromisingly put it, "We didna' care for the VAT."

Wherever I travelled in Britain, there was the usually bright and busy post office, with its red letter box, comforting windows, and its sign waving like a tin flag. In one year, although not entirely in the course of this, my odyssey to the remoter parts of this country, I bought stamps at the most northerly post office in Britain – high up in Shetland at Haroldswick – and the most southerly at Samaris on the island of Jersey. In these odd corners the post office is frequently run on rather less official lines than perhaps its urban bureacrats would wish. There is a story of an island post office, not far over the sea from Applecross, from which no official returns had been made to the GPO in Glasgow for many months. Letters and other reminders met with no satisfaction. A telephone call only evoked the reply, "The Post Mistress is away in the wee boat." Eventually a civil service emissary was despatched to this outlying place and arrived (I fondly imagine him, in pin-stripes and bowler) to find the windy post office perched far out on a cliff, against a raging ocean. He entered to the usual dinging of a bell to find himself at the rear of the everyday crowd of island housewives who used the place not only as somewhere to get their provisions but also as a social centre. It was made plain that he was obliged to join the slow queue. He noticed, as he neared its head, that the post office part of the establishment appeared to consist of a biscuit tin. From this were produced stamps, postal orders, and anything else that Her Majesty's Post-Master General had seen fit to furnish.

Eventually the emissary found himself at the counter, to be faced by the formidable proprietress. "I've come from the GPO," said the civil servant meekly. "You haven't been in touch with us for ages, you know. It's causing some concern."

The island lady regarded him incredulously. It was as if some grave insult had been made upon her person. Then, with a fierce sweep of her hand, she slammed down the lid of the

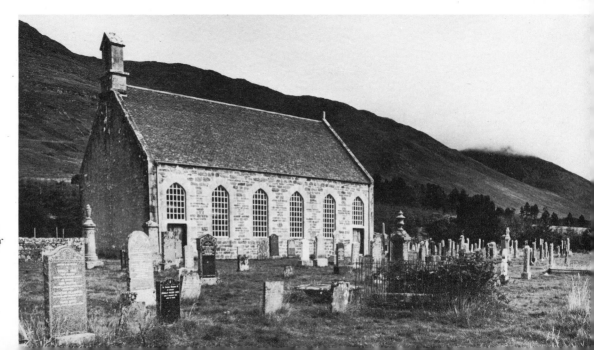

Exterior of the Old Church of Scotland, situated on the opposite side of the bay to Applecross. St Mael Rhubba is buried in the far corner to the right of the picture.

Interior of the Old Church of Scotland, now used by the local people chiefly for weddings.

biscuit tin and thrust it at him across the counter. "Go on," she cried. "Take your post office and be on your way!"

On the inland side of the Applecross peninsula is a valley of cool trees, large and munificent oaks, some pines and small, rustling nut trees. Here at almost the point where the two roads, the old one climbing sturdily over the mountain and the new one wriggling alongside the sea, go their distinct ways, is the ancient churchyard of Applecross, the resting spot of generations going back a thousand years, and at its heart one of the simplest and most remarkable churches I have ever entered.

It was to this light valley in the year 671 AD that St Mael Rhubba, a Celtic priest, arrived to establish a church. He was a magnetic man, brave and wonderful, and he landed his small boat from Ireland somewhere on the shore near the place where I now stood. He was said to have been a relative of the High King of the Irish but he forsook whatever trimmings went with that position and travelled as a missionary to the wild coast. Christianity, then the religion of the kingdom at least in name, had failed to surmount the mountains and Applecross had not been converted. The priest made a sanctuary in that remote place, the peace of which can still be felt today. The feuds of blood that were part of the coastal life were stopped and, having achieved that, he travelled over the greater part of northern Scotland spreading his mission. At the age of eighty, while journeying in Sutherland, he died and, when the news reached the peninsula a party of Applecross men set out on foot across the hills to bring his body back to the place where he was so well loved. Perhaps they used the Coffin Path. Mael Rhubba is buried in the south-eastern corner of the churchyard, his name added to the Catholic Calendar of Saints.

The church he founded, however, adhered to the Church of Scotland in later years. It stands now on the ribs of the abbey that was raised and stood there from the seventh to the tenth centuries. The gate is guarded by a great, old, worn Celtic cross, which was carved in the time of the delectably-named Abbot MacOggie.

But all the peace and settled life of Applecross vanished in the ninth century when the Vikings fell upon it with their customary bloody industry. The village vanishes from all written records until the Dark Ages were gone and the light and life of civilisation began to shimmer again.

The churchyard today is as interesting as most. There are the usual verses and sentiments, carved into the stone but often not quite fitting, so a piece has to be added somewhere. The odd spelling mistake is clumsily amended. It must have been hard to be a stonemason who couldn't spell. There is also the most uncompromising tombstone I have ever seen. Simply a very large and gruesome skull and crossbones. Away with sentiment, even in a churchyard. It's stuffed with McDonalds, McCreas, McLeods, and Livingstones, and especially McDonalds. Brambles and grass have overtaken many of the ancient graves. There are one or two poignant places where sailors, washed dead from the sea, are buried. Birds sing beautifully among the clustered trees, sun makes the old stones as yellow as cheese. It's as good a place as any in the world to be buried.

The church is something different. It is not used now for regular services for the parish – the other churches are well-subscribed – but is a place of worship mainly for young people who climb the mountains as part of Adventure School training. To walk in there is to see something so simple, so stunning, that it stops your steps. No formalised, traditional church this, despite its age and history. Inside it is as bare as a barn, with a barn's simplicity; the walls grey and stark, with a brilliantly white, bare pulpit that soars high into the holy air. There are no pews, just plain, bright wooden chairs, a clear floor and an altar as clean as a kitchen table. On the altar was a bunch of vivid flowers. Some cushions were placed on the floor. The clear panes of the tall, arched windows looked out onto trees and beyond the trees, the hills. A wonderful and moving place. I hope Mael Rhubba and Abbot MacOggie are pleased with it.

Along the low, new road from Applecross where the green land slips down to the ocean's edge, are the ruined crofts of what was once the lovely village of Lonbain. When I was there only three people inhabited them: Donald McBeth and Marie, his wife, and Duncan McKenzie who lives alone. Theirs is a solitary and not very happy existence. They grow a few crops and fish, but the living is far from good.

Perhaps the caravans and the campers who increasingly find their way around the cape to what was once Britain's most isolated community, will bring a new prosperity to the place. Romance is not everything.

EIGHT

Sweet, Rainy Allendale

There was once a man who lived in one of the loftiest and remotest parts of England and spent his time wandering the hills – measuring the rainfall. His name was John Charlton. He travelled through the twin Dales of Allen and over Killhope Law, and along the winding defiles of the valleys between. There must have been much to occupy him, for in these bare uplands and in the tight dales of Northumbria they have rain in plenty.

It had been a benevolent, early summer and as I went through Weardale the sun lit the folds of almost velvet fields. Sheep shone, rivers tinkled and there were flowers in the village windows. Country men sat squarely outside inns and drank pints of Old Peculier, a brew favoured in these regions. Dogs dozed and children raced shouting across fields as they came home from school.

But at the hamlet of Cowshill, the road abruptly lifts its nose and, as if in a sudden fancy or flight, heads for the hills. Alston, the most elevated market town in England, is straight (as far as any road is straight in those regions) ahead, but I took the curling highway, climbing by the yard, until the world of houses, streets, children and Old Peculier had vanished. At once there were only the sky and the earth; earth almost naked, rounded hills enclosed by stone walls and beyond them darker uplands, and then the sky, laden with the daily rain.

The snow posts begin at a thousand feet or so, as soon as the signs of habitation vanish, every seventy-five yards along the single road, marked out clearly with summer-painted bands so that some poor winter traveller may know how deep he is in trouble. This is Durham but over the border in what, despite committees and boundary commissions, is still called Northumberland, the posts were worn and rough from their duties. I suppose the summer-time painters had not yet reached them. What a singular occupation that must be, moving over the mountains painting coloured rings around posts, up there with the rain and the crows, trying to reach the end before the first snowfall, and then starting all over again in the spring. There are stories of post painters who have gone off and vanished for days; like the tale of the gang in some remote place who set off to paint white lines in the middle of the road. *And were never seen again.* Somewhere they may still be painting.

As I drove higher, so the rain came to meet me, expectedly, dotting the windscreen and polishing the road ahead. Sheep stood like spectators looking over the stone walls, chewing

and watching with their dull eyes. I felt the squall suited the landscape. This is no place for fine weather.

As though to perish the thought, at once the rain clouds hurried away and, with sudden pleasure, I saw the valley of Allendale – the East Allen – open up almost magically before me. Tender fields lying green, sheep and cow strewn, below the brown slopes. Trees in thick, June clusters, stone walls and buildings, and streams bouncing from the mountains.

It is not difficult to miss the hamlet of Allenheads altogether, for the road, bending above voluminous trees, runs over its roofs and it remains hidden like a child playing hide-and-seek, almost hugging itself with its secret. Even the sign pointing the way to the Allenheads Inn is concealed by foliage, which no-one has ever thought of cutting back. I was a mile beyond it before I became suspicious and turned back, spotting the sharp, dipping side road that turns off and down, only a few feet into this most enchanting of habitations. On this day, with the sun suddenly aloft and the rain-clouds in retreat on the hills, the traveller might have been forgiven for believing that he had somehow strayed into a village in Provence.

There is a little, tree-hung, irregular village square with an island of greenery at its hub. There are a few stone houses and a shop, all with flower-laden gardens, a single petrol pump, and the serene face of the Allenheads Inn, its benches and tables set outside among the fuschias and the sunshine. It was a happy find to go there first. There was a fire burning in the old bar (they don't really trust even June in these regions) and, as it was the middle of the day, there were a few customers, miners from the few, newly re-opened lead mines, a couple of men from the fields, and a man with a face as strong as iron who arrived on a small, ancient tractor. They drink Scotch Ale (making it a nervous moment when someone says, "Thanks, I'll have a pint of Scotch"). The accents seemed to me to be dark Northumbrian, although the experts

say they are akin to Cumbria across the border. However, for me, that strong voice from what is quite a small corner of Britain is (after Welsh!) the most pleasing sound to the ear.

That morning I had heard on the radio that a horse with the name of 'Virgin Soldier' was running in a race at Lingfield. Having been responsible for a novel of that title, I felt that I had to back my fancy. I asked the young man behind the bar if he knew a bookmaker – and told him why. Soon the turf accountant at Hexham, the nearest town, had a flush of bets from Allenheads, high up there in the folded hills. I hope he put a wager on for himself because the horse (with a lady jockey) ran a brilliant race to win by a head at three to one. Immediately I was among friends.

This place, little and shy, was once an important centre of lead mining. All around, the hills are riven with the old tunnels going miles below ground, most of them disused for almost a hundred years. Beneath the rustic square of Allenheads there is a tunnel, a water course for the uplands, and buried below the patch of green with its few trees at the centre, is a huge chamber housing three great, now silent, water-wheels. They were used as a giant pump to rid the lead mines of ever-encroaching water. Fred Harris, a pleasant, articulate man, who was a lead miner until they closed the mine in which he worked, remembers going down into the subterranean wheel-house years ago. "It wasn't very safe then," he recalled. "The tunnel was dangerous and the roof of the chamber was sagging. But it was worth going down to see the big wheels – twenty feet across, just left like that under the ground." He glanced from the window of the inn. "They're only thirty yards away from us now – down there in the dark. But nobody can go there now. It's too dangerous. All the tunnels are blocked."

One of the strange results of having these great turning wheels just below the doorsteps, was that the hamlet of Allenheads was the first place in that part of the country to be lit by electricity. When even Newcastle, thirty miles away, was a city of gaslamps, little Allenheads shone like a diamond in the night-time hills.

*   *   *

The fire munching away in the grate at the Allenheads Inn, was burning as much for tradition as for warmth and comfort. The lead miners, the farmers and the other inhabitants of these cool, sometimes draughty hills always had what they called a 'cat fire' burning in their hearths – pieces of clay moulded to the size of an orange and mixed with rough coal or peat. These fires smouldered on, summer and winter.

Allendale, being among the hills only just south of Hadrian's Wall – the nearest Roman stonework is at the quizzically named Twice Brewed – it was, once the Legions had gone home, open territory for border wars and raids that continued over centuries. It seems to have escaped the major bloodsheds, although in the twelfth century it was uncompromisingly under the thumb of the Scottish King, William the Lion. It was not until the sixteenth century that it was seriously ravaged, and then by a freebooter called Willie Side-Ears assisted by relatives and friends, notably another Willie, this time nicknamed Fingerless Will. Yet a third Willie, William the Elder, descended on the farms and settlements, in October, 1589, and took off seventeen prisoners who were ransomed at prices ranging from five pounds to thirteen shillings and fourpence. What the odd fourpence meant no-one has told. The horses were set at forty shillings to five pounds and the ransom demanded for a dog was a pound. All the demands were met in the face of threats that the hostages would be 'Fyred and burnt'.

By the end of the century the Elliotts, the Armstrongs and the Nixons all raided the suffering country folk, either separately or in combines. In 1596 they accounted for the deaths of 'above fifty of the Queen's good subjects including six honest Allendale men going to Hexham Market'.

The lead mines which had, naturally, been exploited by the industrious Romans (tribute was paid to Claudius in pigs of lead), fell largely to disuse in the Dark Ages. Awakened by the Industrial Revolution they were prospering and pitting the hills by the mid-nineteenth century, although, for those times, the miners appear to have enjoyed an unusually casual life.

Their labours beneath ground enabled them enough free hours to carry on as small-holders and farmers in their spare time, with owners and stewards apparently remote. In 1845, however, Thomas Sopwith, an engineer who was to have an historic effect on the industry, took over at Allenheads, and his enthusiasm and revolutionary time-and-motion studies resulted, in 1849, in a strike of the disgruntled leadmen. It began on New Year's Day and no work was done until the first of May.

A document survives detailing a strike meeting which, for all its quaintness, casts a long shadow before it. It took place on March the twenty-first at Swin Hope Primitive Methodist Chapel, with a strike leader in the chair – or, rather, the pulpit. The business began with a hymn and a prayer. Then Mr Heslop, the chief man, stood and addressed the strikers. What he said is worth retelling.

He told them, "Now lads my orders out of this pulpit is that every man has liberty to begin

Jimmy Dixon outside the Allenheads Inn with Len Strand, the former owner. He has only recently sold the Inn.

The magnificent water wheel of Killhope.

work, but it is my hope and earnest prayer that if any man do begin work in connection with them that has begun, that you will all have the goodness to pass them and their wives and families without speaking to them; to have no connection or communication with them.

"If they be sick do not visit them. If they are in need of a doctor do not seek them one. If they die do not bury them. If they are fastened underground in the mine do not assist in seeking them out but let them die or be killed in the dark, or go from darkness to darkness in the fangs of the devil to be kept by him without remorse in the fires of hell for ever and ever.

"You are all to torment them while on earth and when they die the devil torment them in eternity. I do earnestly hope that you will one and all do them all the harm you can and say all manner of evil against them in your power. If any of them owe any of you anything be sure to put them to all the trouble you possibly can. Let them be like Cain, deserted by God and forsaken of men. I charitably hope that all millers, shop-keepers, cloggers, blacksmiths and every tradesman, even tailors, deny them everything and if they emigrate to Australia or America if any of you should be there be sure to treat them in the same way."

After five months, deprivation overcame oratory and the strike crumbled. But many of those who took part never again entered the mines. Within days of the end there was the pathetic, but not unfamiliar sight in the mid-nineteenth century, of families gathering their

The sundial near the south porch of the church at Allendale Town.

bare belongings, walking the streets of their town for the final time before sailing for a sad salvation in America. Today there are many inhabitants in New England who have names that are easily recognisable in the Dale of Allen.

*   *   *

Allendale Town, eight miles up the winding valley from the hidden village of Allenheads, claims (although these days, quietly) to be the very centre of Britain. The town's elders are reticent about it and, indeed, Hexham, a few miles north and east, has been mentioned for this distinction, if distinction it is. In any event the fading sundial on the face of the church at Allendale Town records, without further comment, that it stands at a latitude of fifty-four degrees sixty minutes which, it is said, makes it mid-way between wild Cape Wrath in Scotland and Beachy Head far down in gentle Sussex. The arguments have continued for centuries and will doubtless continue until someone paces it out.

The church, set about with nice umbrella trees among the tombs and the ancient yews provided for the arrowsmith, stands at the centre of the little grey-skied town. Its most notable incumbent was Robert Patten, a successful turncoat in the days of the rebellion of Charles Edward Stuart. He took with him six of his parishioners, who owned horses and swords, and joined with the Bonnie Prince's forces. He fought against the English but when captured boldly changed both mind and sides and gave evidence at the trials of various men accused of treachery. He escaped the executioner and lived to write a *History of the Late Rebellion*, which, wisely, recorded the events from the English point of view.

The town stands now as quiet as its churchyard; a row of pretty but sedate cottages, with flowers about their windows, borders its street. Its square is heavy with horse chestnuts, sycamores, limes and fine copper beeches, the grey buildings clothed with abundant green climbers; lupins in the gardens and roses on the wall. There are several pubs, three wise-looking banks and two garages, neither of which sells petrol.

It is difficult to imagine that, in the high old days, Allendale Town had a reputation for gaudy living. This stemmed from the fact that the lead miners were only paid every six months and, human nature being ever-ready for a fling, they tended to celebrate the occasion. The men worked in teams of four, often members of one family, and these partnerships, as they were called, undertook to raise the ore at so much a ton. Every month they would receive 'lent money' cash for subsistence, and the balances were totted up at the end of the half year and paid at the end of the following half year.

If the monthly Money Days were busy, becoming riotous, in the little town, then it is not difficult to imagine the activities of the half yearly days known as 'The Pays'. Every farmer, merchant, tradesman and cheapjack from the three counties, Northumberland, Durham and across the hills from Cumberland, would converge on Allendale Town. The farmers' wives and daughters, decked in their best linsey-woolsey gowns, each with clean white neck-cloths tied over their heads and clogs on their feet, would line the cobbled streets with their bags of corn and other produce open before them. Bills were settled and purchases made. Tinkers, beggars and performers were noisy in the streets.

It did not take long before the inns were full and ribaldry turned sour and ended up with fights among the dungheaps (and the town was noted for its dungheaps) on the pavements. A contemporary evangelist complained that every other house in Allendale Town seemed to be a place where drink could be purchased, although he off-balanced this by noting that there were three temperance houses serving milk, which the miners drank in plenty since they believed it warded off the underground diseases.

The mines brought great fortunes to the owning families and unglamorous lead was not the only produce brought to the surface. Silver weighing 52,386 ounces was mined in 1869, and a cake of silver 12,162 ounces and worth £3,344 and eleven shillings went from Allendale to the Great Exhibition of 1851.

Fred Harris, the former miner from Allenheads, knows as much of the history of the mines as anyone. "Generations of the same family would work down there," he said. "The tunnels were called levels – and each length of level would be named after the man who dug it out and built up the stonework at the sides, so you would get a man going down the mine through a passage he knew his great-grandfather had fashioned. The stonework along the walk was no rough work, it was built with great pride and care, like a fine wall in a garden.

Coalcleugh, the highest village in England, now almost completely deserted.

"Each man would take a candle underground and this would be divided into eight sections, each lasting one hour. After four hours they would take a break for food and when the candle was burned through they came up to the surface and ended their shift."

These candles were the cause of one of the mine tragedies in an industry where there were none of the explosive dangers associated with coal mining. Naked lights could be carried quite safely into the deep earth. But in March, 1856, the miners came off their shift early to take part in the local celebrations after the marriage in distant London of Wentworth Blackett Beaumont, the local MP and mine owner. There were still two or three 'hours' left on the candles and when the men tossed them away on coming from the mine, they set fire to some underground timber and two of their fellows were suffocated by smoke. Predictably, nobody had any stomach for the tea party after this and the prepared feast was distributed to the poor.

Every year, on New Year's Eve, there takes place in Allendale Town, a festival procession with patently pagan origins. A robust bonfire blazes in the town square and men called (for the night anyway) Guisens march, wildly painted and dressed, carrying burning tar barrels. Such occasions help to see through the long, lingering winter.

They also used to have a famous band festival in the town and on one such occasion in the

1870s there was much excitement because Mr Boosey, founder of the London music publishers, had agreed to travel to the remote place and judge the contest. Sadly the day was disastrous. Mr Boosey asked the brass band from Nenthead and that from Carr Shield to play again. The rural musicians imagined that they were playing for first and second place and their chagrin can be imagined when they found that, in fact, they were blowing for *last*. There was violence with instruments used as weapons and Mr Boosey, vigorously manhandled, needed to be smuggled away from the district.

*   *   *

The Northumbrian hills go half way to meet the Northumbrian rain. It was weird, almost eerie, to be travelling among those peaks in June among wintry mists and low, weeping clouds, swollen like bags of laundry; weird but not discomfiting for the skies and the naked hills were full of dark beauty and enjoyment for me. I played Wagner on the car tape recorder and drove through the crags and valleys like a Valkyrie. And there was always the surprising pleasure of an abrupt descent into a pocket in the hills, a cupped place brimming with thick trees, with a couple of tight meadows and perhaps a stone house beside a tumbling stream.

Water gushes from every crack in the landscape, from gorges and through fissures and chasms and from the mouths of the hundreds of abandoned mine workings (the miners had a poetic name for a stream used to wash the lead; it was called a hush), streams and rivers rush down to the road and the valleys as if the mountains were splitting at the seams. Centuries of cataracts and the erosion caused by the mines have uncovered thousands of ancient artefacts, tools, weapons and pottery, some from the very morning of man's life in these parts. By comparison the Roman traces at Old Town, on a hill above Allendale Town, are almost recent. Other relics stand in solitary disuse in the remote uplands, the skeletal walls of farms and homesteads abandoned because they could no longer support the families who worked them. Coalcleugh, the highest village in England, now has only two inhabited houses; the rest is ruins. Here the old counties, Northumberland, Cumberland and Durham, meet indistinctly and the shoulder of the hill called Killhope Law rises above all else on the landscape.

The hamlet of Ninebanks presented a more optimistic aspect, a snug little place with the remnants of an ancient fortress, a pele tower, sensibly incorporated into the cheerful post office. A travelling butcher weighed meat at the back of his van and he and the housewife he was serving both stared, and then waved, at my intrusion as I drove by. The itinerant tradesman's vans were almost the only traffic in the hills that rainy day; the butcher, the grocer, the milkman and (thank goodness for the unexpected) a vehicle apparently transporting the luxury of Suchard Chocolates. Whatever was it doing in that remote, lofty, but down-to-earth region?

Through the valley the West Allen River curls along the most satisfying of landscapes, its torrents suddenly quiet as though pacified by the peace along its banks; rolling sedately by cow-strewn meadows, dividing around treed islands, then scurrying across stones and tipping over child-like falls, before pausing, as if to regain its breath in wide, pooly places, and then journeying on.

I suppose that television has now replaced religion as the leisure preoccupation in these

IN LOVING MEMORY OF
· JOHN CHARLTON ·
OF LAMBLEY & DENTON HOUSE LOW ROW
BORN 13. APRIL 1827. DIED 17. SEP.T 1903
FELLOW OF THE ROYAL METEOROLOGICAL SOCIETY

The memorial plaque to John Charlton on the south wall of the nave of Lambley Church.

The Killhope water wheel, now being restored.

parts. In former times the travelling preacher provided both the expectation of entertainment and Eternity. Wesley barnstormed through the hills with his fire and hope. Non-conformism was always strong and grew stronger after Wesley's magnetism. By 1900 there were only two Catholic families in the entire region. There were others less gifted and famous than Wesley but just as enthusiastic. Thomas Batty, called 'The Apostle of the Dales', propagated Primitive Methodism but was not always understood. He was once attacked by village women who, hearing his sudden singing, were misled by the words 'I am a soldier' and imagined he had come to recruit their sons for the army.

Francis Swindel of Dryburn, a hamlet on the West Allen, was rejected as a Wesleyan preacher, so began his own religious clan, the Bochimites. They held services at a house called Bochim, named after the place, according to the Book of Judges, to where God brought the Israelites when they came out of Egypt. The Bochimites became so popular that a trap-door had to be cut in the ceiling of the main room and the overflow congregation accommodated upstairs in a bedroom. When Swindel died, however, the cult died with him.

Further to the west, across the peaks and fells of Humble Dodd, Dun Hill and Three Knights, within the almost luminous church of Lambley is the memorial to John Charlton, the remarkable man who spent his life measuring the rain. He was a familiar traveller in both the East and West Allen Valleys, a determined, almost ferocious figure, leaning into the wind, climbing the bare hills in his quest for correct and current figures for the Royal Meteorological Society in faraway London. He must, by the very evidence of the place, have been very busy. His memorial tablet is notable for its very fierceness, his powerful face and iron eyes staring from the wall.

Over the high haunch of hills to the south, stands one of the great reminders of the industrious age of the lead mines, the mighty iron wheel of Killhope. It stands now like something in a ghostly fairground, the wind seeping through its spokes, its rim still beautiful and powerful but unturning. In the days of the mines it was moved by the descending mountain streams and, in turn, it revolved the rollers disintegrating the lead ore in the crushing house alongside.

All through Allen Dales and the mountains such great wheels moved long ago. Killhope is the only one remaining.

Thomas Sopwith, whose arrival in Allendale caused such alarm and the miners' strike of 1849, remained as the great engineer and mining agent of the district for twenty-six years. He lived at Allenheads where he was visited by Robert Stevenson, Faraday and Lord Armstrong – the Gunmaker as they called him.

In the mid-nineteenth century Lord Armstrong was loudly experimenting in the Northumbrian hills with a design for a military gun which revolutionised artillery. Before his re-inforced barrel the field guns of the British Army killed almost as many friends as enemies. It was while he was there that he and Sopwith paid a visit to the Killhope wheel. Engrossed in the operation the two engineers toppled together into the rushing torrent that fed the contraption and, according to the contemporary report, 'narrowly escaped being pounded to nothing by passing through the water wheel'. It would have been a strange thing if Armstrong who had spent his life experimenting with gunpowder should have met his end in water.

* * *

I returned, not infrequently, to the warm inn at Allenheads, where there was always talk and characters in the bar. The Strand family, who ran it, made me welcome at their fire and their own family meals. After coming down from the rainy hills it was always a pleasure. A century and a half ago the landlord had his customers' convenience at heart because he installed a unique bath and shower, a drawing of which was found in the inn. The bath-tub incorporates an open fire directly beneath it to bring the water to a comfortable heat, presumably when the incumbent was already in occupation.

In winter the hamlet, concealed in its deep, sly hollow, is often snowed in. The local schoolmaster has taken pictures after a blizzard which have all the white beauty of Antarctic photographs. Three winters ago Allenheads was under thirty-two feet of snow. "Nothing moved for days on end," recalled Leslie Strand, the son of the landlord. "It was just like being the only people left in the world. The miners from the Allenheads mine used to come off shift, come into the bar and stay there until it was time to go to work again. Then we heard that a family in an isolated house needed some urgent medicine for a child."

Fred Harris, the quiet and likeable ex-miner, said he would try and get through the snow by tractor. He left at six in the morning and reached the beleaguered house at noon. It took him a further six hours to get back. Fred laughed. "That was not so bad," he recalled. "But when they finally managed to get a helicopter into Allenheads the damn thing almost landed on top of me! Its rotors threw the snow around and by the time they stopped I was up to my neck in my own drift."

Great falls of snow were recorded down the years in Allendale. But even the most violent blizzard could not keep Jimmy Dixon from the bar of the Allenheads Inn. Jimmy is in his sixties, a craggy, retired miner, who lives alone on a hill over the village. There is no road, hardly a track, to his single house and he transports himself to and from the village by a small, trusty, rusty tractor. Whatever the weather he comes chugging down the hill for his midday pint. "Here comes Stirling Moss," they say in the bar.

Jimmy went down the lead mines when he was twelve. His hands, protruding from the sleeves of his warm donkey jacket, are themselves like lumps of lead. "There was no choice, I had to go down," he said. "My father was sick, he had rheumatic fever and the boss told him that if he didn't turn up for work then I would have to take his place. So I did and they gave me the job of leading the horses down the shaft. God, was I terrified. Three miles underground I had to go. The horses wore hoods so they were blind and they had coats on their backs to stop the chafing from the walls of the shaft." That was his job for life. He remembers seeing broken blue and white plates down in one of the deep caverns. "They were left from the days when the gentry used to have banquets underground," he explained. "They thought it was fun. It never seemed much fun to me. It was always hard and dark down there."

Just how dark I was very soon to find out.

Far underground, if you turned off your miner's lamp, you would be standing in darkness thicker than you could ever have imagined. It is so dark that you can feel it pressing on your face. Deep down there, in the narrow tunnel, there are the unending sounds of water, rushing, running, babbling. A turn of the switch on my helmet illuminated a great hole a few yards ahead, a chasm in the floor, with a stream gushing in its deepness. The only way across it was by a laughable flimsy bridge, fashioned from old, rusty rail-lines. Each step had to be accomplished with inching care, the face, the body and the hands against the rock face. It was not advisable to look down, or anywhere except the rough stone in front of your nose. "That's right," my companion called eerily through the mine shaft. "We're two miles under now. This is where it gets *really* interesting."

I found myself in that fearful and enclosing place by courtesy, if that is the word, of John Salmon, an engineer for whom the lead mine workings of Allendale have an unending fascination. He went down once ("just to try it") and now he has trudged below the surface through half of Northumbria.

He had described some of the mines to me as we stood by the fire in the bar of the Allenheads Inn. In a moment of bravado, or beer, I agreed to let him take me down into the gizzards of the Brownley Hill Mine which gave up its last ounce of lead ore in 1886. It has been

Len and Rita Strand outside the Allenheads Inn.

closed since then. He arrived the following day with a heroic collection of equipment, overalls, deep boots, a miner's helmet and lamp. We drove a few miles across the wet hills, then went by foot down the course of a stream until we reached an aperture, the dimensions of the average front door, embedded ominously in the hillside. "Here we are," said John Salmon as cheerfully as if he were entering his own house. Water ran out briskly. He switched on his lamp and fixed it in his helmet. I did likewise and with a last nervous look at the world, I followed him into the darkness.

We were at once in one of the levels, the long, sloping passage leading down into the belly of the mine. A turn of the head and the helmet lamp immediately illuminated the fine stonework which lined the walls, craftsmanship that had occupied men for a lifetime and their sons and grandsons after them. Not in these mines the rough shoring up by timbers and pitprops. It was careful and elegant. It seemed a pity that such workmanship should be confined to deep and everlasting darkness.

Descending to steeper tunnels the gurgling of water became louder, finally roaring ahead of us. A mighty hole opened up, shadow-patterned by our lamps, and then a side gallery going off into the unknown. Underfoot had been wet and rough since we first entered the mine but now the tunnel diminished to an aperture barely two feet high. It was a case of crawling through, scraping the fifty-year-old stomach over the hundred-year-old mud, pulling with the fingers locked into the rock and then slithering down the other side. The mud soaked into my overalls and left a large cake on my chin. One hand was cut by the sharp rock. Had it not been for my excellent helmet I would have knocked my brains out by then, for the low ceiling seemed to be hitting my head every few yards. Under all the wet and mud I was sweating like fury. I began to think what a strange occupation this was.

John was pressing optimistically ahead, ducking and weaving in the right places like an experienced boxer. He kept calling back to ascertain that I was still with him. My strangled voice echoed through the galleries with the news that I was perfectly fine.

Jimmy Dixon coming down the lane in his tractor from his cottage on his way to the Allenheads Inn.

After a second length of tunnel which could only be negotiated at the horizontal, I heard his voice over my own echoing, panting breath. "Careful ahead. This point's a bit tricky."

God, I thought, if he says it's tricky, then what is it going to be like for me? He had not exaggerated. I emerged into the next chamber and to my horror saw a huge hole in the ground and – much worse – John Salmon clinging like a spider to the rock-face as he edged his way across the chasm on two, old, buckled, *moving* railway lines. "It's perfectly all right," he said reaching the far side. "Just don't look down."

I was glad he could not see my sickly attempt at a brave smile. I tottered towards the hole, the pounding of water – water that even *sounded* icy – coming up from the stomach of Northumbria. Placing my feet on the rails I began to edge across. My trembling set the rails vibrating. My nose was against the wall and my arms and hands spread out on each side. I could not even allow myself a frightened swallow in case the jerk of my Adam's Apple disturbed my balance and sent me plunging to Eternity. After hour-long minutes I reached the other side. Achievement glowed in my chest. "I'm glad you managed that," observed my guide.

"It wasn't too difficult," I boasted.

"Good. There's an even more tricky one along here."

Actually the second hole and rail-line bridge did not seem so frightening. All at once we were in a series of comodious caverns. I began to feel glad I had come (apart from the thought of getting back).

John telt along ledges and in crevices. "Sometimes," he explained, "you can find matches, candles and other oddments, left by the miners. And I've found clay pipes. They enjoyed a good smoke underground."

The lead mines had none of the explosive dangers of coal pits and naked lights could be used freely. There was also a good flow of fresh air even down in the deepest apertures. When the heavy winter snowfalls isolated the Allendale villages it was common to carry food and other supplies through the tunnels which ran out and connected in all manner of directions.

We came to a wondrous part of the mine, a chamber and a succession of exposed galleries where the walls glinted with minerals. Still on their little railway lines were two metal trucks used to take the ore to the surface. They stood, misty ghosts, where they had remained since the final shift in the Brownley Hill Mine had gone to the surface nearly a hundred years ago.

From that point we began to make our way back, over the chasm, through the tight places, until eventually after almost three hours below ground, we were trudging up the last level and the door glowed ahead.

Out into the afternoon I stumbled, smiling at the sunshine pushing through the wet clouds across the hills. It lit the green everywhere. I took a deep, satisfied breath.

When, a week later, I departed from Allendale, and descended the road to Weardale, where summer remained on the fields, I felt a little sad at leaving my friends in the hills. It was still cloud-clung, still raining; the streams and rivers tumbling, the uplands bare. I was glad I had been there. I had stood on its highest places and in its secret pockets.

I had even been down a lead mine – and it's not often that you can visit a place from the *inside* as well.

NINE

A Place Called Odd

Spurn Head is one of the oddest places in Britain. It waggles, like a reversed, beckoning finger, out into the whirling estuary where the wide-spread River Humber meets the North Sea. Every day – every hour almost – it moves a little, fidgets, just a few inches, until, at the end of a year, it has taken up a new place; at the decade it is noticeably adrift, and every century it has completely removed itself to another place. At uniform intervals of two hundred and fifty years it has been washed away altogether, sent sprawling into the beds of the river and the sea, only to reform gamely in small islands which eventually become another Spurn Head. The present two-and-a-half centuries is almost up.

It is a place of sand and mist and ever-moving water, of gales and gulls, of rare grasses, flowers and brilliant butterflies. Once, during the First World War, soldiers manned a gun on its very tip. There was a comic little railway which connected them to civilisation. Three-and-a-half miles away, and on the railway used to run a truck *propelled by a sail*! That is one of the happiest thoughts, images, I have discovered during my journey through Britain. I can just imagine these soldiers, jolly with beer, being blown along the helter-skelter of the track on wild nights, the sail bucking and cracking, the gunners hanging on. There was one sharp bend in the track, where the sail had to be luffed. Many times the odd-wheeled ship (or full-masted train) was wrecked there.

Today, to follow the railway, is to realise how much the headland has moved since those days sixty-five years ago. What had been a straight run, apart from the single, epic, elbow bend, is now running in all directions except in the original. In some places the track careers almost at right-angles to the sandy land, at others it burrows into dunes and marram grass at a sharp angle, and in some areas it has tipped into the sea. Nothing remains the same on Spurn Head; not for long.

The misty and singular peninsula is, notwithstanding its isolation and frequent loneliness, within sight of the wharfs, the cranes and buildings of the fishing city of Hull. It lies to the east of the port, tacked on to the very conclusion of what is now called Humberside, but to most is still doggedly the East Riding of Yorkshire. The folk who inhabit the villages in the flat, green mainland, the root of Spurn Head, even count themselves a people apart from the rest of Yorkshire. The Clublys, the Stothards, and the Biglings, who form a stronghold within the

populace, even now say they are 'East Enders' and their dialect, when issuing forth into the bar of the White Horse at Easington, defies understanding even by those people who live within a few miles. It's that sort of place.

I drove south from Beverley, the old market, racing, and churchy town, over the hamlets of the green plain to reach Spurn. It was a sharp and sunny day. There had been a dry spell in a rainy summer and the fields shone, the houses preened themselves like ducks, and the splendid inn signs of the North Country Brewery (the best I have ever seen) stood like a picture gallery along the way; enough to catch the eye of the most arid tee-totaller.

Easington, Skeffling, Patrington, Welwick and Out Newton are settled, and have been for Yorkshire centuries, in that flat triangle of meadows and ditches between the North Sea and the maw of the Humber. Sunk Island is now inland, although they murmur that the steeple of a church can be seen offshore; Kilnsea is the last hamlet before you take the tight road to the ever-moving sands of Spurn Head.

The villages were still half asleep for it was early and a Sunday. A bell from a church, sitting amid meadows, nodded a reminder of the day, sheep gnawed, and a man on a horse with a small milk churn fixed to the saddle just like a drum, clopped along the lane. The sky was bright and wide and warm. Then I came to Spurn Head.

At once the scene was changed. Now, all became mystery. A glove of mist enclosed the hand that reached out to the sea. It lay, still, along the flat sands, giving a line of war-time tank-traps the aspect of strange warriors marching from the water. A foghorn groaned and then I saw the form of a great vessel, a tanker no doubt, a creeping city out in the estuary.

My road diminished to a single track and the single track diminished into fog, but then a

Left, the seaward side of Spurn Head, looking towards Spurn Point. Right, the Church at Patrington seen from the south with a local cricket match going on in the foreground.

slice of sun slid through and touched the river and the sea, only a few yards on either side of me. Islands of vegetation moved slyly, scarves of mist advanced again, the horn hoo-hooted like a baritone owl. I was glad when the small, busy figure of a lady called Brenda Jackson materialised through the mist.

She was out in this place charged with looking after the birds, the plants and the flowers for the Yorkshire Naturalists Trust, who now own the three-and-a-half miles of Spurn. The regular warden was away, at some remote place (in Wales for a change) and she was thrilled to be there, alone in the little hut between the eroding sea and the eroding river. The winds and the clouds were her company.

Next to her temporary home is a cobble hut which used to be the coastal bailiff's house. "He doesn't exist now," she explained. "It was his job to take the dues from the people who came with carts, years ago, to shovel up the pebbles and sand from the seashore. They were used in building and the takers paid by the load. Then somebody realised that the sea was taking away enough without people doing it too, so that was stopped." The Industrial Revolution had finished on Spurn Head.

"I haven't been here for some time," said Mrs Jackson. "And I'm amazed at the way the sea has taken so many great lumps from the land." We walked up the dunes, past a heligoland bird trap, a long construction like the ribs of an aeroplane, used to catch seabirds for ringing. On the backbone of the dunes, looking straight out to the misty sea, it was easy to see how the contour of the land had shifted even quite recently. Massive whorls like the bendings of an earthquake patterned the shore. A bird-watchers' hut had, prudently, been moved back in stages to safety so that it was now yards inland from its original place.

"I'm afraid I'm a botanist at heart," said Brenda Jackson, curiously a little fey about the confession. It was almost as though she feared I might laugh at her, or know more about it than she and begin to cross-examine her. Seeing I had no such knowledge nor designs, she quietly touched a plant near the bird-trap. It was oddly exotic to be in such a northerly situation, almost a stray from the jungle, with a long, lush, pendant lolling from it. "The Duke of Argyll's Tea Plant," she announced as though making a formal introduction. "One of Spurn's own plants. A small, mauve flower, delicate and dainty, and with cream stamens." She said it like a couplet.

Apparently encouraged, she led me on over the sands. "And this flower is called the Scarlet Pimpernel, which is also called the Shepherd's Looking-Glass because it oddly opens when the weather is going to be bright." Her eyes were sharp with enthusiasm. The sun had come out of the mist. "And this is sea-sandwort," she said pointing again. "In the old days it was a delicacy, used as a pickle. I think the recipe must have been lost. And there's the sea-holly which ladies love for flower arranging, although it is quite rare in other places. In Elizabethan times the roots were used for making children's sweets called eringoes."

She was in full flight now, darting over the dunes, finding rare and interesting flowers and plants at every step – the Pyramidal Orchid, the pink Storksbill, the Restharrow, a relative of the common or garden pea. It was difficult for me not to smile at her eagerness. At almost every yard she found something worthwhile. What a wonderful thing that, in this world, there are still people who can do that.

*   *   *

Spurn Head has forever been a place of lighthouses. As the sands have shifted, so have the lighthouses tumbled; some are now below the sea. St Catherine's on the Isle of Wight was the first recorded lighthouse in Britain and Spurn Head was the second. It was built, appropriately, by a hermit, lighthouses being places of singular solitude, after the sandspit known in fourteenth century maps as Ravenser Odd had been washed away in its due time and gradually been replaced by a reformed cape called Ravenser Spurne, later known simply as The Spore (from 'spur') and, by Mercator on his map of Britain in 1564, as Spun Head.

In an elegant petition to Parliament in 1427 Richard Reedbarowe 'Heremyte at the Ravensersporne' pointed out the 'many diverses straites and daungers bee in the entrying into the river of Humbre out of the see where off tymes by mysaventure many divers vesselx and men, godes and Marchandises be lost and perished, as well by Day as be Night, for defaute of a Bekyn.'

Henry VI granted him his bekyn so having 'compassion and pitee on the Cristen people that ofte tymes there perished.'

The solicitous and solitary Richard Reedbarowe, however, was not the first to live on the shifting sands of Spurn. His first-recorded predecessor was one Wilgils, a monk, who established a minor monastery, probably no more than a cell there about 670 AD.

Near John Smeaton's lighthouse grows a profusion of Scarlet Pimpernel which opens only when the weather is going to be fine.

Right, John Smeaton's lighthouse from the seaward side looking northwards.

Wooden groynes on the seaward side, looking towards Spurn Point.

Three hundred years later, when the spit had moved its customary mile westwards, Egil, the Icelander, was wrecked there, and the stragglers of the defeated Scandinavian army, routed by Harold at Stamford Bridge. embarked from the beaches as the English king was hurrying south to death in 1066.

By the late thirteenth century Ravenser Odd (the 'Odd' being a cape or headland) was a prospering port boasting a market, a fair and (from 1304) a *Member of Parliament*. But the sea and the river made their regular claim and forty years later the constituency and the town were two-thirds tumbled to the tides. By 1360 the gulls and the seals were playing among the ruins. Now the town of Ravenser Odd lies below the ships three-quarters of a mile offshore. There are no legends of people hearing church bells ringing as the tides change.

Henry Bolingbroke came ashore at Spurn in 1399 looking for (and eventually gaining) the throne of England. His welcoming was confined to one hermit. Edward IV, also heading for London and the crown, landed on the shingle in 1471.

In 1602 the sea and the river were again advancing on the headland and Parliament was told of the great 'Dekay of Ravenspounne'. Soon all was awash, the tides and the shoals moved across the sands and man retreated to safer ground. It was said that a landowner on Spurn Head could always reclaim his property – if he could wait a century.

Left, the home of Redvers and Doris Clubly at Easington, situated on the southern edge of the village on the road to Spurn Head.

After that the history of Spurn can be followed by the history of its lighthouses, so many of them lying now blind beneath the sea.

By the late seventeenth century Spurn was once more poking its vigorously growing nose out into the waves. A London man called Justinian Angell thought it might be a fine place for a lighthouse. He built one but by the time it was complete the land had altered again and sailors complained that it did more harm than good. So he built another light to rectify matters and Angell's High Light and Low Light adorned Spurn Head, but only for a while.

A table of the fortunes (or misfortunes) of the various cape lighthouses, compiled by the Hull historian G. de Boer for the East Yorkshire Local Historical Society, carries a sorry catalogue of phrases which tell all too well of the folly of building anything – even a lighthouse – on shifting sands. Tracing the lighthouses from 1674 to 1895 it has one column headed 'Date of Erection' and another ominously 'Date of Destruction'. The catalogue of catastrophes is recorded with such phrases as 'moved', 'surrounded by water', 'taken down', 'moved back', 'disused', 'lantern removed' and 'washed down'. Sometimes the lights failed through lack of coal to burn and ships were wrecked.

John Smeaton, that considerable engineer, built two lighthouses in the nineteenth century; one has now gone forever, leaving an almost prehistoric circle of lightkeepers' dwellings which can still be seen today, the other sits useless and decapitated on the beach half a mile from the present nose of Spurn . . . awaiting the inevitable.

*   *   *

There is a house with a watchtower that looks across the table of green meadows and marshlands and on to Spurn Head. It is just beyond the village of Easington on what might be called the mainland. In it lives John Redvers Powell Clubly and his wife. He was born in 1900 (Redvers after General Buller of the Boer War and Powell after Baden-Powell, hero of

Mafeking). All his long life he has known Spurn Head. "I always wanted this house," he explained. "Ever since I was a lad. I liked the watchtower. It used to belong to the coastguard, but now it's mine." Inside the front door is a passage lined and decorated with fragments of glass from Smeaton's High Lighthouse.

He is a large, grey man. Once he must have been powerful. He was a champion darts player renowned throughout the North Country. "Years ago," he recalled slowly, "I used to shovel gravel on the Spurn, eight men shovelling it into a sailing barge. We reckoned to load a hundred tons in three hours and a half. Three pence for a hundred tons we got. In all weathers too."

We talked of the great storms that have charged in from the North Sea across the flat land. "In 1906 we had eleven feet of water in our house at Hedon," he remembered. "There was a horse and a donkey swimming in our stable."

He has been a lifeboatman too and describes violent nights when they galloped the farm horses down to the Head to pull the lifeboat out to sea. And a beachcomber. "You'd never believe the things I've found along that beach," he said. "During the war I found a foot in a boot. I took it to one of the army people, an officer, and he said I'd best go and bury it, so I did. It's a very funny sensation burying just a foot in a boot. Another time I found a dead man in one of the creeks. Full of shrimps, he was. I've never touched a shrimp since."

His wife went from the room and returned with Redvers Clubly's most prized beachcombing treasure – a prehistoric mammoth's tooth, the size of a large tomcat. "Just found that one morning, dug it up," he said. "Amazing what you can find in these parts. I sent it to a museum but they said they'd got enough of them."

John Redvers Clubly does not use his first Christian name because Redvers is more notable and there is another John Clubly in the village, his senior by one year. I found him among the cabbages in his cottage garden, a twinkling little man whose parents were both Clublys. "There's a lot of us in these parts," he said. He remembers well the gun on Spurn Head and the little railway wagon, propelled by a sail which used to trundle the three miles to Kilnsea, the first 'mainland' village.

"Once," he remembers with a dry, old chuckle, "they moved one of the big guns from Spurn Head and they brought it back on the railway. Right in the Narrows the train broke down and there was the sea and the Humber washing all around their gun. That was a laugh."

At Christmas the young lads and girls from the flat land villages would walk out to Spurn Head to sing carols to the coastguards and their families and the lighthousemen. Old John became pensive. "That was wonderful," he said very quietly. "The wind off the sea, and cold, and sometimes a moon, and us singing carols and walking all the way home, lads and lasses holding hands."

After the First War, while the railway was still running straight, before Spurn fidgetted again, the little engine and its trucks used to run to and fro. "Edwin Hodgson was the driver of the engine and a man called Hammond was the engineer. I remember them even now. The engine squeaking and rattling along the lines and the little truck – the Drury Car we called it – bouncing and swinging behind. We used to go down to Spurn for fun, like an outing, the girls all in the Drury Car and the boys hanging on to the outside."

John Clubly's uncle, who was Tom Wilson, helped to build the lighthouse which (for the

Above, the sand and grasses at Spurn Point.

present anyway) blinks from Spurn Head. His father used to carry paraffin from Kilnsea for use on the light. "He used to take it by horse and cart across Hummabank," he said. It meant Humber Bank. "When he got over there he used to have a few drinks with his friends and many's the time I've seen the horse and cart coming back across Wormsand you'd think without my old dad. But there he'd be, drunk and sleeping in the bottom of the cart."

*   *   *

Left, the lighthouse at Spurn Head.

Years ago a distressed ship off Spurn Head brought the sound of a warning gun, and the heavy horses from the inland farms would be taken galloping down the narrow road to haul the lifeboat to the sea.

The jetty on the river side at the mouth of the Humber, from where the pilots leave and the lifeboat is anchored.

Today the path they took, like the meandering railway, wanders in strange fashion, sometimes heading straight into the sea, having to be built up and added to and straightened after almost every stormy winter. But it is a road worth walking. It goes by an almost primeval landscape of moulded rocks and whorls of boulder clay, some of which were washed down here in the most ancient times from the Pennines and from Scotland and Scandinavia. There are sudden bays, so small as to be secret, with a surprising copse here and there, thick-stunted trees full of sounding insects, brilliant butterflies and hiding birds. In the course of one day a hawkbilled moth and a snow-bunting in its summer plumage were witnessed. A rare feast.

Out to sea, and at any point the ocean and the river are never more than a few yards to the left and right; old groynes and sea defences, breached and defeated by Nature, stand up from the waves like toothless wrecks. Redvers Clubly told me they don't make the barricades the proper way now because they build them of concrete. The wood of the old days bent and 'gave' to the sea.

The Narrows at Spurn Head is well named, the sea and the river being only fifty yards apart and forever trying to reach each other like lovers kept distant. One day they will succeed. There is also a skulking shoal called Old Den which was once, in the olden times, an island upon which there were buildings. No more. The fish now swim in and out of the doors.

Spurn Head owes whatever semi-permanence it has to the grasses and the reeds which, miraculously seem to root and flourish in the most dry and desperate soil. In 1849 Parliament paid for loads of chalk to be transported to the odd headland to stabilise it; ships entering and leaving the Humber were finding it shifted faster than the revisions which reached the navigation charts. A captain, meticulously going by the book, might find himself staring into a coastguard's window. The chalk bank gave some substance and held the Humber at arm's length. It can still clearly be seen today, its whiteness forming the base of a seashore rockery, with rare plants, flowers and grasses sprouting prettily from its niches.

The present Head of Spurn is a blunt, flotsam-strewn beach, beyond the new, sturdy coastguard station, the lighthouse and the jetty used by pilots going out to ships waiting in the Humber. Some of the coastguard children who live down there were playing in the sand in the growing sunshine as generations have before them.

It must always have been a wonderful place for childhood; the treasure hunts among the litter that the sea brings up almost daily, the racing and games in the wavy dunes; the secret bathing bays and paddling beaches; school within sight of the ships; storms heard from a warm bed; the birds and the wild animals. Grey seals and the 'little whales', the porpoises, appear in the frothy waters where the Humber meets the sea; the porpoises, in their travelling circuses, plunging and curling through the waves, the seals lying indolently on sandbanks basking a while before lolling into the water again. The stoat and weasel go about their sly business among the dunes and grasses; Spurn has its own peculiar race of mice; rabbits can be seen sitting on the beach like elderly holiday-makers, fur-coated against the wind, and foxes sit down to a supper of fish. Brenda Jackson spent a glad, late hour the evening before my arrival watching a vixen and her cubs, out for a dusk walk, pausing to make a meal of a dead gull. The little terns nesting on the headland, jealously observed by the conservationists, have been haunted by accidents. One year the foxes made a feast of the young birds; the next a helicopter landed squarely among the nests, blowing them away with its rotors; then the sea roared in during the third nesting season and ended the domesticity of the small sea swallows.

There is a wreck on the beach facing the North Sea, a trawler doomed one night long ago. Parts of the hull lie slotted in the sand, every year diminished by salt and tide and silt. Many others lie offshore, together with the lighthouses of former days and that vanished part of Ravenser Odd. The remnants of groynes long washed away stand out from the sea like ghostly arms calling for assistance. Driftwood comes ashore in fantasy shapes. The bar of the White Horse at Easington is decorated with a carnival of wood, all in the accidental shapes of animals.

Spurn Head is something to almost everyone. The delight of the lover of ships at seeing the great towering vessels passing off-shore is matched by the triumph of the botanist discovering a secret flower or the ornithologist at the new season's bird migrants. The history seeker may plod happily about his business, scarcely noticing the fisherman reeling in his line on a deserted shore.

It is a place to discover solitude and quiet joy, always remembering that its time, according to its shifting history, is almost up. The two and a half centuries is almost gone. Spurn Head may not be there tomorrow.

TEN

October In The Hills

Although it is many years since I have lived in Wales – since childhood in fact – I can never go back and be among the hills and the soft meadows of the south without a smile appearing on my face. As I journey I can feel it growing, idiotically. It is the smile of someone going home.

Driving from England across the wondrous Severn Bridge is worthwhile in itself. (It may not be structurally faultless, as its almost constant repairs and refurbishment indicate, and it may bend like a bow in the wind, but it is still slenderly beautiful and travelling upon it is never without a sense of airy excitement.)

As I drive, having wrestled to find twenty pence in change for the man in the toll booth at the English end, I have a feeling of crossing a frontier more definite than anything I have known even between, say, France and Spain. The widespread Severn is as much a divide as the border between this country and the United States of America. From the moment I am above the girders I find myself involuntarily, and illegally, attempting to stand in the driving seat, trying to look over the fringes of the bridge at the great, grey river. Although I never fully succeed (and perhaps from a road safety point of view it is just as well) I do get tantalising but wonderful glimpses of the eddies and currents, the shoals and runs, and once I saw the Severn Bore itself, moving along the surface like the dark edge of a tropic storm.

When the ancient poets called it Sabrina I imagine they must have been viewing the sweeter, upper reaches, for here where the Severn meets the Bristol Channel it is different – nothing short of majestic. Like a sea it stretches from misty headland to misty headland, birds make considerable journeys across, there is an island with a ghostly lighthouse. And never yet have I seen a ship, or a boat, or a vessel of any description.

But the best is at the end. For, having made the mystic journey, the bridge goes on its downward slope and the road runs quickly into Wales.

My route usually takes me to the town where I was born, Newport, no longer wearing the suffix 'Mon', but properly claimed by Wales and in the county of Gwent. And not before time either! It stands on the estuary of the River Usk, the only river, so my father used to say, with the bed on top. Like the Severn, though, the Usk becomes decent, indeed delicate, a few miles up the valley to the north of Newport. That first day my primary object was to reach Brecon where the Welsh Book Council were enjoying a festival and had asked me to give a lecture. If I add that the venue for this extravaganza was Brecon Barracks, that I dined satisfyingly at the long polished table in the Officers' Mess, and that there was a long night in the Sergeants' Mess with an old army comrade I had not seen in twenty-nine years, then it may be gathered that the visit was entirely convivial. Twenty-nine years cannot be recalled in five minutes, nor without lubrication. One of the few things I remembered with any clarity the next morning was the padre playing pool (that miniature sort of snooker) to such effect that an opponent was heard to comment, "I knew he was a man of the cloth – but I didn't think it was green baize!"

The next morning Wales was bright and clear, even if I was not. It was the perfect autumn day, the road west following the feet of the hills. Trees were red, yellow, silver, copper and vivid green; the slopes, buttoned with sheep, were thicker, more velvet than even in summer. Rivers and streams bounced wildly along the edge of the route. There was little traffic. It occurred to me then that this road, the A40, had its root running from the West End of London and out through the western suburbs. I had a mental picture of what it might be like now at this time, the morning rush hour.

In an unhurried time I reached Llandovery in mid-south Wales, quiet and grave, with the ruined keep of its castle standing up like the trunk of an old tree. This town was to be one of my cornerstones for I was going to explore the mountains of the Dyfed-Powys border, the rough rectangle encompassed by Llandovery, Lampeter, Tregaron and Llanwrtyd Wells; what the Welsh would call tidy little towns.

The road out of Llandovery – still the A40 which travels from Shepherds Bush to the Atlantic Ocean – is plain, unexciting, but at Llanwrda Post Office, by the white war memorial, strange and stark with its figure of a spectral soldier, it turns firmly west and into the exquisite country I sought. Every few yards the road impishly changes direction, dodging through heavy trees, over busy rivers and across the toes of the increasing hills. There were rosy apple orchards, unofficial meadows, cottages red with autumn ivy; cottages so comfortable as to appear positively smug, looking under the eyebrows of their low roofs, their windows friendly (and often with a Welsh jug and basin framed there, a perfect still-life, for the evaluation or delight of the passer-by).

Gardens were brimming with flowers, staring over walls like brilliantly dressed spectators. Every tree glowed, every leaf a separate dab of autumn colour. Birds sang and meadows gleamed in the sun, hills sniffed at the blue hem of the sky. Still, I thought, now the summer had gone we should be entitled to some good weather.

Somehow I always knew that I would like Lampeter and that Lampeter would like me. I was not wrong. Another tidy Welsh town, as they have it, the main street lined with shops called Davies. They stand two, three, four next to each other, and there are more across the street. Even when the exotic words 'Bon Marche' are over the window, the more homely name of Tom Davies is present also, Tom before the Bon; Davies after the Marche.

At one time they had a famous horse fair here when dealers from all parts of the country came to town to buy Welsh ponies. They used to gallop them up and down the main street to see that their legs were in working order. In the Black Lion Royal Inn, a satisfying Georgian hostelry facing the main street, they have a copy of a painting by Thelwell, that wonderful conveyor of the horrors of juvenile horsewomen, which is a beautiful and sober scene of the

Sheep grazing on the hillside in the valley of the Afon Berwyn.

Lampeter Horse Fair in 1909. The street is lined with flanks and tails and studious men stand debating or bargaining with their hands deep in their breeches pockets. An odd feature of the painting is the background formed by the Black Lion Royal Inn itself. The landlord, Henry Dickinson, and I had dinner one night and he described how, after studying the painting, he had gone, puzzled, into the street and carefully counted the small windows on the third – the top – floor of the hostelry. There were five, as indeed there are in the painting. "But," he said mysteriously, "we only have *four* rooms up there. We have tried to locate the *inside* of the fifth window but we can't." Naturally there are stories of an old murder and a haunted room. . . .

   With the foresight of a true pioneer, I set out first to make a journey around the perimeter of the region I planned to explore. It was, as I have said, a slightly askew rectangle cornered by Llandovery, Lampeter, Tregaron and the modest (and now dried up) spa of Llanwrtyd Wells. The roads connecting these places totalled roughly sixty miles. Between Llanwrtyd Wells and Llandovery was the well-used trunk road; between Llandovery and Lampeter, the pretty curly road I had already travelled; between Lampeter and Tregaron, *two* roads, a main route and a shy, almost timid, lane that ran parallel, like a small boy jogging alongside a big brother; and between Tregaron and the starting point of Llanwrtyd Wells a glorious mountain road, wriggling across heights and valleys, laden with mists and silence, travelling from isolation to emptiness, from beauty to enchantment, from delight to wonderment. And back again.

   Taking the minor route from Lampeter to Tregaron I found, with a smug satisfaction, that it was intertwined with the silvery River Teifi. Shredded by shallows and shadows it noses between its banks, busy as a dog, hurrying over clicking stones, swaying beneath trees and hiding playfully below small, grey bridges.

There were few buildings, just farms lying against the hills as if they had been cut out and pasted on the landscape. There were animals, sheep and cows occupied with their perpetual lunch, but in ten miles the only human I met was a man driving the world's slowest vehicle, a hedge-cutting tractor. He crept along like a hedgehog in no hurry, the machine chopping the summer growth from the hedgerows with great efficiency and much noise.

There was no room for his machine *and* my car in the tight lane and neither was there room for doubt as to who was going to have to move. Cautiously I backed up until I came to a joining lane, even narrower, and turning into that I waited for the slow-progressing hedge-cutter to go by. It took several minutes, which I used up by admiring the gurgling river and remembering that this, the Teifi, was one of the last habitations of the beaver in Britain. Then the cutter came nearer and I abruptly realised that my car was being machine-gunned by flying lumps of wood, part of the hedgerow that was being violently shaved by the contraption. It was like hail on the roof and a piece of beechwood, large enough to put on my log fire at home, came bouncing onto the bonnet. I backed up hurriedly. The tractor driver, with the slow smile of a man who knows full well he is in charge of a secret weapon, acknowledged my retreat with a kind wave of his countryman's hand.

When he had gone out of range I turned down my original route again and, after weaving through a further corrugation of hills and vales, I arrived at the village of Llanddewi Brefi, where St David made the ground rise up beneath his feet. It is still risen.

The story is that David, whose mother was said to be a nun called Non and his father a king called Sant, was preaching here to a great crowd who, because the ground was flat, were unable to see him. At his prayer the earth rose beneath his feet and everyone was able to hear and marvel. To complete the miracle a dove appeared and sat with aplomb on his shoulder.

Today, the church built upon this spot is still at the summit of a brief hill, with the ground falling to the small, nice village on one side, and to the waters of the Teifi rushing through a nave of trees on the other. George Borrow in *Wild Wales* mentions the rooks about the square tower who 'fill throughout the day the air with their cawing'. They – or their descendants anyway – are still there and still calling in the silent afternoon. He found Llanddewi Brefi a place with a remarkable air of solitude 'where a man of the world might settle, enjoy a few innocent pleasures, make his peace with God and then compose himself to his long sleep.'

The solitude is still present, accentuated in a sad way because the strong-looking church is locked and closed. In the porch I found, pinned to the wall, like a writ to the mast of a ship, a letter from the Ecclesiastical Authorities promising to do something about the absence of a vicar as soon as possible. It was dated ten months before and the vicar of Tregaron told me that there had been no incumbent at St David's miraculous place for two years. A great pity.

According to Borrow he was shown in the church a silver cup, kept in an old chest, which was the gift to the parish from Queen Elizabeth in 1574. The timeless traveller's comment is worth repeating today: 'I thought to myself "I wonder how long a cup like this would have been safe in a crazy chest in a country church in England?".'

In *Wild Wales* he repeats, too, the legend of the giant humped oxen, one of the mythical team

From Golygfan viewpoint, looking west towards Tregaron down the valley of the Afon Berwyn.

of the godlike Hu Gardan, which came broken with sorrow to die at Llanddewi Brefi. Indeed, he points out, the word 'Brefi' in Welsh signifies an animal bellowing or lowing. Hu Gardan, the King of the Summer Country, a land in the east, came to Wales and civilised its people as he had done in other places from the Crimea to Scandinavia. His chariot was drawn by the mighty oxen team who met their match when they tried to pull the Magic Old Crocodile from the Lake of Lakes. The Crocodile won the tug of war and some of the oxen died. The beast that went to Llanddewi Brefi did so in sorrow and humiliation and there died, moo-ing its heart out. According to George Borrow, the great horns of the animal were once to be seen in the church, but by the time he arrived in the 1850s they had powdered and vanished.

I left the village to its peace, the only sounds on the sun-dappled afternoon were the high cawing of the rooks, the barking of a lone dog sounding across fields and the busy rattling of the river. Tregaron is just a few miles away, another of those decent, little towns, with a statue of Henry Richard, one-time Member of Parliament, standing in oratorial stance outside the Talbot Hotel. He was so vocal and ubiquitous that in Parliament he was known as the

'Member for Wales'. The river wriggles through the town and the more serious mountains rise at its back. It was once a great stopping place for the drovers who moved, yard by yard, from the pastures of West Wales to the English markets, taking their flocks of sheep and cattle herds across the mountains a yard at a time. They had no choice but to travel slowly for the animals grazed the whole way.

These men were a tribe of their own, familiar with rough ways and great hardship. They knew every path across the highest places, even through the snow. Apart from delivering their livestock, sometimes to Smithfield in London, after a journey stretching into weeks, they earned some side-money by delivering letters and parcels from the remoter parts of Wales to people in England.

Every year there was Hiring Fair in Tregaron, when the farmers, drovers and labourers came into town to arrange the year's work. It was a time of modest gaiety, with lights and bonfires and sideshows. The story is told of a local woman who, in recent times, immediately after the fair, went on her first trip to London. Leaving Paddington Station and seeing the everyday lights, she exclaimed to her companion, "There's lucky I am, there's a Hiring Fair on in London too."

From the square at Tregaron the mountain road begins – the wonderful, exultant road that climbs and dips in glorious loneliness all the fifteen miles to Abergwesyn and then down to my other 'corner post' at Llanwrtyd Wells.

In truth its start was not very exciting. It exited from the town by the wall of the saloon bar of the Talbot Hotel, climbing a little through gardens and houses. Not for a mile or more does it give any indication that it is going somewhere remarkable.

Then, as though at last making up its mind, it abruptly leaves the lower ground like an aeroplane becoming airborne at the end of a runway. At once there are no more houses and gardens, but lovely, empty, windy peaks ahead, and autumn valleys falling richly on either side. The road is narrow, fixed to the green-sided hills like a rope ladder. Before me opened out a long and graceful valley, a river, the Afon Berwyn, wriggling and rolling along its meadows, the meadows themselves cut off abruptly by the switchback of the hills. From that distance it looked like a Victorian cardboard tableau, each edge of hill standing out against another height more distant and then another, until in the furthest place, against the fine blue sky, rose the real uplands.

Colour was everywhere. Vivid reds and velvet green on the slopes, soft lighter green along the floor of the valley, with the river bending like silver wire, the trees in all their late shades with powdery little copses at the river bends.

Slopes went like drawbridges, steeply up and down. In the distance the mountains were bald and blue; those walling the valley through which I travelled were patterned with sheep on the upland pastures. Stone walls ran up and down the slopes, miles of walls which must have taken years to build. It seemed amazing that in such a wild place men should go to such trouble to build boundaries.

About three miles from Tregaron, and much higher, where the air had a wintry edge, a track led off the road to the right and there, at a vantage point called Golygfan, I looked back over the miles of wonderful valley, in the reverse direction from my first view.

Right, waterfalls beside the road from Pumpsaint to Rhandirmwyn.

Astonishingly, the scene from here was even more satisfying than from the other end of the valley. It was possible to see how the hills form corners and barriers, rising to sweet isolation and then curling around and down to the next fat meadow, with its trees and the binding, bending river, the string that held it all together.

The most distant aspect from this high platform is the range of mountains to the west, so far and so misty that they might be in America, or Heaven for that matter! As I looked – realising not for the first time what a privilege I enjoyed being alone in such a place, matching its solitude with my own – a sight much nearer caught my glance. Now my pleasure was complete for in the valley that dropped away almost beneath my toes, far down and yet in mid-air, was a splendid buzzard. It loitered on unseen breezes, moving its wings and then stilling them, letting the wind do the work. It was hunting and, as I watched, warm with joy, it ranged imperially over the whole bowl of the valley. At first it was in the middle distance, sitting up there, watching for a possible lunch far below. Then it took itself off, soaring until it was a dot against the highest of the peaks.

When I believed it had gone forever it appeared only fifty yards away, much lower now, having seen something moving in the trees. When it moved it was the only movement in the world as far as I could see. Eventually it vanished from my sight around the elbow of the next hill. But it was not alone up there. Three miles further on another buzzard – or perhaps the same – rose from the roadside and whirled away at my approach.

By then I was high up on the road. Around was the most dramatic hill scenery; dark, misty, even in the sun, falling steeply into equally dark valleys. It was as though the roof had been taken off the world.

Against the face of an escarpment far ahead, I could see the drifting silver tail of a waterfall. There were streams and torrents all around, beside, over, and under the narrow road. I was way beyond the treeline with nothing between the land and the sky except me. It was at that point I saw the telephone box.

Now I love the idea of telephone boxes in remote and unexpected places like this. I have seen them on deserted islands and in ghostly dis-inhabited villages. In America, on the wild seashore of Cape Hatteras, off the Carolinas, I once stopped my car next to the loneliest call-box I have ever seen. A giant storm was raging and in that narrow isthmus the sea was pounding in over the lowland to both right and left, the wind screaming unchecked and the rain bucketing down. I went into the call-box and within two minutes I was speaking to my wife sitting cosily at home in Hampshire, England. It's a wonderful thing, the telephone.

Here in the Welsh mountains the telephone box was at a crossing of the single track roads. It stood, like a hopeful hitch-hiker, with water, cataracts and streams all around, the only other visible structure an old railway wagon used to store winter feed for stranded upland sheep. I felt almost duty-bound to stop and go in. I did so but I discovered I had no change to make a call. Nevertheless I took the number and on some dreadful, biting, winter's night, I intend to ring it. Can't you imagine the box, with its solitary light, far out there in the snow, with the lonely ring-ring, ring-ring, and nobody to listen but the sheep. On the other hand, would it not be odd if *someone answered*?

The road spun out and I reached its end, the cosy spa town of Llanwrtyd Wells. What a

The Camddwr flows past Soar-y-Mynydd churchyard.

journey it had been. It was the first time I can ever recall being breathless while driving a car. I went into the Drovers Rest at the corner of the little town's main crossroads and had a pot of tea and a bun, with scarcely less enjoyment than those drovers themselves, who long ago, had refreshed themselves more stoutly there after the long trek across the mountains with their herds.

Llanwrtyd Wells was another of my 'corner pieces' – a place with four hotels, a relic of its days as a spa – which now makes its living from fishermen and pony trekkers, a change from wheelchairs and walking sticks.

The healing waters ran out a few years ago and now all that remains of the fountainhead are the remnants of a few somewhat lavatorial buildings. The sulphur spring was said to cure all manner of ills, including the scurvy of its nineteenth century discoverer, a Mr Jones. The inhabitants of the valley, however profitable the source was to them, called it the 'stinking spring'.

Llanwrtyd Wells has taken its loss well. It's a serene little place, its square almost continental, its shops endearingly window-dressed in the manner of the late 1930s, and its war memorial a building of stout proportions, licensed, it proclaims, 'for billiards'. Framed outside was a nice letter from the lady-in-waiting to the Queen Mother thanking the villagers for their good wishes on Her Majesty's eightieth birthday.

Once more I drove south to Llandovery and then west to Lampeter. The fine October day was drifting away like an ebb-tide. The valleys were strung with mist, the roads became quirky and the mountains mysterious. I went, with all the anticipation of George Borrow, who had stayed there many years before me, to the Black Lion and Royal Inn, in anticipation of a good meal, a bottle of wine and a warm bed in which to pass the chilly mountain night.

In this central fastness of Wales many people speak Welsh as their first tongue. In Lampeter

The entrances to the Roman gold mines at Pumpsaint.

it is worth loitering in the shops to hear the conversations, even if you don't understand a single syllable. A customer in a sweet shop, for instance, will reel off a whole string of rising and plunging Welsh and finish off the order endearingly with the words 'chocolate bon-bons'. In the homely and excellent dining-room of the Inn were two dark-eyed, black-haired sisters, waitresses, who spoke English with such an accent and precision that it was patent that for them it was very much a second language. Henry Dickinson, the landlord, who is from Swansea, told me, "There are many people in this region who have to think carefully before they speak any word of English. They have had to learn it the hard way, by listening. It does not come easily."

In the bar that night I saw a notice which said that on the following morning there was to be held a sale of antiques in Lampeter at the Victoria Halls. It was a chilly morning, the sort where your footsteps sound loud on the pavement. The hall was easy to find; it was just a matter of following the clatter of cups and saucers. Many of the potential bidders were already there, drinking hot tea and eating pies. It was just ten o'clock. The rattle of these cups was only drowned by the rattle of potential buyers examining the crockery to be auctioned.

To call it an antiques auction was possibly using a little latitude. There were goods ranging from an old fashioned sweet-shop bottle to a pair of fins from war-time bombs (from which of the protagonists the catalogue did not stipulate). There were also some bits of china and brass, and some jewellery. There was a great army of jugs (Wales is a country of jugs) and one in particular to which I took a liking. I thought I might bid for it: a Mason's ironstone jug with a nice dragon handle and a pleasing blue and white pattern.

The auctioneer, a robust and jovial man, ushered everyone into their seats and requested that dogs and children should be kept reasonably hushed. He launched into the bidding as heartily as any of his kind and cheered immensely when he came upon a lot described by the catalogue as a Jubilee Mug of Queen Elizabeth the *First*. Alas it proved to be the wrong Queen Elizabeth and he had to settle for one pound twenty-five.

My jug was among the early lots but even before we reached it I realised that I was facing difficulty. Almost everyone in the room was called Davies, Jones, Evans, Hughes or Thomas. Each successful bidder called his name and then, in the Welsh fashion, the nickname by which he was known or the locality in which he lived. I did not get my jug; I backed off quite early in the face of a whole tribe of Thomases who apparently have a family weakness for Mason's ironstone. Had I won, what would I have shouted? 'Thomas, Hampshire', or perhaps 'Thomas the Writing'. It was something I could not face.

I was heartened, however, once I had left the hall, by the prospect of another day in this fine landscape. It was dull and rainy but the hills seemed all the greener. I took the road, which the wonderful wanderer George Borrow had taken, to the east to the village of Pumpsaint, passing through Cwmann where the traveller had remarked in *Wild Wales* on the presence of three inns and the distrustful nature of the populace.

Pumpsaint is old Welsh meaning 'Five Saints', an appellation received because of the presence of a large stone above the village where five saints, Gwyn, Gwyno, Gwynoro, Celynin and Ceitho, once rested for the night of a storm, their shoulders against the boulder. The imprints are still there for all to see. Some say they put their feet on the stone, in which case they must have had outsized feet.

Pumpsaint, for all its holy stone, has another, greater – if more secular – wonder. For it is here in this quiet Welsh valley that the Romans mined gold. They did not discover it. That was the men from the dim ages. But the Romans, as in everything, put the gold-mine on a sound, commercial basis. It can be seen now, just beyond the Saints' stone (which, in all probability, was a special boulder brought from some distance and used in a stage of the gold-mining operation. So much for Gwyn, Gwyno, Gwynoro, Celynin and Ceitho). It is a sylvan place, even in the autumn of a rainy day, an amphitheatre hollowed from the side of a green hill, half hidden among birch, beech and muscular oaks. There is the ubiquitous stream wriggling through the rocks, the descendant of the watercourse that the Romans used to wash away the surface soil and reach the precious metal – and to clean it once it was mined.

The rockface that rises from the floor of this bowl is streaked with colour, predominantly bright yellow. It goes in veins and strata, vivid but not so vivid as the patterns within the large cave there. There are several openings in the rock but this is the largest and most obvious. Cautiously I entered.

Being the sort of person who is rarely prepared for anything, even when on a journey of exploration, I had no torch with me. Near the entrance to the cave, where the dull light seeped in through the shrouding trees and boulders, I could see the strong streaks of gold in the rock. I ventured further into the tunnel. It was much darker in there. I could hear my own breath echoing. *Then I saw six yellow eyes watching me.*

It was a moment of surprise if not actual shock. "Puss?" I asked carefully. "Is that a pussy cat?" It was. Three in fact, a mother and two half-grown kittens. They came from the darkness in friendship, poor furred things, mewing with pleasure at seeing some other creature. I took them back to the car, where they sat on the back seat, quite at home, and between them ate a bar of Cadbury's milk chocolate, which was all I had.

The other entrances to the gold-mine are blocked with gratings. One has a few lines of

Left, water and trees along the path which leads to the cave of Twm Shon Catti. Right, the saints' stone at Pumpsaint.

railway and a bogey-truck inside, much like the ones I had seen deep in the ground of Northumbria. It was pressed against the grating, a bit like a wild animal at the zoo. University College Cardiff sometimes go prospecting down there, their mining students working the rock where the Romans left off. I suppose, if they strike lucky, they could end up as the richest university in the world.

The Romans, using their military engineers, began mining the Dolaucothi gold in AD 75 and went on for about seventy years when the workings were abandoned. The site is the only known Roman gold-mine in Britain. With the great disrespect they had for obstacles the Romans built two aquaducts, one four miles long, the other seven miles long, to bring the washing water to the site. Their barracks, granary, defence works and, of course, their bath house have been unearthed, as well as a wooden water wheel, a panning cradle, the remains of sluices and washing beds, weapons and a fine hoard of Roman jewellery.

One of their relics stands decoratively in the middle of a flower bed in the garden of the Dolaucothi Inn, at Pumpsaint. A piece of carved masonry, like a small column or support, it was found when the landlord's sons were digging the garden. Clive Yarnold, the landlord, is a lively student of the history of this region, although he comes from Sussex.

The gold-mine, he said, was opened several times after the Romans left, the latest occasion in 1938 when a company called Roman Deep Ltd, extracted sizable quantities of gold. Unfortunately, the machinery for processing it was only to be found in Hamburg, and the events of the following year soon stemmed this out-let.

He has a record of a murder at Dolaucothi House, a mile away, in 1876. John Johnes, the local landowner and MP, was shot by his butler, Henry Tremble, in pique because he had refused to let the man take over the licence of the Dolaucothi Inn. It was strange to be reading it, sitting in the bar of the very place described.

Charlotte Johnes, the rich man's daughter, kept a diary. There is an entry for 18th August, 1876, an ordinary day, and then the words: 'Here there is a long and terrible interval'. The following entry, more than four months later, on 29th December, 1876, described the killing on 19th August. Charlotte, herself, was severely wounded by the berserk Henry Tremble firing off a shot-gun, and was unconscious when her father succumbed to his wounds. But she heard an account of his last moments from her maid.

'Darling Papa said: "I am dying. Henry Tremble shot me. Mind he is taken". He was sensible and very calm. He never uttered a harsh word even against his brutal murderer . . . he died as he lived all his life – a saint with a blessing on his lips.'

The paragon gone, Tremble then attempted several other murders, but only succeeded in shooting the family dogs. He went to his home, Myrtle Cottage in the village of Caeo, and, when besieged by the police, did the only sensible thing he had done all day. He shot himself.

Today Dolaucothi House is no more. Its gatehouse can still be seen, white across the fields. It is now a farm. The family fortunes dropped after the murder, although the house remained until the Second World War when it was used as a small munitions factory.

For all its explosive history the house came down fairly sedately. It was finally demolished after it had fallen to disrepair.

There were two reasons for my wanting to return to the innermost hills. The first was to find the hidden cave of the legendary Welsh outlaw, Twm Shon Catti.

Looking south-west across Llyn Brianne towards, on the left, the top of the dam.

Twm Shon is the Welsh way of saying Tom Jones. Catherine was his mother's name and so he was called Catti to distinguish him from the many other Joneses. He was a sort of Robin Hood, robbing and riding, until the fortuitous marriage to a rich widow (he is said to have pulled her hair through a barred window to persuade her to wed) bought him respectability. He became High Sheriff of Breconshire, and was said to have never sentenced a thief to hang unless he could not possibly avoid it.

When he was in his wild days he lived in a narrow cave in the mountains, from which he could look down on the rumbling River Twyi and the surrounding land. It was said that no-one ever found his cleft hideout. And, personally, I don't wonder. Because I did.

The track is known well enough these days, of course; anyone will tell you where it starts, less know where it finishes. It runs enchantingly at first, through slim woods alongside the lovely river, hills rising on each side, some bald, some thick with trees. One, clothed such, was shaped like a tri-corn hat. I had seen it from the distance and now, I discovered, I was climbing it from the far side. And, in middle age, on a rainy afternoon it was a climb enough.

But it was worth it. The trail wriggled through bogs and boulders, up among the trees and the mosses, with the river always calling from below. Before I had started the ascent, when I was still following the watercourse, I turned a rocky corner and came face to face with a standing heron. We regarded each other with mutual surprise; then, I swear with a dignified sigh, he took off and flapped greyly away like some frock-coated clergyman.

It took me the best part of an hour to reach the cave. The rocks became more difficult, the path less easy to follow, the rain thicker and the footholds less secure. I had the passing thought that if I fell up here it would be some time before anyone found me, although my car was parked down in the valley. Having always found famous last words of interest, I mentally

composed a brief, compelling sentence, to put on my pocket tape recorder if the worst came to the worst. But it did not. The words will have to wait until another time.

Eventually, high among the birches, with the occasional family of sheep regarding me with cautious curiosity, I found the cave. Frankly it was a disappointment, for, whatever form it had when Twm lived his outlandish life, it has collapsed and changed now. The rocks and boulders have tumbled and only a tight passageway remains. Twm would have to be a dwarf as well as an outlaw to exist there now.

Getting down was almost as difficult as getting up. The rain had soaked through my trousers and shoes and socks. My Wimpey navvy's coat was heavy with moisture. My hands were scarred. Eventually I regained the low level and then it was just a matter of getting through the bogs alongside the river. I renewed my acquaintance with the heron and this time he did not even bother to fly away, but gave me what I can only recall as a pitying look.

Not unthankfully, I reached the end of the trail at the mountain road again. There was the faithful car waiting. Soon I would be in a hot bath – and dinner-time beckoned.

To my astonishment I came suddenly upon a man, older than me by ten years I would say, who was just entering the trail. It was now getting dark. "Excuse me," I ventured, "You are not thinking of going up there are you?"

"Up where?" he asked reasonably.

"To the cave," I said. "To Twm Shon Catti's cave."

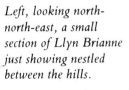

Left, looking north-north-east, a small section of Llyn Brianne just showing nestled between the hills.

Right, the reservoir of Llyn Brianne showing the constant jet of water at the bottom as it feeds the Afon Tywi.

"No, mun," he said. "I'm just going behind those trees to spend a penny."

.   *   *   *

The country is never less than romantic. Here the wizard Merlin was born, and among these hills and forests of sisal oak Llewelyn the Last fought Rhys the Less; not so much a battle of losers as their names suggest.

But if hills echo history, the sight of a great lake lying among these hills is the echo of solitude. The lake here is called Llyn Brianne and it glowers among dark pine forests in the bowl of the mountains. It is a huge reservoir (for Liverpool) but even its mechanical harnessing has something lovely and magical about it, for a massive dam traps its southern end, and water slips hundreds of feet down a giant chute – looking like a perpetually unrolling carpet – and explodes in high-flung spray at the foot. What a sight and what a sound – and, when I was there, none but me and the sheep to watch it and listen to its majestic booming.

A road curls along the contour of Llyn Brianne lost high above its surface. From there even sunlight on the water looks cold; currents and winds corrugate the surface and all around is the frowning fir forest. A mile beyond the lake the landscape becomes beautiful again, lofty but warm. At a place called Soar-y-Mynydd a beautiful collar of trees, with a river running at their

Looking south down the valley of the Doethie from Nant Llwyd.

roots, stands about a white chapel. No other habitation is in sight. It is the most moving place. Solitary but cared for, its round-topped windows throw back the sun, the trees are brilliant and more softly luxurious than any in the hills. People came from the isolated farms for many miles to worship here. On summer Sundays a service is held there still. There are only four tombstones in the sloping grass that goes down to the busy river.

There is a single farm called Nant Llwyd, surely one of the most isolated in Wales, beyond the next hill, reached by a bumpy track. It was once worked by six bachelor brothers called Jones. Today only two, John and David, remain to raise sheep over the hundreds of upland acres. They go out shepherding on horseback and they have a farm lad who rounds up the flocks from the back of a motor-bike, a bumpy and spectacular occupation.

I climbed the track and John Jones, a round-faced, cheerful man, welcomed me into the farmhouse kitchen where the rural postman was enjoying a midday bowl of cawl, Welsh soup. David was out riding the hills, rounding up wandering rams for it was the tupping season.

"Our grandmother came from a farm called Fanog, which is now under the waters of Llyn Brianne," said John.

He spoke careful English, but the sounds were Welsh. "The first winter she and my grandfather had it, they had such terrible weather that they thought that they would never be able to pay the rent when it was due in the spring. Most of their sheep died and they only survived by selling the skins at sixpence a time."

John went to school in the vestry of the little Soar-y-Mynydd chapel. He and his brothers were the only pupils and the teacher lodged at the farm. They learned their English there and from wandering labourers and tramps who roamed about the mountains during the depression of the 1930's. They learned to work with the sheep almost as soon as they could walk, or ride, whichever was the sooner. The menfolk from each isolated farm would help their neighbours in rotation in the busy seasons.

John remembered a one-eyed shepherd who came to stay with them once. "Our father told us off one morning for not getting up early enough – not until the old shepherd was out with the lambs. My brother pointed out that he could never be awake as soon as him, because the shepherd only had one eye to open!"

For weeks in winter the farm at Nant Llwyd has been snowed in. Snow often appears in November and does not leave until May. In the blizzard winter of 1947 they were cut off for thirteen weeks, and during that time the youthful John walked eleven times the twenty-two mile round journey to Tregaron bringing food to the farm on his back.

The following day before I left Wales again, I met John and his brother, David, in Llandovery where they had been at a horse sale. David is taller and quieter but with the same round and pleasant face.

We stood at the bar in The Castle Hotel by the market place. They spoke fondly of their years at their isolated farm. "During the war," said David, "our family had its own Home Guard company – on horseback. There were no uniforms, only great-coats. The weapons were shot-guns. When it was over my father was very proud leading his little company in the Victory Parade at Lampeter."

We talked about the solitary chapel where they had gone to school. "Did you notice the few graves in the grass?" asked John. I said I had. "Did you see the strange thing?" he continued. I had not. "One stone," he said, "says it was the first grave in 'this sequestered place'. But the stone next to it has a date two years earlier."

After an hour I left them and drove east towards England. It was a bright, cold morning. Almost the end of October. And as I journeyed I saw on the highest uplands the first snow. The white fingers of winter.

Above, sun-lit trees surrounding Soar-y-Mynydd. Right, the churchyard and chapel with its adjoining vicarage.

ELEVEN

On The Bank

At night, when a large wind advances up the Channel and the waves are 'biting', as they say, the people of the Dorset coastal villages lie beneath their thatch and listen to the sounds of the Chesil Bank, a mile distant, as it snores, groans and wheezes like a restless man in bed.

There is no other place like it. Ten miles of brown pebbles fifty feet high, running straight as a sword from Portland to the lovely and friendly village of Abbotsbury, the sea pounding one side, its other sheltering long lakes, or fleets; a place of wild birds and grand swans, where I once saw a lone flamingo.

The scientists have no explanation for the Bank's uniqueness. How it came to stand there, how it forms, throws itself back into the sea and promptly reforms. Nor can they explain the phenomenon of its graded pebbles – as big as oranges at Portland and becoming smaller for every mile west, until at Abbotsbury they are the size of beans. Fishermen of former days could come ashore on that deserted coast on the blackest of nights and know exactly where they were by feeling the size of the pebbles.

Although I had for seven years lived within sixty or seventy miles of this wonderful place, I first saw it from a distance of twenty thousand feet. I was on a morning flight to Miami, on the first of January, and as the plane climbed from London to its cruising height I watched the coastline I recognised lying far below in the first sunshine of the year. Poole Harbour with its little herd of islands was slipping under the wing. Then the curve of Weymouth Bay and the protruding nose of Portland Bill – and then Chesil Bank. It was an ideal vantage point to view its straightness, the fleets reflecting the sun, the green Dorset hills rising quickly but not blatantly from the shore, the grey villages snug in their valleys. At that moment I would have willingly gone there instead of Miami. It is not an unfamiliar emotion with me; I remember as a soldier, a young man who had never been anywhere, standing on the violently rolling deck of a troopship taking me to Singapore and seeing the Isles of Scilly on the storm-swept horizon. My heart ached to go there, but I was bound for further places, and it was years before I achieved my ambition.

This time it was much quicker. I went to Chesil Bank (some call it Chesil Beach) several times over one summer, and again for a memorable two days and a night in the early winter. It is nothing if not romantic; old, full of stories, still wild.

It is one of those parts of Britain – like the coast of Suffolk – where a single turn off a busy main road takes the traveller into a different and enchanting country. In the case of Chesil Bank the turning is just beyond Dorchester on the main western road towards Exeter. It is like Alice stepping through the looking-glass. At once, in yards, old Dorset closes around you. The roads become lanes, the hedgerows are thick and beyond them, viewed with happy surprise from some unexpected rise, are the exquisitely domed hills of England's most secret and lovely county.

Of my journeys there, I loved the last best of all. It was afternoon when I travelled west, down into deep Dorset; empty, winter Dorset. The light was rich. The numbers on the black-faced church clock at the village of Martinstown glowed gold in the sun. There the houses have small stone bridges over the stream that runs outside their gates. At Winter-bourne (a name given in these parts to a spring which rises in winter) the same stream curls slyly by the side of the road.

It was odd, although perhaps not so odd, that on two occasions when I drove this way in summer, rain fell thickly and there was fog on the higher ground. Today, in December, everywhere was clear and bright. The sky looked a little worn, pale, as it does late in the year, but the rounded fields were full green, or rich brown after ploughing; steeples and smoke rose succinctly from hidden villages, rooks and crows called over the afternoon and trees rattled.

I passed some huntsmen (and women) going home. The first was a powerful man on a big horse. He wore a black coat and a black top hat, just like an undertaker.

At Portesham, at the top of a rise, you catch your first glimpse of the Chesil Bank – a straight line in the distance, caught between two nearer hills, so that it appears like a bridge. Eagerly, as though anxious itself to get there, the road hurries down the modest valleys until it arrives in the cheese-coloured village of Abbotsbury.

Left, looking down from the hill fort onto Abbotsbury. On the horizon is Weymouth. Right, Abbotsbury, with St Catherine's Chapel on the hill just beyond the village. Looking west-north-west from Chesters Hill.

If I could choose one place in this country (and that means one place in all the world) to live it would be Abbotsbury. It is perfect in its setting, nice to know, and wears a smile of undemanding friendship. It is like a pretty girl, unspoiled by the knowledge of her beauty or the attention afforded her. It has a single stone street, many of the houses carrying small clues that they were built from stone originally set in the great, ruined priory. At one end the street leads to the splendid swannery, which since the time of Elizabeth the First has been sheltered by the haunch of Chesil Bank. At the other it rises steeply and travels one of the most stunning coastal routes in England, with a sharp turn leading again to the Bank, a lane down which, not so long ago, the villagers used to run when a wreck was on the beach, her cargo for the asking.

All around the fields and woods fold and refold in small hills and vales. Immediately above the village, on a single velvet hill, stands a chapel, St Catherine's – just one room, but built tall and importantly. It stands out against the sky like a lighthouse. It is from there that the whole of Abbotsbury can be seen, heard, almost *felt*. I first climbed to it on an August evening, a stiff climb from the back garden of the inn, only to discover a notice which said that the key to the chapel was kept at a house down in the village.

But the view that serene evening was worth the ascent. Abbotsbury was spread about the foot of the hill, on three sides; on the fourth was the long, green drop down to the sea.

To my right was the sturdy church, its tower square against the blue evening sky. Then the single wall remaining of the priory, standing like a great hand, and beyond that and a reeded pond, the most majestic barn in the whole of Christendom. Half in ruins now, but the other half still standing – and still in use – it was used in the fourteenth century by the monks of the wealthy abbey at Christchurch for the storage of grain. It measured 270 feet from end to end, all hefty stone, with a great timbered roof. It is an astonishing building, as long and as high as a big ship.

The village houses, some substantial, some only cottages, but all of the same fine, pale stone, curved below me; the inn, the jovial Ilchester Arms, was almost at the centre. There was bright washing hanging on lines, a man worked in a vegetable garden, children played on the opposite hillside where the mediaeval tracks, used by the busy and commercial monks of the Abbey, are still clearly showing. Village sounds drifted up, caught by the evening air and carried casually to me: voices, barely discernible, the snoring of a wood-saw, cows lowing in the meadow directly beneath me. The church clock sounded seven, measuring each strike like a breath.

Before going down the slope to dinner, I went to the back of the hill and looked out over the late sea. It was blue but shadowed. Far out were two small boats, but otherwise it had no interruptions right to the evening horizon. There was a grand view of the Chesil Bank there also, pointing like a finger at misty Portland. Inside its straight bank were the petrol-coloured waters of the fleets, hundreds of swans lying close to Abbotsbury, white as foam on the shore.

Turning back I gained the landward flank of the hill once more. Without hurry I took the downward path, delighting in the changing stance of the village at every pause I made. The sounds and the very smells of the evening were entrancing, not the least of them being the aroma of dinner wafting up from the kitchen windows of The Ilchester Arms.

In most of my travels I have been fortunate in chancing on the right place to stay. I seem to have a nose for a deep bed, a convivial bar and a satisfying table. The Ilchester Arms (The

Right, looking north-north-west along Chesil Beach from the Isle of Portland end.

*Remains of the domestic
architecture of the old
Abbey at Abbotsbury.*

Earls of Ilchester, the Fox-Strangways family having been the gentry of Abbotsbury for centuries) fulfils all these requirements. It has, in addition, a ghost whose presence I have felt, a former sailor as a cook, and a delightful landlady who is Bread Pudding Champion of Dorset and has a plaque to prove it. What more could anyone ask?

Joan Thorneycroft, her husband John, a grave humorist whose glasses steam when he laughs, and Richard Derrick, the sailor home from the sea, run the inn together. The bar is the sort of place to ensure a lifetime's contentment for any reasonable man. The food is a happy memory and the company also.

Richard Derrick, a black square of beard on his chin, was pulling the pints one night and describing, with colourful detail, how he was once arrested in Hampshire and charged with stealing *daffodils*.

"How was I to know they belonged to somebody?" he pleaded. "And that somebody being the Lord of the Manor. They looked lovely, there in the field, so I hopped over the fence to pick a few to take on home, see. Next thing I knew the police are calling at my door. Somebody'd seen me and now it turns out they was *private* daffodils. I didn't know now, did I? I said to the magistrates – oh yes, I was charged all proper like and stood in the dock like the worst of them – well, I said to the magistrates, I reckoned on their being *wild* daffodils, being in a field."

St Catherine's Chapel,
dominating the
surrounding countryside.

It was bizarre, if not an exactly sensational case, and ended with Richard being found guilty and being asked if there was anything further he wished to say to the magistrates. He said there was. They told him to say it, whereupon he spread his big arms theatrically and began to recite: " 'I wandered lonely as a cloud. . . .' "

"Somehow," related Richard sorrowfully, "they didn't seem to appreciate that. I got fined twenty quid."

We had some memorable times in that bar, evenings that somehow lengthened into early mornings; cheerful, firm company with dear John Thorneycroft wiping his glasses because he had laughed so much he couldn't see.

When I was there in the winter, and the fire was red in the grate, the night went on until about three o'clock, whereupon I went to my bedroom at the end of the house. It was a fine room with a single beam, black with age, running the whole width, twenty feet or more. Because it was out of season the rest of the rooms were shut off. In fact the Thorneycrofts had specially aired this one for me.

I got into bed, pleasantly warmed with whisky but by no means awash, being very lucid, and lay drifting towards sleep. The street outside sighed in the night wind as streets do. I listened to hear the singing of the Chesil Bank but there was none that night. *Then I heard the cry.* Not a scream but a distinct cry – almost above my head. A frightened cry, but truncated, cut off before it could reach its crescendo. Hurriedly I sat up in bed. Then heavy footsteps crossing the ceiling above my head. Down the old wooden stairs they clumped. Cautiously I got out from the sheets and went out, through an adjoining room to the landing.

There was a light burning there but no sign of any person. I attempted the old cliché, 'Is anybody there?' No answer. Then I went along the corridor and looked up the stairs. It was black up there. I'm not by nature a nervous person – but I decided to end my explorations at that point. Perhaps I had imagined it, although I was sure I had not. Perhaps it was someone in the street. But the street of that blameless place was deserted except for the wind. I went back to bed. Almost at once the thudding footsteps crossed above me again. That was the moment I decided on the well-known formula of putting one's head under the bedclothes and closing one's eyes tightly.

In the morning my story was greeted with understanding. Things had been heard before. Richard had experienced the same mystery. One night there was an eerie gunshot and on another a cowbell which hangs in the bar began ringing of its own volition – and in front of five witnesses. As for my adventure – well, they told me that, in fact, everyone else had slept elsewhere that night. I had been ALL ALONE in the inn.

That same day the Thorneycroft's daughter, Lindy, showed me over the twelfth century Abbots House, next to the church, where she lives with some friends. It is a wonderful stone house, full of excitements and mysteries. They had been carrying out alterations in the loft and there, under the eaves, they showed me a mummified cat which may have been there for centuries. It is an old Dorset custom to leave a dead cat under the roof. It is reckoned to keep the ghosts away.

In the pulpit of Abbotsbury Parish Church are two bullet holes, relics of the Civil War. There was a fight within the church, occupied by the Royalists, and a fiercer engagement outside. Eventually the Parliamentarians, under Sir Anthony Ashley Cooper, prevailed. The Royalists surrendered. Then, while the victorious Roundheads were crowded into Abbotsbury House next to the church, intent on plunder, the gunpowder magazine in the cellar blew up – either by sabotage or accident – and winners and losers went sky high with it. The solitary wall, standing incongruously by itself, is all that remains.

In the porch of the church today is a stone figure which must have stood there when the bullets were flying. It represents an abbot, one who may well have seen the original abbey built in his lifetime eight hundred years ago. The features are worn to nothing but he is a tall, strong person, robed and holding a bible. He stands patiently while the years roll on, like an eternal usher.

The church, the single admonishing wall of the great house, and the breathtaking Mediaeval barn are grouped at the eastern end of the village. Skirting them is an ancient way which leads down to the enclosed waters of the fleet and the marvellous swannery. Since the days of the first Elizabeth there have been swans here. Today there are about eight hundred, nesting, breeding, sailing in white convoys with the wind in their wings.

For almost three hundred years the Lexster family have been swanherds at Abbotsbury. Fred Lexster is the latest – and most probably the last – of his name to hold the profession. Known as 'Lecky' in the village he's seventy-seven years of age, wears a pair of swan feathers in his hat and beams a knowing Dickensian benevolence over a pair of spectacles worn low on his nose.

"My son decided he didn't want to follow on," he explained when we talked of the generations of his family who had tended the swans. "He's gone to be a fisherman. It's a pity but that's what he wanted. He tried it but he decided it didn't suit him. I can remember coming down here to work with my grandfather. There were fifteen hundred swans then." He thumped his walking stick thoughtfully on the ground. "You know, we're the only family called Lexster left in Britain. It came from Norway in the beginning."

He surveyed the white herd spread out over the water and on the low grass banks on the landward side of the fleet. Chesil Bank rose like a brown dam on the other side. Among the swans was a single pink flamingo.

"Came over from France I expect," said Fred Lexster. "Seems to be at home, don't he. The others think he's a swan with long legs."

Even though he does no heavy work at the swannery now, Fred is down by the water most days watching the birds and talking to anybody who asks questions. It's not just the swans that are his concern but all the wild seabirds which come to the sheltered place.

"When I were eight years-old," he said, "I came down with my old grandad and I learned all the birds. The warblers and the waders and the terns. And in the winter the wild duck. We used to lie quiet and see the water filled up with duck. Twenty different kinds. I've spent my life ringing duck – and I've had rings back from nineteen countries. Three or four years ago I had a ring from a teal, all the way from Archangel in Russia. That's a good distance."

During the war Fred was in the Royal Observer Corps, watching for enemy aircraft approaching across the Channel. The most extraordinary incident of those days concerned one of our own fighter pilots.

"He went and had a rush of 'igh spirits," remembered Fred. "He flew right across the bank and machine-gunned all the swans. He killed some of them and injured a lot more. But I saw

The dried out body of a cat found in the eaves of one of the old Abbey buildings near the church.

him through my field glasses and I got his number. Twenty minutes after he landed he was in hot water. He had to pay up for the damage.''

Fred has had many memorable moments in his outwardly quiet life. One was when, as a young man, he met Thomas Hardy. Years later he sang an old Dorset song in the film *Far*

From the Madding Crowd. He's met Augustus John and George Bernard Shaw when they came to see the swans. And then there was the amazing day when Sir Jacob Epstein came to the swannery. "He asked me to hold a swan for him – while he measured its wings. I caught one of the big birds and he measured every feather of its wings. If you look at St Michael and the Devil – which he did for Coventry Cathedral – St Michael's wings are modelled on the wings of that swan."

A few yards inland from the spot where Fred Lexster watches the swans over the little glasses on the end of his nose, is a thatched building that was once the house of the Duck Decoy man. In a great tidal wave of 1824 – the only occasion when the Chesil Bank has been fully breached – the house was destroyed and the water reached a height of twenty feet, even today commemorated by a marker on a pole near the door.

That infamous night is still remembered along the coast as if it happened only last winter. The villages of East and West Fleet were drowned, the sea coming over the Bank in a thirty-foot wave.

Today the row of sweet cottages in Butter Street, the only habitations in East Fleet, run down to what was the church. It has never been restored after that fateful flood but remains a solitary chapel, surrounded by broken gravestones and dark pines.

Within, it is a small, peaceful place, a white cell with an altar flanked by two ancient brass tablets, memorials to the Mohun family who lived in the great house at Fleet. The family and the house were the centre-pieces for John Meade Falkner's famous adventure story, *Moonfleet*. A commemoration tablet to Falkner who died in 1932 is on the south wall of the chapel.

The Mohun brass tablets – from the early 1600 s – are intriguing. Maximillian Mohun, in armour, is seen kneeling with his modest wife and his sixteen children arranged behind. His sister Margaret with her husband and seventeen children form up on the tablet at the other side of the altar. They face each other like two teams. They are buried beneath your feet as you read their memorials, in a vault they shared, in the old smuggling days, with barrels of brandy, tobacco and other contraband concealed from the eyes of the excise men.

If the old church at Fleet is full of interest then the 'new' church half a mile distant is almost dreamlike, in summer lying in exquisite tranquillity beneath the shadows of great trees. There is something wonderful about it, withdrawn, mysterious. It is the sort of sight to stop the traveller in his very step. It has a luminous beauty, somehow enhanced in winter when the trees around it have changed. Then it takes on what can only be thought of as a pale glow. By moonlight it is beyond description.

Alongside the fleet, isolated from the small village, is the place John Meade Falkner called Moonfleet Manor in his famous story. Today it has become a hotel but it still retains the aloof atmosphere that it held when it was the seat of the Mohun family. They lived there in some glory with the great black 'Y' on their coat of arms apparent everywhere. Then, and today, the Dorset people called them the 'Moons'. Fishermen using the coast along the Chesil Bank find it useful as a seamark, for there are few other buildings. To them it is known as 'Mother Moon's'.

In the bar of the hotel today is a framed excerpt from *Moonfleet*, a rousing tale of smugglers and wreckers, rivalled in English literature only by *Treasure Island*.

The swannery at Abbotsbury.

Falkner dedicated his novel to 'All the Mohuns of Fleet and Moonfleet'. In the opening chapter he writes of the fleet as ' . . . a lake of brackish water . . . good for nothing except sea-fowl, herons and oysters, and forms such a place as they call in the Indies a lagoon; being shut off from the open Channel by a monstrous great beach or dike of pebbles. . . When I was a child I thought this place was called Moonfleet because on a still night, whether in summer or in winter frosts, the moon shone very brightly on the lagoon; but learned afterwards that 'twas but short for 'Mohun-fleet' from the Mohuns, the great family who were once lords of these parts.'

Nowadays, the Mohun family arms can still be seen in the village and in Moonfleet Manor itself. But it has its most curious relic on the gates of what was once the entrance to the estate. Coming from the north the narrow road passes the stone plinths surmounted by two, pink gauntletted arms bent at the elbow and waving flags. The first reaction is that this must have been some embellishment to a railway level crossing, for the arms and flags have a definite railway look about them. But a glance at the neighbouring house, a modern bungalow built on the site of the old gate house, shows the Mohun coat of arms in stone above the window, and above the black 'Y' are the flag-waving arms.

If the Mohuns ruled the land around the fleet then the Fox-Strangways family at Abbotsbury have outlived them. Sir John Strangways was the Royalist who held the village from the King in the Civil War (one of the many little battles of that war which is not mentioned in

The old church at Fleet which stands almost on the banks of East Fleet. The church was flooded in the 19th century.

the six volumes of *Clarendon's History of the Rebellion*). It was the skirmish which ended in the great house blowing up, taking friend and foe to eternity in a moment. The ancient charters and records of the monastery went also. Sir John and his son Giles escaped the blast but were imprisoned in the Tower of London for three years. They survived to return home to Dorset. To the west, up over Abbotsbury hill, which tops the wide, wide seascape, and down again, are the hamlets of Swyre and Puncknowle. Going out there that winter's day was exciting. What had begun as a sunshine morning had transformed itself into a blizzard by noon. Driving up the hill was like going into the Himalayas. Sheets of snow came over the rise.

Two swans at the Abbotsbury swannery.

Then, on the plateau, I saw the whole length of the curling coast in the grip of the white storm. The snow fell from the horizon of the sea, all across the width of Lyme Bay and threw itself against the high Dorset cliffs like spray. There was nothing for it but to stop and watch. The windscreen of the car was getting blocked anyway. It was wonderful and wild. The sea lay grumbling and grey under the thick clouds and the white curtain that fell from them. The Chesil Bank was rimed and crusty, and the fields leading up to the hill on which I stood soon became webbed with white.

Then, as if the storm had only been permitted on sufferance, a strata of lighter sky appeared across the sea, growing and lightening, pushing the snow clouds before it briskly. Within ten minutes the blizzard had gone and the sky was pale and sunlit again. Only the streaks of snow along the hillside road were evidence that it had ever been. Over my shoulder I could see it hurrying east, like a fugitive, towards Weymouth.

When I reached Swyre it was like spring. The sun touched the windows of the low cottages and shone on the bell of the old schoolhouse which is now someone's home (what a happy idea to retain the bell in its neat belfry). The churchyard has an array of railed gravestones all

Above, Chesil Beach looking north-west with Moonfleet Manor Hotel (formerly Fleet House) in the middle foreground, facing Gore cove and West Fleet.

Right, looking south-east over East Fleet with the Isle of Portland in the distance; Chesil Beach is disappearing towards the Isle of Portland where it terminates.

rusty now, the lettering on the stones mossed and illegible. It looks strangely like an abandoned zoo, the old railings disused cages.

Across the lane from the church is a bulky farmhouse that was once the home of a shipper of wines, John Russell. One night in the late fifteenth century he was called from his bed by a messenger. A Spanish princess and her husband had been wrecked along the coast. They were safe but someone who spoke their language was needed. John had acquired a knowledge of Spanish while buying wine and he rode immediately to help them. As a reward he was summoned to the court of Henry VIII and so began the dynasty of the Russell family, the Dukes of Bedford. His memorial plaque is in the village church.

Another family, the Napiers, have their memorials in the neighbouring village church at Puncknowle (pronounced 'Punnle' by its inhabitants). In fact, it would not be exaggerating to say that the church *is* their memorial for they are on every wall. It is a small, peaceful place where the bellringers stand immediately within the door so that the Sunday morning worshippers can appreciate their labours.

The Napiers – identified mostly by initials – are entombed around and in the church. The family's main memorial has a line of Latin and another of Greek with the final warning in English: '. . . Therefore this marble affords no roome for fulsome flattery or vaine praise.' So there.

Another of the family tablets stands on the west wall, immediately over the final, short pew. It is so positioned that the unhappily grinning skull with which it is adorned, is fixed at the head level of anyone sitting in that pew. Two worshippers would find it grimacing between them. I don't suppose that particular seat is very popular, except possibly with village children.

Undoubtedly the most touching thing about this church is a note written in smudged red ink under a helmet of armour which belonged to some far-off Napier. A notice draws attention to the helmet, a gauntlet and a spur. The red ink note adds apologetically: 'The gauntlet and the spur have been stolen'.

Outside it was still spring-like. Rooks were noisy in the fine large trees within the walled churchyard. The sky was pale and clear, the air keen. Across the road from the church the inn frowned under its thatch. An old man came by and stopped me to ask if I knew where Mr So-and-So lived. Since he was so obviously local (he had a stick and patently could not walk far), I took this as an excuse for a conversation. He didn't take long to launch into it. "I don't know what the world's coming to. . ." he began. We stood in the street, with the cawing rooks speckling the sky, the timeless village sitting among its gentle fields and trees. For fifteen minutes we discussed the troubles of mankind and easily put them to rights. And we were quite undisturbed. There are still places like that in England today.

*   *   *

Time and again it was the great Chesil Bank that drew me back. The very breadth of the sea there – nearly always empty of ships – is worth surveying; the way it bends and patterns, the way the winds frisk it, the formations of the sky and the swooping of the birds. Where it rises to almost fifty feet immediately beyond the high water mark, it drops seven fathoms almost as

The figure of an abbot in the porch of the village church at Abbotsbury.

Looking over the cannon to the dogs' graves at the sub-tropical garden that borders the Chesil Bank at Abbotsbury.

soon as the unwary would step into it. Only a hundred yards off-shore are dozens of ancient cannons jettisoned from ships being driven ashore in heavy weather. The guns were the easiest things to get rid of in an attempt to lighten the ship. They lie on the treacherous bottom, all in neat lines as they were thrown. Even closer to the shore are more guns and all manner of materials from sailing ships who failed to escape the trap. Sometimes things are washed up but mostly Davy Jones keeps the locker door tightly shut. Because of the dread currents very little of this debris will ever be recovered.

Admiral Thomas Hardy (the 'other' Dorset Hardy) called that area of sea 'Dead Man's Bay'. His memorial now stands on the modest inland hills within sight of the Channel. Out there, off the Chesil Bank, are generations of wrecks, from Spanish galleons to the submarine MI, which lies on the bottom with her crew, hatches cemented – an official war grave. Five weeks before the invasion of Normandy in 1944, nearly seven hundred Americans died in the same area. They were aboard two landing craft, rehearsing for the D.Day assault when a squadron of German E-Boats from Cherbourg attacked them. Of the men who died that April night very few had ever seen the enemy.

Some odd relics of the sea can be found today in the enclosed sub-tropical garden that borders the Chesil Bank at Abbotsbury (it is said that the pebbles of the bank retain the heat of the sun like some natural storage heater and so provide the temperature which makes rare plants, trees and flowers flourish so near that wild and exposed shore).

There, together with the splendid old palm trees and ancient camellias, are set a battery of ships' cannon, Spanish, their noses pointing dumbly towards the sea. They were washed up on the beach just below the coastguard cottage occupied by John Kelly, the curator of the gardens. It was he who told me of the lines of guns still lying just off-shore. He does not come from these parts but he is the sort of man who fits very easily into such a place.

I had first met him and his young wife, Nicky, in the cheerful bar of The Ilchester Arms. He had trained to be a doctor. "I found my heart wasn't in it," he said. "So I became a gardener instead. But I love the sea almost as much, and in this job I have some of both."

He has indeed. The warm, enclosed feelings of the deeply foliaged gardens, his work among the rare and absorbing plants, while a few yards down the lane the sea is bounding across the pebbles. "When we first came here we were given the coastguard cottage overlooking the beach as temporary accommodation," he said. "But we found it wonderful there, the sea right at your doorstep, so we said that there was no need to find us any other home. And that's where we have stayed."

Alongside the guns is a row of small gravestones. Beneath each is the body of a dog. Three are the first golden retrievers ever to be bred. Lord Tweedsmouth, a friend of the Fifth Earl of Ilchester, and a frequent visitor to Abbotsbury in the late nineteenth century, crossed a flat-coated retriever with the now extinct Tweedwater spaniel and the result was Tess, the first golden (or yellow) retriever and the mother of the whole breed. Stella and Aura, the next two bitches, are buried alongside her. The place is one of pilgrimage for golden retriever owners.

The other grave has a different story. One winter morning in early 1915, the body of a dog was washed up on the beach just below Abbotsbury Castle. The engraved story on the tombstone tells what happened: 'Bruce, an Airedale terrier, who stood to the end with Captain Loxley, RN on the bridge of *HMS Formidable* when sunk by a torpedo three miles off Portland. January 1st 1915.'

The castle is gone now. Fire damaged it (some sight that must have been, a blazing castle along a lonely shore) and it was eventually demolished in the 1930's. The remnants of another fortification, from the earliest time of man in Dorset, can still be traced on the rising ground behind the hump of Chesil Bank.

John and Nicky Kelly live out there now, in their coastguard cottage, the great, wide bay outside their window. Perhaps the final word about Chesil Bank, a unique place, should come from John. "When the wind is coming up the Channel at the right speed, in the right direction," he says, "then the sea starts to bite into the Bank. It shifts, it groans and turns. It even sings. On a wild night you can hear it outside our window. It's worth being here just for that."

TWELVE

The Merman And Other Stories

Many years ago fishermen who had been out in the North Sea returned to the little Suffolk port of Orford with a merman in their catch. He was kept a prisoner in the stout keep of Orford Castle until one day he escaped to the sea again. Today the merman is a story often told along the flat and windy coastline. People believe in its truth, for this is a place of tales and mysteries. Legends thrive in places of rough winters, where the wind blows about the roofs and the fire is bright. The people will tell you, for instance, that at Butley, three miles inland, a man is buried in a solid silver coffin. But no-one knows quite where.

I went to Orford twice during my travels in search of the hidden places, the visits, in two winters, separated by nine years. At that season on the coast of Suffolk there comes a thin, cold wind, skimming across the reeded land and low islands; there are majestic storms, or blizzards, when life can scarcely move outdoors; there are sudden, soft skies, days of surprise which would have delighted John Constable.

To travel there late on a wintry evening was to sense at once its isolation. The road from Ipswich to Great Yarmouth was laden with traffic, headlights shimmering through East Anglian rain. But once I had turned away from the main route and gone through the homely streets of Woodbridge, I entered the blackest of nights with trees clattering above and hedges tight as walls on either side of the road. Even in the few hamlets there seemed hardly a glow.

After ten miles the road enters Orford and stops abruptly at the doorstep of the North Sea.

I went to the Crown and Castle Hotel, remembering its roaring open fire of nine years before. The fire had gone, replaced by an imitation; not enough of the smoke went up the chimney, they said. But the old inn, its next door neighbour, the great and ghostly keep of Orford Castle, has character and comfort enough. It stands at the conclusion of the endearing square of the town, with shops and houses arranged happily around the King's Head Inn, a smugglers' rendezvous, at the far corner and the amazing, great church beyond that.

That first wintry night, with the wind looping over the Orford housetops, I walked through the deserted square and then down the road that leads to the quay and the Jolly Sailor. It is a low, little inn, so deep into the ground that you have to step down to the bar. At one time there was a tradition that locals only used the back door. Because of alterations to the structure they now have to enter the front door like ordinary mortals. They grumbled at first, but now they've become used to it. The beer still tastes the same.

It's truly an old place, this, with a great wooden table especially built for clog-dancing. Around that table, for generations, have sat the old men of Orford, playing shove-ha'penny (with *real* halfpennies). They have leaned on their elbows year in and out, so long someone even took the opportunity to paint the scene. The picture is on the wall: fine, riven faces, flat caps, knowing eyes. They sit around the shove-ha'penny board like aldermen in council. These days the old men generally meet at midday but one, Harry Smy, was sitting at the table, pint between palms, in exactly the same position as I had left him nine years before. It was a different pint, of course (a good *many* different pints), but Harry was unaltered. He's into his seventies now. Sixty years ago he went down to London. "I din' like un," he philosophises, "so I never went again."

*　　*　　*

The following morning was splashed with lemon-coloured, winter sunshine. I walked through the square again, savouring its silence; Quay Street was as little populated as it had been in the darkness of the previous night.

In the silence of the moment it was possible to hear the slap-slap sound of the water long before I reached the abrupt end to the road on Orford Quay. The gulls seemed to have it to themselves, walking about, preening, and sitting shouting from the roof of the Harbourmaster's little office. Suffolk grass comes right down to the fringe of the water here. The harbour, or anchorage, is protected from the onslaughts of the full-grown sea by the flat bulwark of Orfordness, a long spit three or four hundred yards out across the dun, choppy water. It is so low it scarcely raises its nose above the waves. To the south, no more than a mile, is Havergate

Orford, seen from the river. On the left is Orford Castle and on the right St Bartholomew's Church.

Boats pulled up on the shingle beach near Orford Quay. In the distance is Orfordness with its lighthouse, which separates the River Ore/Alde from the sea.

Island, an enchanting place of waterways, lakes and banks, the haunt of hares, giant coypu rats and one of the rarest birds in Britain.

Between the oddments of land the anchorage was strewn with small boats, their snouts chopping up and down like animals at the trough. The horizon was clear, cold and featureless. Somewhere across there was Denmark. It was easy to appreciate how Romans, Danes and others, including, naturally, the rapacious Vikings, found the low land of East Anglia so inviting. They came into the estuary here (today the river is called the Alde from Aldeburgh to Orford and, with a nice distinction, the Ore from then on) and found themselves, once local resistance had been subdued, in a comfortable country.

Today the horizon from Orford to Woodbridge is a patchwork of sand, marsh, wild areas of furze and, surprisingly, daunting forests of close pines, dim enough to make you think of wolves. The rivers, the Deben to the south and the Alde twenty miles up the coast, slice deep into it with sudden streams and ditches crossing it like a defence system.

Farms are large and villages small. According to old Harry Smy in the bar at The Jolly Sailor, farming today is too much like hard work. When he was working it was pleasant and leisurely. "Us took our time," he said. "When it started rainin' we git us inside, and we stayed there till it stopped. 'Tis all too much of a business today, bor.''

The fortunes of Orford have moved with the sands and the tides. In the days of Raleigh and Drake, Orford was a countable port. In 1727 the local pride and confidence was such that a sailor's address to King George the Second read:

> *If the King ask – who are you, then*
> *We humbly answer 'Orford men'*
> *Who else dare ask, we answer bluff*
> *'We're Orford men and that's enuff'.*

It thrived even into the eighteenth century. It was known as *Oreford-Nigh-The-Seas*.

Sometimes the seas were more nigh than others. Eventually the silting of the approaches to

Looking up Quay Street towards the Church of St Bartholomew in the distance.

the harbour, limiting the draught of ships able to enter, and the growing of the port of Ipswich robbed Orford not only of its trade and prosperity but also of its Mayor and the title of Borough. Its regalia, constables' truncheons, long staves and money bags, the town silver and seals, the handles in the form of silver oars, are now in the charge of Major John Steurt-Gratton, who holds the ancient post of Claviger. He keeps them in the bank at Woodbridge. One day, who can tell, they may be taken from the safe and used again.

The miniature town bears its loss well. It preserves a quiet dignity, almost an aplomb, with nothing moving quicker than the sea. Behind the Square there is a pattern of tight, straight lanes. There is a story that a local man of some influence once had the little village houses of these lanes demolished because the inhabitants made too much noise.

They lie almost beneath the elevated doorstep of Orford Castle like the excavations of an ancient place. The mound on which the tall keep stands today is likewise ribbed with old and buried fortifications. Built by Henry the Second, it remained a major military factor in the defence of East Anglia for two centuries. It had its battles, although the local populace, far from being defended from its walls, were not infrequently terrorised by the garrison. But it would be just another castle in a country of castles if it were not for the amazing story of the Orford Merman. The merman was caught in the nets of the Orford fishermen in 1167 and

Red brick houses in Quay Street, seen from the road.

taken to Sir Bartholomew de Granville, the custodian of the castle. According to the first person to relate the story, Abbot Ralph of Coggeshall, the merman was 'naked and like a man in all his members'. He was covered in hair and had a long shaggy beard.

In an attempt to get the creature to tell his history Sir Bartholomew used contemporary logic and had the poor merman hung up by his legs. But he would not, or could not, speak. He was kept in a dungeon and ate eagerly whatever was put before him, raw or cooked. Further indignities were tried and when these failed he was, curiously, taken to Orford Church to see if he showed any religious feelings. He did not and was returned to his cell. Eventually a day was proclaimed when the merman was to be returned to the sea so that his aquatic prowess might be observed. Strong nets were spread off-shore intended to prevent his escape, but once in the water he had no trouble in evading them and swam out joyfully while the townspeople watched from their beach and boats. Some distance out he treated them to a display of his swimming and diving skills and then, to everyone's amazement, calmly returned to the land

to be taken back to his dungeon. There he settled down for a further period of several months, closing his eyes to sleep at the moment of sunset and opening them at the first beam of sunrise. He was guarded but only loosely and one day, when the sentry was late, he vanished from the cell and was never seen again. He had heard some call from the sea.

*   *   *

To go inland from the town is to go into a quiet and ancient country. Stone Age people worked the soil here, leaving their flints to be found in plenty today, and long before they arrived it is said that the land was joined to Europe and the Rhine flowed through it. I went to Chillesford, a silent hamlet now, but one where the archaeologists and anthropologists hurried eagerly when a whale's jawbone was found in a pit behind the church. It was from pre-historic times. The local people were not astonished. For generations they had been casually picking up fragments in the fields; bones and fossils and petrified starfish. To reach the pit the searcher must circuit the calm, old Suffolk church. It stands with its attendant graves and trees on a brief rise of ground. Ducks and geese noisily inhabit a pond by the road. In a space behind the church, and between it and the pit of the whalebone, are the mass graves of the villagers of Chillesford who succumbed to the Black Death.

The placid village had had its bizarre moments. In 1874 lightning struck the tower of the church, and when the anxious vicar and churchwardens climbed to the belfry they found that one of the two bells had melted into a shapeless mass. The village also had a fine windmill, seen for miles across the country and used as a navigation mark by ships coming into the haven at Orford. A carelessly left lantern turned over one night and set the mill afire. It was a spectacular moment with the blazing sails of the mill careering around in the wild and windy night, watched by the awestruck inhabitants.

The next hamlet, Butley, has the remnants of a once-powerful abbey, and the extraordinary story of Michael de la Pole, Earl of Suffolk, who died at Agincourt. In that notable encounter the French lost hundreds in dead, the English a handful, some say as few as forty. Two noblemen died for England, the Duke of York and the Earl of Suffolk. The story is that the Earl of Suffolk's body was brought from France and carried through the villages of Suffolk *in a silver coffin* to be buried at Butley Abbey. No record of the exact burial place has ever been discovered, although the records of Butley Abbey since the twelfth century are available in detail. There have been attempts to find it but no spade has yet uncovered the silver casket.

In the pleasant library at Woodbridge there is a transcription of the daily records of the monks of Butley, itself lost for many years but re-discovered before the war among some papers in the Bodleian Library. They include a roll-call of monks and their duties within the abbey community: William Cookson, surveyor and outrider; Edmund Burwell, keeper of the garners and corne; Thomas Marryn, barbour; Simon and Thomas Pullen, keepers of the sculbote (the boat used at the landing stage). Other brothers were employed in 'makyng candyles' and 'keepyng fysshe' while poor William Pawling is described as 'lame and febled'.

Only the gatehouse remains today as a sign of the industry and glory of a great abbey. It has, needless to say, a ghost – the shape of Robert Bremmor, Prior of Butley who, having aroused the wrath of Henry VIII, committed suicide in 1509. He was buried in unconsecrated ground,

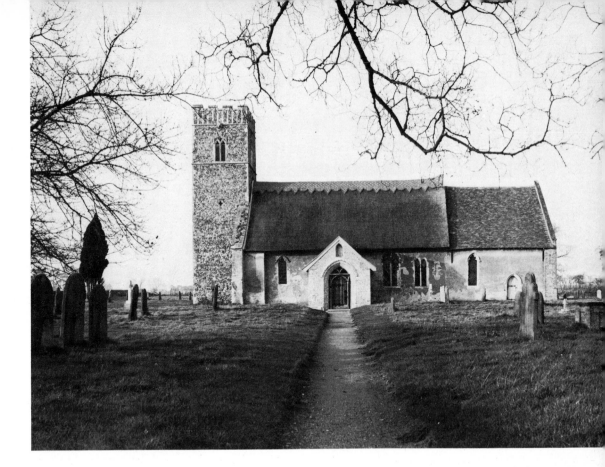

St John the Baptist, Butley.

six feet outside the abbey walls, but in the following year, with Papal authority, his body was disinterred and reburied in the confines of the churchyard. That was in June. In September it was decided that there had been a serious error and poor Richard was again disturbed and re-buried outside the wall. It is scarcely surprising that he has since found it difficult to rest and now mournfully haunts the scene of his unhappy priesthood.

It was rather a doleful day at Butley. Moody rain was drifting across the winter fields when I reached the Oyster Inn at the crossroads. A rural funeral moved across the dulled land, a hearse and a few cars, to be met on the narrow road by a procession of farm vehicles. There was much manoeuvring of tractors and cars and (at the same time), although it was difficult, the respectful doffing of caps.

That evening I went to the Oyster Inn, there since Elizabethan days, famed for its beer and quoits. Edward FitzGerald, the translator of Omar Khayyám, used to drink there with his Suffolk friends, and wrote in praise of it. It was a place where the real men of Suffolk, with the voices of Suffolk, met and drank.

I went into the bar at eight on that damp evening. Hanging on the plain walls there were the village quoits teams of old, holding the metal rings of their sport. A small but lively fire burned in the grate but there was no-one there to warm themselves. Old, wooden chairs ranged around the walls. The bar was unattended.

Eventually a quiet lady appeared and I had a drink. Vera Noble is the licencee now, as her mother was before her and her grandmother before that. I chatted with her about Butley Abbey and the story of the man in the silver coffin. Oh, certainly she knew about the silver

Chillesford, viewed from the churchyard of St Peter's.

coffin. Everyone in those parts did. She remembered an unrewarded search party digging in the grounds of the abbey.

I glanced around at the empty chairs. Where were the cheerful drinkers, the rural men with their earthy good humour, that had brought fame to the Oyster Inn? "What time do the regulars come in?" I asked. "There won't be anybody in tonight," she said. "We don't get many in here now. The young people all go away and the old ones don't live for ever." The empty chairs looked oddly like silent men sitting around the fire.

*   *   *

The very name of Shingle Street, like that of Allendale Town in Northumbria, was enough to make me want to be there. I was not disappointed. It proved to be windy and romantic, a row of irregular houses and a converted coastguard station, boldly facing the salty cold of the North Sea. Shingle slopes from the front doors down to the waves and the beach, not unlike Chesil Bank in Dorset, are formed of great humps of brown pebbles. The sea was sulky, grey to the horizon, but the sky was so apparent you could almost feel it. No wonder Suffolk painters delighted in their clouds, no wonder Crabbe wrote with such exquisite freedom, no wonder Benjamin Britten found music here in the very air.

I walked the vacant beach, the sharp wind on my skin, the sea so dull and yet never without its own brooding fascination. Far out it broke in grey surf on a reef as edged as any in the South Seas. There were few birds that day, a tern skimming through the air currents, a single gull coasting above the sullen waves, although on the inland side of the pebble bank, beyond the Shingle Street houses where green marshes begin, I did see an extraordinary encounter between a green woodpecker and a cat. Puss had apparently strayed into some preserve of the bird and was being dive-bombed noisily. The cat, as if apologising for the mistake, ran from the reeds and headed home towards the houses.

It was enjoyably solitary there. The houses, as irregular as washing, hung on a line, white, pink and blue, of varying heights and shapes. Boats were pulled up, turned up or covered from the winter, and there was a rusty windlass on the shingle. At the end of the street, set back a pace from the shingle, was a Martello tower, now a dwelling, one of a broken line stretching down the coast, built when it was thought that Napoleon might attempt an invasion across the lower North Sea instead of the obvious route across the Straits of Dover.

The coastguard cottages stand at the other end of the street, once, not very long ago, the centre of a tragedy of the sea. On May Day, 1914, seven coastguards took a small boat and made the easy voyage up the river to Aldeburgh where they spent the day before embarking in the early evening to return to their station. Off Orfordness a freak wave overtook their vessel, capsized it and five of the men were drowned.

The story is related in a framed poem now in the bar of The Jolly Sailor at Orford. At this distance its innocent melodrama seems to have more than a touch of William McGonagall, but the sadness of the story comes over graphically. It was composed by W. S. Montgomerie who signed himself 'The Blind Organ Grinder of Westleton.'

> *When from Shingle Street the Coastguard and their boat to Aldeburgh came*
> *Seven brave and jolly jack tars who ever sailed the main . . .*
> *Leading boatman David Bignall is alas no more,*
> *Walter Finnis and McCauley died within sight of home and shore.*
> *Their comrade Sidney Lakin did like British sailors die*
> *With their chief brave H.S. Maugher – and the flag is half-mast high.*
> *Homes now sad and lonely who have lost their head and stay,*
> *While poor McCauley's sweetheart amost weeps her heart away.*
> *For their banns have just been published and the wedding day is soon,*
> *Now her heart is well nigh broken and her life is filled with gloom.*

That night the weather blew wild around Orford and I had to lean into the wind on my way to The Jolly Sailor. Once inside, the door shut, it was full of the special warmth that is peculiar to maritime pubs. There were some young men there who were working on the coastal walls, shoring up the bits of East Anglia which are constantly nibbled away by the sea. They were wanderers, adventurers, travelling wherever there was work of their kind. They had been on bridges and down in tunnels, all over Britain and out among the oil wells of the Persian Gulf.

They were lively and ready with graphic reminiscence. One told us he had once worked in a pub known as The Murderer's Arms. Yet all admitted that they had never read a book and only one had ever written a letter. The old men of the village, at their ancient shove-ha'penny on the board that has been used since before anyone there could remember, drank as slowly as they conversed, sometimes pausing and listening with slow-growing grins at something the younger men were re-telling. There was a lad in a fisherman's jersey, tatoos up his broad forearms who drank quietly and another man who had been hunting the giant coypu on the off-shore mud-flats. There was another drinker, a man from an industrial town far away who said he was taking his annual holiday and that he always came to Orford in December and it was there he meant to retire. It was a good company but not an unusual one for The Jolly Sailor.

Sid Harper used to be the landlord, as his father was before him, an expansive man who, on my first visit described with some relish how, during the great floods of 1953, when half the east coast was drowned, he found himself swimming around among floating barrels in the cellar of the pub. He rescued most of the beer.

Sid died last year. It was the end of a tradition at The Jolly Sailor. His father was a famous

Shingle Street, looking north-east towards the coastguard station.

man in those parts, in the days when the great, silent, sailing barges used to come regularly into the haven. A painter called into the pub one day and old Harper's portrait ended up in the Royal Academy.

Pat Buckner, once a prison officer, is now the landlord. He is a large friendly man, in the same mould as the lamented Sid. He has inherited a hostelry that is full of mystery and history. It is one of those places that seems to have grown into its special landscape. Inside it has settled like a face settles in old age. A shot-gun on one of the beams has been there so long it appears to be part of the beam itself. For longer than anyone can recall one of the curiosities of The Jolly Sailor has been a small glass case which houses a pair of Chinese muff dogs. They were brought from the Orient by some Orford sailor in Victorian times, two tiny but perky creatures, hardly bigger than mice. Ladies in the court of Henry VIII used to conceal dogs such as these in their fur muffs and they were specially brought from China to be this curious fashion accessory. Also in the bar is another tiny dog, preserved for posterity after killing a rat three times its size. The rat is also displayed, although whether the dog died because of the fight or was butchered so that he could take part in the taxidermist's cameo is not clear.

On another wall is an advertisement calling for the men and boys of Orford to volunteer for the Royal Navy, where they could expect good pay and prospects. They were required to present themselves at HM Coastguard station for selection.

But more fascinating is the strange painting that decorates one wall of the landlord's bedroom, discovered there after fifteen layers of wallpaper had been removed. It is painted in oils directly onto the plaster, a gallant scene of English and Dutch ships, their sails full, their pennants streaming. It was concealed since the seventeenth century and came to light only

The Jolly Sailor, situated at the bottom of Quay Street, just before the quay.

during renovations to the inn in 1947. The Jolly Sailor, like the King's Head and the Crown and Castle in Orford, has a firm place in the story of the Suffolk smugglers. Will Laud and his lover, the adventuress Margaret Catchpole, used the inn in their journeys and, according to tradition, the body of Laud was laid on a table in a small room there after he was shot dead by a Prevention Officer on Orford Beach. He and Margaret lived on Havergate, the flat island across the channel from Orford Castle, where they could easily spy the approach of the Customs boat.

Pat Buckner showed me the leaflet circulated throughout East Anglia after Margaret had duped the authorities – and not for the first time. It says: 'March 26th 1800, escaped from the county jail at Ipswich last night or early this morning, MARGARET CATCHPOLE, a convict under sentence of deportation for felony or horse stealing. She is about eighteen years of age, swarthy complexion, very dark eyes and hair, hard favoured, about five feet two inches high, and escaped in a convict's dress which she has probably changed and may be disguised in men's apparel. Whoever shall apprehend the said MARGARET CATCHPOLE so as she may be brought to justice will be entitled to a reward of twenty pounds granted by Act of Parliament.'

Eventually Margaret was apprehended and transported to Tasmania. From there she sent to her former mistress a stuffed lyre bird. It is now in the Ipswich museum, a memento of a singular lady.

The King's Head is the oldest inn in Orford, standing at the gate of the church, its origins probably not far removed from the earliest times in the town. It was heavily damaged in a fire in 1969 and has since been well restored. Orford inns have been prone to accident; in 1963, after a flooding of ten years before, The Jolly Sailor's roof was blown off by a freak hurricane.

The large church, which would dominate any other place, here sits with odd shyness at the corner of the village, partly screened by the haunch of the King's Head, and partly by its own trees. Orford's landmark is the elevated keep of the castle at the other end of the square. It, therefore, comes as something of a surprise to realise how large the church is. It is gigantic for a town of this size, half-concealed like some reluctant giant by the trees and roofs of its own town. The fine square tower is splendidly apparent from the bottom of Quay Street but, even on entering the churchyard, the true magnitude of the building is hidden.

Only when you go through the porch and open the inner door, as I did, on a cold and empty winter's morning, do you realise the space and magnificence of the building. St Bartholomew's, Oreford-Nigh-The-Seas, as it was known, is of breathtaking proportions and airy beauty. The first church was built in the late twelfth century and the stumps of this are still to be seen to the east of the present structure. What happened to this building no-one knows. It was certainly of some significance because Henry II ordered its building, to match his new castle at the other end of the town, and the stone was brought in barges from Caen in Normandy. Wimar, Rector of Sudbourne, who had charge of the souls of the Orford people, wrote that when the church was complete the Christians of the town should no longer have to go to Sudbourne to pray – 'to tread the sandy road for pious purposes'.

That early chapel's successor is a cavern of a church, none the less compelling and beautiful for that. My first reaction on going through the door was to stare up and around me in disbelief. The roof flies high, the pillars rise like fingers to support pointed arches, echoing light from the windows. It is not a church merely to visit, it is a place to explore.

Three bells, sitting like robed bishops on the floor, immediately took my attention. They were brought down from the tower in 1830 when it was deemed too insecure to bear their weight and, although the tower has been solidly restored, they were never replaced. In that wonderfully quaint intimacy that bells possess, each bears a legend of its founder. The triple bell, the smallest of the trio, is set with the words: 'Miles Gray made me, 1639'; the second says: 'John Darbie made me, 1679'; the large tenor says: 'Tho. Gardiner, facit. 1745' and adds the names of two churchwardens, I. Harries and E. Ellis. The founders have their just and simple memorials. Alongside the bells, mutely realistic, is another memento of Orford's history – the town stocks, weathered wood with room for the legs of two malefactors. Here, also, is a massive wooden locker, a churchwarden's chest, which bears the burned date 1634.

Between the times of the casting of the first and second bells the church had a visit from Cromwell's inspector, William Dowsing, charged with demolishing undesirable ornaments in churches throughout Suffolk in 1643. He made Orford one of his first calls, for his journal reads: 'January 25th 1643. We brake down 28 superstitious Pictures and took up 11 popish inscriptions in Brass; and gave order for the digging up of the steps, and taking of 2 crosses of the Steeple of the Church and 1 of the Chancel, in all 4.' Quite a day's work for Master Dowsing, even if he couldn't count. And what offence could the steps have caused?

If Orford has a fame, far outdistancing any of its small and intriguing history, it is because of its bird life. The Sandlings, the gritty land that runs in from the coast, with its sly waterways and its great areas of gorse, are inhabited by a whole nation of familiar birds. If the wind is still, the curlew calls, a heron drifts across the Suffolk sky, mallard come in whirring squadrons from the sea.

But for all this inland life it is Havergate Island, lying low a half mile off the coast, that attracts the eye. Here the great geese honk, teal and shellduck live in colonies, and to the delight of the ornithologist, the rarest of all, the avocet, not only visits but also breeds.

Not inappropriately the man who keeps his eye on this island treasure house for the Royal Society for the Protection of Birds, is called John Partridge. He is a lean, modest and pleasant man, a former sailor who journeyed to Tahiti and New Zealand, before returning to work on the rather less adventurous Orford Ferry. His father, Reg Partridge, had been bird warden of Havergate for twenty-five years. They used to say that he knew every beak and feather and he taught his son, taking John across to the exposed island and teaching him to watch the entrancing life there. One day he went to Norwich for a day's outing and died in the evening. John took over his job at Havergate and has been there ever since.

We had fixed a meeting on the quay and I stood waiting in the snowy wind, watching a tractor manoeuvring itself onto the ferry to be taken across to Orfordness where a farmer was using the land vacated by the watchers of the Ministry of Defence. I saw a man in a pram dinghy rowing briskly out into the choppy anchorage to get aboard a stubby blue boat. I guessed it was John Partridge and I was right.

I must have presented a curious sight because I had borrowed a red woolly hat from Miss Mary Puttergill, the good-natured landlady of the Crown and Castle Hotel. I had a sheepskin coat but with the snow already drifting in the air I wisely thought I needed to cover my head

230 / The Hidden Places of Britain

and ears. This was all she had, her 'fishing hat', and, although slightly on the large side, it did the job splendidly. Nevertheless I must have appeared rather odd as I waited for John on the cold quay. To his credit he did not even allow himself a smile at my expense.

If my embarkation to the small boat was awkward, then my leaving it after the twenty-

Birds on one of the mudflats on Havergate Island; in the distance is Orford and the castle.

minute voyage through the chill and choppy channel was grotesque. I had no rubber boots and to leave the little vessel six or eight feet from the sandy shore and wobble along a narrow plank, clad in my bulky sheepskin coat and bright woolly hat, must have been a moment to remember.

Islands come in all sorts. Some, like Skellig Michael off the coast of Ireland which I climbed one hot day long ago, rise straight out of the sea and seem to sniff the clouds, an ocean mountain; others, like Lundy, are tubby, like a large cow grazing, or are strung out like boats in tow, with small hills and gradual beaches. Havergate Island barely raised its nose out of the sea. It is horizontal and combed by the wind, a long cutlet of land at no point, except for artificial dykes, rising more than a couple of feet above the water. The sea was brown, the land low and grey, the sky almost black with sleet. The wind curled unchecked across the land. It was a wonderful place.

From the top of the dyke near our landfall I could see the forehead of the Castle Keep at Orford and I realised what a fine seamark it must always have been. The comfortable roofs of the town crowded together to the north of the keep and the church tower, splendid at a distance, like a sword against the darkening sky. Other than that the only vertical object in view was the lighthouse out on The Spit, as the locals call Orfordness, sitting up in its red and white striped football jersey like a substitute player waiting to take the field. Once a beacon – a blazing tar barrel – was sited at the castle to warn mariners of the dangers along the half-hidden coast. Then, one October night in 1627, thirty-two ships were sunk because the light failed. Another light was established out in The Spit, one of the first keepers being a lady, Mrs Bradshaw, the widow of a lighthouse man. In the first six months of her custody, there were more complaints from captains navigating the coast than there had been in the previous twenty years. She was summarily removed. In the town records of Aldeburgh is her notice of dismissal and her acceptance of a pension of £20 a year, unduly generous in the circumstances.

Of the many vessels that came to grief along the Orford coastline, the *Queen Esther*, wrecked in the nineteenth century, has a memorial more permanent than most. The figure-head was washed ashore on Orford Beach and taken secretly inland by a landowner who used it to frighten poachers on his property. Today Queen Esther's Grove is still the name given to the place, and is marked so on maps. (The Ordnance Survey Map of Orford, incidentally – Sheet T.M.44 – must be the biggest cartological fraud in history. Apart from one triangle in the left-hand corner, which takes up less than one-eighth of the area, the entire sheet is just blank blue and marked informatively: 'North Sea'. It still costs the same as the other Ordnance Survey maps!)

Havergate, it has been suggested, takes its name from 'haver', the old English word for goat. Goats are there no longer but many other animals run free and untroubled by humans. Hares literally abound (but no rabbits since myxomatosis), stout and weasel live without aggravation. The only species hunted by John Partridge is the giant coypu rat, from South America, bigger than a large tomcat, who were bred for their fur in East Anglia and escaped to the wild before the war. They bred profusely and are still widespread throughout the region.

Yet the blunt-nosed coypu is of no threat to the many birds of Havergate for he is a vegetarian. "It's the other damage he does," said John Partridge. He pointed to the banks of one of the island's many waterways. "See there. That's where they've been digging. They

*Orford seen from the
ramparts of Orford
Castle. On the left is the
tower of St
Bartholomew's Church
with the harbour at the
end of Quay Street to the
right. The River Ore i
separated from the sea by
Orfordness.*

destroy the sides of streams and ditches and before long you've got a flood. And they breed like mad. A female can have a litter of six, and in six months they themselves are mating."

John sets traps for the coypu. I was reminded of Arthur Markwell, landlord of The Sorrel at Shottisham, whom I had met on my first journey to Suffolk. He was employed part-time by the Ministry of Defence to keep the rabbit population under control at one of its private establishments on the coast. He despatched the rabbits with a catapult. Since a boy he had been a dead shot. He showed me the catapult and the small pebbles he used as ammunition. "Always was a good shot with this," he ruminated. "Didn't pay when I went in the army, mind you. They made me a sniper!"

A flight of nine Brent geese, like a formation of plump bombers, came over the marshy land to descend on one of the small lakes at the island's centre. We watched teal and widgeon sitting safely in the lagoon.

John was searching the flat landscape through his field glasses. "There," he breathed quietly. "There they are."

He handed the glasses to me. I panned them carefully across the dull water in the distance. There they were indeed – the whole colony of avocets, the rarest of sights. There are ninety pairs which breed there now, a miraculous number. People come vast distances to see them; what the Louvre is to some, the Smithsonian Institute to others, so Havergate is to the people of the birds.

A spotted redshank arrived and sat cautiously on the debris of what had once been a house. Now it is level with the ground, just a few scraps. It was in this place – called The Red House – that John Luff, the villain who masterminded the smuggling life of Will Laud and Margaret Catchpole lived. The marks of boundary fences are still to be seen on Havergate for it was once used for grazing cattle. They used to be brought across on boats and left to live out there in wild privacy.

Today the birds and animals have it to themselves. For several hours during that day of sharp weather, we walked and watched on the island. When I slipped on a bank and slithered in a pond of mud, lying there in my red woolly hat, John contrived to remain serious and helped me to my feet.

As we were about to leave, heavy with mud and stiff with cold, John's accustomed eye caught the flight of a bird coming low over the reeds and waterways, disturbing the shell-duck and the widgeon. "A hen-harrier," he said with satisfaction. "See it." Once more I looked through the field glasses. There it was with the arrogant attitude of the bird of prey. We watched it hunting and, as we left Havergate for Orford Quay, it came at us, skimming the waves of the Channel, beating the winter air with its wings. There was a note of triumph about it, as though it had succeeded in driving us away.

We reached Orford and it was time for me to go. We went into The Jolly Sailor and had a pint; then I put my bag in the car and began to drive back towards the crowded world. It was snowing now, sweeping across Suffolk on the unchecked wind. As I went across the winter land I reflected on what I had once heard someone say: that to go to Orford you had to *want* to go there. It is impossible to pass it casually because the road leads to nowhere but the sea. It is necessary to make a special journey.

I was glad I had.

THIRTEEN

The French Lieutenant's Woman

It is possible, indeed easy, to pass into the calm and secluded country between the Berwyn Mountains of North Wales and the border with England, by driving west on the uncomplicated road from Oswestry in Shropshire. But it is not the proper way to go.

The true traveller should only enter this arcadian region by making a great loop to the north, turning down towards Bala in the chest of Wales, and then climbing over the great pass through the Berwyns. It is as difficult and as exhilarating as any road in Britain, except for the other pass, further south, by means of which you can get out again.

Winter was mild, despite the forecasts by a Canadian Commercial Weather Company (how would they know?) that we were set for the coldest December and January for years, that there would be rigid rivers and the coal would be scarce. But God decided otherwise. Christmas was so spring-like that I played tennis before the turkey and, although there were keen spells of frost and some large winds, by the middle of January the sun was shining benignly as if it had never considered doing otherwise.

There had been, it is true, that very week, some snow at random in the north, but as I journeyed down towards Mold and Bala through the centre of Wales, it was as cheerful as April. The only snow was crowning the mountains to the east – and it was over those mountains I was going. Rain had washed the Welsh fields to a bright green, trees stood bare but optimistic, people sat blatantly in the open.

I took a sharp and narrow turning from the main A494 road to Bala at the village of Druid. At once I was in deep, almost Devonian lanes; it was like travelling in a trench. In Devon, during the war, the Americans were unable to drive their tanks along these lanes so they simply filled them in with earth and drove along the tops.

The River Dee, its back thickened by winter water, like an animal putting on protective fat, runs widely through the valley which also houses the road. At Cynwyd it seemed as broad as the Thames, streaming quickly under the entrancing stone bridge, wide enough only for one vehicle at a time and with alcoves for pedestrians to avoid whatever is coming across. Below it the river had outgrown its banks. Willows stood up to their knees in brown water like paddling people.

Pleasing countryside unfolded, an unspectacular but a lived-in countryside with a smile on its face. The sun was out for the day, it appeared. In the villages lads were strutting about in their red and white scarves and woollen hats and shouting to each other, for Wales had defeated England in a famous rugby match in Cardiff the previous afternoon. At Llandrillo I saw a notice, one of the more nonsensical of the bi-lingual signs that national pride requires must be displayed throughout Wales. It said: '*cyfleusterau cyhoeddus*' and underneath the translation: 'public conveniences'. The arm of the signpost must have been two yards long.

Beyond Llandrillo I saw that the river had flooded the fields, leaving trees looking lost and lakes and bays and inlets according to the shape of the land. Much of the water was stationary, in the overflow areas anyway, and I could only see the river by the middle stream moving sinuously among the still lakes. The vale spread itself like a man stretching his arms. All at once it was a mile or more wide, the Dee having, with surprising modesty, retreated to the middle meadows. From the elevated land on my side, I could look across the flattest of landscapes with the complimentary hills rising without histrionics on the far side, patched with woods and clothed with fields with white houses spaced along their flanks. Sunday morning crows and cattle, and a man walking phlegmatically towards Llandrillo were the only moving things to be seen. He looked as if he might be going home after the night before.

Then I found the road changing its mind again. Within a mile I was among timbered hills – mere mounds compared to the mountains towards which I was heading – with farms and hamlets lying on the flat. Just before the village of Pale (pronounced Palais, as in Hammersmith) the route curls into a splendid vale, lined by some of the tallest trees I have ever seen, great, thick-girthed pines stand beside the road, the sun filtering through them. The river follows the valley (or is it the other way around?) and the villages are strung along its course like beads on a string. The road takes the easy way also and at one time there was a railway, but that is no more.

Here I saw the sign. It said Llangynog, like a name from *Gulliver's Travels*. I turned the willing car up the immediately steep incline by the stony Bryntiron Inn. The Berwyn Mountains were at once arranged for my inspection. From this point they looked jagged, dragon-backed, prehistoric. A notice in Welsh and English said: 'Snow and ice on pass'.

The road wasted no time. It put its nose in the air and began to climb. Mossy stone walls gave way to conifers, with deciduous trees standing naked alongside them. The bare trees were wet with wintry rain or snow, and the sun shone through them making them shine. The dull conifers stood by glumly. It was strange how some trees can look more beautiful than others, even when they don't have the benefit of leaves.

The river, like a faithful friend who keeps appearing to remind you of his presence, did some eye-catching tricks in the steep clefts on either side. There was a hairpin bend in the road and a tidy little house sitting by the water as it rumbled over a terrace of cataracts. What a good, pleasing place for a house, I thought. It was the last habitation I was to see for some time.

Up and up we went, the road, the car and I, entering a lovely if desolate world of rocks and rivers, tough mountain heather and gorse, with the sun piercing a hole in the gathered clouds, like a peeping tom at a keyhole. Bunches of snow began to appear at the side of the single road. Descents and chasms came into view at every yard; the world rolled away from beneath my feet. I saw a lone hawk against the leg of the mountain in the distance. It was solitary and

Looking due north down Hirnant Valley.

wonderful. The road was called the B4391. It is remarkable how a living road can differ from its mere impersonation on a map. On the Ordnance Survey the B4391 looks prosaically like any road through Bala, Buxton or Burton-upon-Trent. The shading of the high and low country on either side of the rivers, marked like the veins in an old woman's face, are only drawings on paper. The altitude figures, as the road climbs, are the same as the figures used on the tills in supermarkets.

Maps are fine as maps, but they're not a patch on the real thing.

I passed two buildings, bereft and deserted, high up on the pass; once grafting farms, I suppose, where the winters must have been long and solitary seasons, but now empty and used for the shelter of sheep and their winter food. The snow thickened against the sides of the road and then began to fall heavily against the windscreen. The sides of the mountains were clear of it, but each top had its white pate. At 476 metres (I prefer my mountains in feet, but the Ordnance Survey thinks otherwise) I might have been on the top of Everest. I drove cautiously in case the car should begin to slide. It would not do to break down up here, to end

The church at Pennant Melangell, situated half way along the Tanat Valley. Behind the east end of the church projects a small room known as the Cell y Bedd (the cell of the grave), in which the reconstructed Romanesque shrine of St Melangell is situated.

up in a hole, especially one several hundred feet deep. While I went so, and when I was really feeling alone, a small animal – a stoat or a weasel – ran across in front of the car, scampering through the snow at my approach. Since there cannot be much traffic up there, he must have been lying in wait for me. Perhaps he liked to live dangerously.

In this white landscape I observed a sign coming up through the foggy snow. I had crossed the border into Powys. I wondered, up there, who would have cared. The snow ceased and the fog increased, blotting out the depths of the long rift valley on my right. I was looking out on the clouds like the pilot of a lost plane searching hopefully for a landing ground. It was an exhilarating experience. I drove right into the clouds and out the other side. There was an enormous slab of rocky mountain just discernible on the starboard wingtip, in sight for one moment then vanishing into vapour. A waterfall, silent because of its distance, fell headlong, and doubtless shouting, into the pocket of the earth. In front of me I could see the heads of more hills looking over the clouds, white-haired like old men. I thought that perhaps one of them might be God.

But that was the climax. I had gone through the pass, with the highest point, Moel Sych, far out, hidden on my left, and now the road abruptly decided to descend. It went down quicker than it had risen, curling and curving narrowly, so that I had to watch it rather than the scenery. I passed some sheep, each with its extra overcoat of snow. Then the mist cleared entirely and I was looking out on clear rocks and tumbling scree. Then a house with a lock of smoke rising cheerily, then some trees, and then another house. The road was hurrying as though it wanted to get home. In no time I was rumbling over the noisy wooden bridge at the village of Llangynog, lying in the palm of the Berwyns. A pleasant place at which to arrive. At the New Inn I stopped, had a pint and asked the landlord if there was anything to eat.

"How about a nice plate of roast goat," he suggested. "And three veg."

The roast goat tasted like strong lamb. Its very presence on the menu made me decide that this was the place at which I wanted to stay. Yes, they had a room, and in no time my headquarters was established and I was ready to explore this hinterland that sees few of the tourists that trudge through Snowdonia. Certainly in January it had the serenity that it must have known forever.

My unerring nose for a good hostelry had not failed me; it had led me to The New Inn, as it had done to The Ilchester Arms in Dorset, to the Allenheads Inn in Northumbria, and the Jolly Sailor in breezy Suffolk. There must be some name for this talent; an inn instinct, perhaps.

The homely house at Llangynog has been there since the middle of the eighteenth century, welcoming travellers who came over the pass in the Berwyns, a considerable task in the horse days. It stands almost beside one of the hundreds of streams that roll and wriggle through those folded valleys, under the very lee of the first of the mountain range, rising up from the outskirts of the village with great piles of slate and rock poised there in dangerous-looking formation. On my first afternoon I heard a sullen rumble and looked up with a stranger's anxiety to the towering slope. Another rumble. Was the avalanche shifting? A young man, who turned out to be the landlord's son-in-law, was splitting wood with a huge axe. At my suggestion he stopped to listen. He had never known the mountain mass to shift, he admitted, and he had lived in the place all his life. Then came the rumble again. His face brightened. It was merely a car going over the noisy wooden bridge at the start of the village.

The landlord of the New Inn at Llangynog, like so many of his kind whom I had met in these travels, comes from far away and from a different world. Alex Williamson had been a computer man living in Slough, making the M4 motorway run each day, up to his neck in the human race. His wife had also worked in London.

"One day," he recalled, "I knew I was weary of the whole thing. The driving and the pressure. And then I had the misfortune to have to pick up the bits from a road accident and that reinforced my feeling that I wanted out."

His wife felt the same. They went on their annual holiday and discussed their future. "We decided to do something different," he smiled. "Just as long as it was not involved with pubs, and so long as we did not have to live in Wales. *Anything* but those two things. And that's how we came to have a pub in Wales."

His two daughters went with them. The younger was serving the roast goat on the day I arrived. The elder met the young man I had seen wielding the axe and they were married

The shrine of St Melangell c. 1160–70.

within the year, the wedding being something of a riot in a valley that is not without its social highlights.

Vera Williamson does the cooking and runs the inn when Alex takes time off to build his boat. "Vera and I are going to sail the Mediterranean," he promised. "When the boat's finished." That should be simple – once they've got it to the sea, *over the Berwyn Mountains*. Even Noah might have backed down from that prospect.

Vera said, "People here are wonderful. The place is full of characters. You should have seen the wedding. Old Robert the bell-ringer lost his false teeth." She is a jolly-faced woman and she laughed hugely at the memory. Then she said seriously, "If there is one thing the people around here are very proud about, it's the little Church at Pennant Melangell. Even St Paul's or Westminster Abbey is nothing compared to that. St Melangell actually lived there, you know. She is the patron saint of hares."

Not having been aware before that hares had their own saint, I was at once curious and set out to see the amazing place. It is two miles from Llangynog, along a tight lane that jumps over streams and bends through thick trees. It was raining heavily now but nothing could detract from this little place the full sense of peace which has been with it for a thousand years. Pennant Melangell has only two houses and a couple of farms. It is enclosed in a cosy valley which travels for miles until stopped by a massive wall of mountain which I could see in the distance through the rain. The silver cord of a waterfall hung down it.

Even with the thick rain running down my neck I could do nothing but stand and admire the sweet place. The church has three great yews, under each of which, so the local story goes, is buried a cache of gold coins. Nobody has ever bothered to look. One of the yews is so widespread that its shelter forms a convenient storehouse for the tools and boards of the grave-digger. I sheltered there too and studied the church. Its simplicity, its serenity and the slight jauntiness of its modest tower, shaped like a little hat, are wholly endearing. In the older part of the churchyard the forebears of the village lie beneath tombstones so awry and tossed about that they looked like wrecked ships.

It has roots in the eighth century for it was then that the fairy-tale miracle of St Melangell and the Hare happened. A hunt was taking place, with the followers of the Prince of Powys, pursuing a hare across country and into a copse. When the huntsmen approached they found the dogs whining and unwilling to go further into the trees. They pushed on and found a young girl praying and with the hare peeping out of the folds of her garments. The dogs were backing further away and the horses were frightened. One of the huntsmen lifted his horn to blow and the *instrument stuck firmly to his lips*! The discomfort of the man was nothing to the amazement of his friends. Brochwel, the Prince, was convinced that some miracle was afoot and he called the hunt off. He was told that the girl had lived in the copse for fifteen years without seeing a human soul. He immediately granted her the land at Pennant where she founded a church and a convent.

She was an Irish Princess, it was said, who had fled from her country to escape an arranged marriage. She became the patron saint of hares, and local people, even today, are loath to catch a hare. If they see one being pursued, they may shout: "St Melangell protect you!" And the hare will certainly escape.

Outside the Tanat Valley Inn, the other hostelry in Llangynog, there is a painting represent-

ing the miracle. It is charming enough, although the young saint looks a little like Snow White and the approaching huntsman like her Prince. The hare looks authentic.

That night in the bar of The New Inn, with a scented woodsmoke fire in the yawning old grate, there were three men who had brought a cargo of coal and fresh vegetables from Bala, over the top of the pass. It seemed like a difficult journey for commodities that could quite easily be obtained along the easy road from Oswestry or Welshpool. Yes, that was right they agreed, but they didn't mind coming over. It was nothing when you knew the pass well. And anyway the pubs were shut on Sunday on their side of the mountains.

They conversed in rural Welsh, with Alex Williamson and I standing helplessly by. Every now and then a recognisable word would float out – Liverpool or Aston Villa or Coronation Street. As I had been told further down in Wales, in Lampeter, the inhabitants do not speak Welsh to exclude or confuse English-speaking people but simply because it is their true language, the tongue with which they are most comfortable. English is hard work.

As the evening went by the local men spoke English, in deference to me (a Welshman who speaks no Welsh), as they put away the pints and talked about some of the characters in the valley. "There was John Bryn-y-Gwern," said one young man. "John Jones, that is, but he was called by the name of his house. He was born on the longest day of the year, June 21st, and he died on the shortest, December 21st."

That was not by a long way the only remarkable thing about him. He was an eccentric, living in his house on the hill, clear of the other habitation, travelling down for his drink or his shopping on a folding bicycle that was army-surplus from the First World War. He had a disabled arm so he had the brake put down by his foot.

Graham Lewis, the young forester who is married to Christine Williamson, smiled at the memory of John Bryn-y-Gwern. "In his house," he said in his careful Welsh voice, "John had two of everything. Two wheelbarrows, two pails, two kettles. Everything. And the whole place was fixed up with an amazing system of pulleys and strings and wires. He could pull a string from his bed and shut the light off in his sitting-room or close the front door for the night. He could even shut his hens in their coop by tugging a pulley next to his pillow. He had a chimney pot in his kitchen sink to stop the water splashing and he had made a special harness for his wheelbarrow so he could wheel it with one hand."

One day Ernie the grave-digger, who was John's friend, went up to the house and found the old man fuming that his radio had gone wrong again. Between them they pushed the snout of a vacuum cleaner into the back of the ancient set and pressed the switch. Then they tried the programmes again and reception was perfect.

Ernie, the Llangynog grave-digger, is a tall man with a busby of white hair. He's another village character, known to wear a top hat to the graveside, and then slip into the vestry and emerge with a pair of dungarees over his best suit to fill the earth into the hole. "Aye," laughed one of the men, "at Graham's wedding he was offering cut price grave-digging to the guests. He used to watch his friend, John Bryn-y-Gwern, getting older and had been known to suggest that he might like to start contributing towards his burial before he actually died."

Someone related a tale about a minister from the valley who decided to go up into the hills, to a remote family who had a reputation for being on the wild side. When he reached their hut, intent on preaching the gospel, he found that the rooms were almost in darkness although the sun was shining brightly outside. Over the years, as each pane of glass in their windows had broken, it had been replaced by a slate from the mountainside. Their abode had become darker and darker but they had never noticed it.

Most of the people in the village, particularly the Jones and the Lewises, are related to each other. They got to telling about how one of the local Joneses, a farmer, hired a decrepit traction engine to work a big saw. Somehow, once the thing had started, it got out of the rhythm and went faster and faster and no-one could stop it. The watching workers stood transfixed while it worked up a fearsome head of speed. Then, as a man, they bolted to safety. None too soon either, for with a bang like a field gun the blade of the saw broke and flew like a terrible boomerang into the air. "Nobody ever saw it again," said the teller. "Just vanished, man, just vanished."

Graham Lewis nodded his head. "That's right," he confirmed. "And I think I knew what happened to that saw blade. Just there is that peat bog. I think it dropped into the peat and just sank."

Then there was the itinerant labourer who earned a lot of money during the sheep shearing season and went to England for a binge. He returned to the little caravan which was his home with a sore head and an empty pocket. He had no food to last him until he earned his first money, so he cut a switch from a hedge and went into a field where he proceeded to chase an innocent pig. It made a great squealing and the farmer arrived and wanted to know what was going on. "That creature," said the labourer, "has just been into my caravan and eaten all my food. Every morsel." The farmer replaced the phantom food.

One tale generated another. Graham remembered a boy from Llangynog who was harrowing a field at the foot of the mountains. When the middle of the day arrived he let the horses graze and sat down himself to rest. Along came the meddling minister who asked why he was lazing about when he should be working. "But the horses have to rest," explained the lad. "There's nothing for me to do."

"Nonsense, boy," reproved the minister. "Just because the horses need a rest it doesn't mean you have to slack. You're a strong boy. Pull the harrow along yourself."

The following Sunday the lad's father appeared at chapel with a bag of potatoes which he handed to the surprised minister who asked what they were for. "For you to peel," said the man. "Give you something to do while we're praying."

*   *   *

To see the slopes of the Berwyns on a fine January morning was a delight. The rosy winter sun caught the many colours – the reds and browns of the gorse and heather, the black and brown and grey of the rocks, the topmost snow against the winter-blue sky.

At breakfast, before the early fire in the bar of The New Inn, I met Robert, the famous bell-ringer. He was hardly as I expected. Instead of a large muscular man, able to pull the bell-rope with power, there, sitting reading the morning paper and drinking a cup of tea, was a thin and mild fellow, grey, small-faced, almost lost in a large overcoat. His speech was deliberate, delivered with great politeness. "We only had the Welsh at school, you see," he said. "No English at all. I had to pick up what I know from English people who came here."

He thought for a while. "Funny really, it is," he said. "Because there was no English and yet we used to play cricket in the field by the school on summer evenings." I had a mental and idyllic picture of the scene, the boys playing, the shouts in Welsh. I wondered if LBW has two L's in Wales. "Never been so far as London," said Robert. "But I've seen it on the television, of course. Very nice it looks. But I don't suppose I'll go now." He was born in the cottage opposite Pennant Melangell Church and remembers snowy winters when the hamlet was isolated even from Llangynog. "In those days," he said, "people used to get stranded on the pass over the mountains. My father used to help to get them down."

We talked of his bell-ringing. He likes the bell at Pennant Melangell best. The one in Llangynog is much heavier and not so fine. At Llanfyllin, to the east, the church bells are said to be the sweetest in all Wales.

That morning I went to Llanrhaeadr-ym-Mochnant which takes its name from a waterfall – one of the seven wonders of Wales. It is a grey, thoughtful town, where William Morgan was vicar between 1578 and 1588, and worked by candlelight to translate the Bible into Welsh for the first time. His translation is the basis for much of the modern Welsh language.

A view of the Tanat Valley, with the village of Pennant Melangell in the distance. The River Tanat flows past the village.

The shops do not seem to have changed their window displays for half a century, which, to me anyway, is pleasing in a nostalgic way. The post office sells Wellington boots and walking sticks.

To reach the waterfall is a journey up a narrow defile for four miles, each marked off by a finely-worked stone, not unlike a small tombstone set into the arm of the vale. It is an enchanting valley, crowded with beech and birch and with yet another Welsh river bouncing across its stones and in and out of the leggy trees. There is a house by a bridge with all these amenities at its front door. The road climbs briskly in the direction of Moel Sych, the peak of the Berwyns, although it never gets there; after four miles there comes a dull roar and you know you are approaching Pistyll Rhaeadr, the great fall.

Compared to Niagara, I suppose it's a mere trickle, but I've been to Niagara and I could hardly see for the tourists. Here we are alone, the waterfall and I. Leaving the car I crossed the river that was charging away and I looked up. The surprised water tips from a ledge 240 feet up, dropping in a wonderful cloudy column until exploding on a ledge two-thirds of the way down.

I went over the footbridge (a single iron girder) below the cataract. The roar filled my ears and the spray wet my face. I could see from there that after striking the intermediate ledge, the fall flew through a natural arch, built by Nature as delicately as anything in a cathedral, before toppling the remaining distance onto the water-worn rocks below. It must never stop raining in that place; the rocks, the ferns, the trees, were all soaking.

A story is told about an archbishop who was taken to see the fall. Unfortunately, it had been an exceptionally dry summer in North Wales and the cataract was reduced to a quarter its normal flow. So that the visitor would not be disappointed some local men went to the top on the previous night and dammed the river with rocks. By the time the archbishop arrived a good head of water had collected above and this was released at the appropriate moment. Down came the fall in full fury.

"It's a wonderful sight," enthused the archbishop.

"Yes, a true miracle," murmured the local vicar at his side.

Leaving the mountain-side I drove towards Llansilin and once more the horizon changed. I entered the softest of valleys stretching far out towards England. It was like some hidden heaven, and again I seemed to be entirely alone. The road was deserted, sheep loitered on the mild hills and cattle among the farms in the plain. The sun came out to light the scene for me.

At Llansilin I found a garage housed in a small, corrugated iron hut. Petrol was dispensed from a prehistoric handpump on the wall. The mechanic was philosophical. "Gives me a strong muscle in my left hand," he said. "He's trying to get it changed to a proper pump. He may do soon. You never know. It's been here about fifty years."

I asked the way to Sycharth and he seemed puzzled. Then he realised. "Oh, that old mound," he said. "Somebody lived there. Somebody famous." He remembered then and told me how to find it.

The somebody famous was, in fact, Owain Glendawr, the grandest of all the Welsh Princes, who had his stronghold here almost within sight of the English border. A prophet is often without honour in his own country, even when the country is Wales. I had long wanted to see this fortification, the place called by the ancient song ' . . . a wood fort on a hilltop. Next to Heaven . . .'

It no longer towers; in fact it is difficult to see until you are almost there. Then it comes into view behind a farmhouse, a long mound and another on top, platforms of grass. It looks out on a peaceful setting which can have changed only a little since the great Prince set out on his wars. There was not much to see, but I was satisfied. I went away happily – not knowing that something even more romantic and more than unusual was to come my way that winter's day.

* * *

Llanfyllin is another small and peaceful town with a large red-faced church, famous for the

Pistyll Rhaeadr waterfall.

sweetness of its bells. It also once had a dire reputation for drunkards. There were many public houses along the street and a saying grew which is still remembered today: 'Old ale fills Llanfyllin with young widows.' But there is a far more romantic tale to be told.

Across the road from the church is a pleasant house of the usual Georgian proportions. It is called The Council House and is thought to have been used many years ago as a debating chamber after fire had destroyed the Llanfyllin town hall. Today one corner is taken up with a pharmacy and grocery store. Upstairs is one of the most astonishing rooms I have ever entered.

In 1812 there was brought to Llanfyllin, a suitably inaccessible place, a disconsolate group of French prisoners of war. They were not enclosed in a camp or compound but were put on parole and allowed to live and do some work in the town. The effect that these young Frenchmen had upon the isolated community is not difficult to assess.

The room above what is now the pharmacy and grocery store was the lodging of a Lieutenant Pierre Augeraud, who was twenty-five years-old, five feet eleven inches tall, had brown hair, an artistic touch, and was desperately lonely.

He set to work to paint upon the walls of the room fairy-tale, almost mystic, representations of his home country. Mountains, lakes, ruins, and some symbolically solitary figures standing looking at the landscapes of which they themselves are part. The hues are predominantly blue. The French lieutenant probably used sheep-dip as part of his colouring.

While he was thus occupying his captivity, dreaming of his homeland, he would often look from the window of his comfortable prison and see a pretty young girl walking through the churchyard opposite before turning along the street towards the town. He learned that she was the rector's daughter – and from that window he fell in love with her. His presence had not gone unnoticed. She glanced shyly up at the tall, framed figure; the glance became a wave and the wave a smile. Soon they were meeting secretly.

One version of the story is that they ran away together and were brought back – him in irons, her in disgrace – to Llanfyllin; another says that the girl's father, the rector, found them in each other's arms. Whichever is true, the rector was furious that his daughter should be consorting with an enemy (and she was not the only girl in the town to have formed such a relationship with the prisoners. Had he not preached against this perfidy in his own pulpit?). Pierre Augeraud was quickly sent to another part of the country and the weeping girl locked up in the rectory.

It might have ended there, but the lieutenant was in love. When the war was finished he was repatriated to France, but could think of nothing but Wales and his loved one. For her part the girl had on several secret occasions gone to the room and stood looking and wondering at the strange paintings he had left behind.

At the first opportunity the Frenchman returned to Wales. At Llanfyllin he discovered that the rector had died and that his widow and daughter had moved to Shrewsbury. He went there and the couple fell into each other's arms. The rector's widow, with no doubt a silent apology to her husband's ghost, allowed them to marry and they did and lived together, happily, in Wales for the rest of their lives.

There is a final quirk to the story. When the French lieutenant died he was buried in the same vault as the rector who despised him so.

Looking
west-north-west across
Lake Vyrnwy from
Lake Vyrnwy Hotel and
showing the delightful
Victorian water-towers.

Over the years the story has had many embellishments but Pauline Page Jones, who with her husband owns the house and the shop, has the roll of French prisoners on parole in Llanfyllin in 1812–13. They were captured in the Spanish town of Badajos in the spring of 1812 at the beginning of Wellington's Peninsular Campaign. Number sixty on the list was Lieutenant Pierre Augeraud who was taken on April 7th – the day after the three week siege of the town ended. His description is given and also his regiment – the 58th infantry.

Pauline Page Jones, a personable young woman, who runs the store and, in addition, is the

Registrar of Births, Deaths and Marriages for Llanfyllin, as was her mother before her and her grandfather before that, has an enormous and fascinating book, handed down in the family for generations, tracing their lineage back to the twelfth century.

She finished serving her customers with Surf and sugar and took me up to see the amazing paintings. And amazing they are. To stand in the room – Pauline and her husband sleep there in a brass bedstead – is to be lost in wonder. There are twelve panels round the walls, some flaking now (although steps are being taken to restore them), so vivid and so romantic that

The early 19th century landscape paintings in the upstairs room of The Council House at Llanfyllin.

they could not fail to entrance anyone with a single line of poetry in their heart. The scenes are operatic – seascapes and hills, a broken building, lone figures, an unending sky. I have rarely been more surprised or thrilled at a discovery.

The window is still there. A large Georgian frame looking out directly onto the church. I stood and gazed as he must have done one hundred and sixty-nine years ago. It would not have astonished me to see a ghostly girl appear on the path to look up shyly, to smile and wave before passing on. What a lovely story.

It was by the fire in the bar of The New Inn that I first heard of the other pass over the Berwyn Mountains. A young and amiable couple who have come to live in the valley told me of it. They are attempting to be entirely self-sufficient in their lives, growing their own food and making their own clothes. They told me of the southern pass over the Berwyns, alongside Lake Vyrnwy first, then taking another steep and single mountain road that eventually reached Bala. It was early afternoon and the winter light was dimming. I thought I must be on my way before I was caught in the dark in the hills.

I had already been to Lake Vyrnwy, a long waterway, damned at the beginning of the century to provide a reservoir for distant Liverpool. A village and church had to be drowned in the process but, very sportingly, the Liverpool Corporation Waterworks Committee rebuilt both nearby and out of the reach of the water, and, in fairness, a good job they made of both. The small, rotund church is perched high above the lake, among the trees, and apart from its belfry has a cheerful little chimney, a homely and unusual touch, I thought. The village is arranged on the other side of the lake and between the two is a massive granite dam, almost Egyptian in its proportions and prospect. It could have been the work or whim of some ancient Pharaoh.

Proof that this engineering achievement was completed in more leisured and careful days, is further provided in a water-tower, so striking that it would not disgrace a castle by the Rhine. When I first saw it the day was full of drizzle and mist and it sat on the flat, iron water, a mile away, all turrets and pinnacles like a set for a Wagner opera.

It loses nothing on closer inspection, either. Its several pointed roofs are topped with spires and one with a charming weather-vane. They don't build water-towers like that any more.

A road encircles the entire lake but at its furthest point away from the dam, an off-shoot climbs to the right and immediately through a collar of trees into the mountains again.

This time the pass was even narrower and the way just as stunning as on my first journey. As the road climbed higher, so the great, desolate, deserted valleys opened out ahead. The afternoon light was running away quickly. The road turned and curled, clinging onto the side of the hills like a desperate climber. Then it began to sleet and quickly the sleet turned to hail. At one point I had to stop the car just to look. Ahead of me was a huge, brown, pudding-backed hill, and across it drifted a magical curtain of hail. White beads, millions of them, hanging across its face.

It fell dark quickly and the way was difficult, not to say dangerous. I was relieved to find myself going downhill, down into the flatlands beside Bala Lake. All at once I was out of the wilderness and on a road with other cars, lorries and buses.

I drove quickly now, towards home. But I was happy enough for I had found another hidden place and it had found me.